New Social Ties

Also by Deborah Chambers

WOMEN AND JOURNALISM (*with Linda Steiner and Carole Fleming*)

THE PRACTICE OF CULTURAL STUDIES (*with Richard Johnson, Parvati Raghuram* and *Estella Tincknell*)

REPRESENTING THE FAMILY

New Social Ties

Contemporary Connections in a Fragmented Society

Deborah Chambers
University of Newcastle upon Tyne, UK

First published in 2006 by
PALGRAVE MACMILLAN
Houndmills, Basingstoke, Hampshire RG21 6XS and
175 Fifth Avenue, New York, N.Y. 10010
Companies and representatives throughout the world

PALGRAVE MACMILLAN is the global academic imprint of the Palgrave Macmillan division of St. Martin's Press, LLC and of Palgrave Macmillan Ltd. Macmillan® is a registered trademark in the United States, United Kingdom and other countries. Palgrave is a registered trademark in the European Union and other countries.

ISBN-13: 978–0–333–98407–9 hardback
ISBN-10: 0–333–98407–2 hardback
ISBN-13: 978–0–333–98408–6 paperback
ISBN-10: 0–333–98408–0 paperback

This book is printed on paper suitable for recycling and made from fully managed and sustained forest sources.

A catalogue record for this book is available from the British Library.

Library of Congress Cataloging-in-Publication Data

Chambers, Deborah.
    New social ties : contemporary connections in a fragmented society / Deborah Chambers.
        p. cm.
    Includes bibliographical references and index.
    ISBN 0–333–98407–2 – ISBN 0–333–98408–0 (pbk.)
    1. Social networks. 2. Social structure. 3. Gender identity. I. Title.

HM741.C435 2006
302.3′4—dc22   2006046377

10 9 8 7 6 5 4 3 2 1
15 14 13 12 11 10 09 08 07 06

Printed and bound in Great Britain by
Antony Rowe Ltd, Chippenham and Eastbourne

Contents

Acknowledgements

I would like to thank my friends and colleagues at the University of Newcastle upon Tyne in the media, communication and culture team for their support and for creating a dynamic research culture: Chris Haywood, Tony Purvis, Liviu Popoviciu, Gareth Longstaff, Jayne Goble and Wayne Webster. I wish to acknowledge my gratitude to Olwyn Ince, who provided helpful research assistance. I extend thanks to Estella Tincknell and Joost Van Loon who collaborated in the research on youth and sexual morality discussed in this book, published in the *British Journal of Sociology of Education, Gender and Education* and *Feminist Media Studies*. I also thank Sharon Lockyer and Mike Pickering who published a version of my research on media representations of single women in their edited collection, *Beyond a Joke: the Limits of Humour* (Palgrave Macmillan, 2005). I am grateful to friends and former colleagues from Nottingham Trent University, including John Tomlinson, Chris Rojek, Andreas Wittel, Richard Johnson and Mike Featherstone for support and to my dear friend, Sandra Harris, for inspiration. I'd also like to express gratitude to the following people for their valued friendship while I was writing this book: Lesley and Adrian Musto; Karen, Martin and Claire James; and the Tuscany tribe: Kate and John Penrose, Mavis and Peter Solomon, and Hilary Beaver.

Introduction

Social and personal ties are undergoing significant changes in Western societies, provoking public anxieties that traditional associations of family, neighbourhood and community are fragmenting. Academics, politicians and policy makers have expressed concern about a decline of community values and personal responsibility. Various factors have been identified as possible causes including globalisation, spatial and social mobility, the welfare state, the women's movement and quest for gender equality, a decline in marriage, higher divorce rates, and the rise in single-person households. How are people relating to one another during an era when high importance is placed on individual self-reliance and choice in relationships? With a focus on gender differences and identities, this book addresses this question by examining how the 'individual' is being conceived in relation to the 'social' in contemporary Western society.

Conflicting views about changing informal relationships have provoked a re-evaluation of the very concept of the 'social' and sociality. Western utopian ideas, such as communitarianism, invest in the nostalgic appeal of traditional community ties by comparing an imagined ideal past with a socially fragmented present. Pessimistic interpretations of recent changes in social ties have emphasised the rise of institutionalised individualism and the erosion of traditional forms of social unity such as kinship and community. In contrast, the emergence of new kinds of social cohesion is being recognised by postmodernist thought in which social ties are characterised as fluid and permeable. Information and communication technologies such as Internet, e-mail and mobile phone use, are supporting new ways of thinking about and experiencing relationships and belonging.

New social ties and the friendship ideal

This book examines shifting social and personal ties through the lens of friendship. As an example of a new approach to belonging, the concept

1

of friendship acts as a catalyst for the exploration and questioning of ideas and values linked with a whole range of new social connections from local family, neighbourhood and community ties to disembedded and global communication networks sustained via new information technologies. 'Friendship' has extraordinary appeal today as a fluid and ubiquitous term. Social and cultural theory has tended to neglect friendship ties. Yet among policy makers of Western nations this informal, but often intense and intimate bond is now being recognised as an essential social resource, as part of 'social capital' in the organisation of wider social support networks. 'Social capital' refers to forms of social organisation that augment co-operation between individuals for mutual advantage. It is a value used in social policy to measure and monitor the 'productivity' of social ties, defined in terms of friendship networks, participation in clubs and membership of voluntary associations: from sports leagues to church groups (Putnam, 2000) . How new kinds of informal relationships are being constituted are crucial questions at a time when the traditional forms of social collective care, once provided by the welfare state, are subsiding. Changing ideas about friendship, identity, communication and belonging in Western society are, then, the subject matter of this book.

Friendship ties are beginning to be viewed as an expression of intimacy that replaces the sense of social integration associated with the concept of 'community'. The book addresses the question of whether informal friendship networks are growing in order to compensate for the decline of intimacy and commitment elsewhere in society. Are weak family and neighbourhood ties giving way to friendship as an important authentic emotional and social bond? While friendship shares certain characteristics with 'community', it also conveys positive values about the voluntary nature and self-expressive aspect of relationships. For example, the metaphor of friendship is being used to describe today's more transient yet intense social bonds: the 'pure relationship', 'friends as family', 'family as friends'. Within a postmodern shift of emphasis from kinship and community networks to personal bonds, friendship is being privileged. It functions as a model relationship and a modernising impulse. The friendship ideal, as a chosen relationship that transcends obligation, seems to fit neatly into a society characterised by expressive individualism. It represents a shift from *obligation* to *choice* in modern confluent relationships (Pahl, 2000: 120).

While the contemporary appeal of the term 'friendship' corresponds with today's emphasis on self-individualisation, it also represents the acute ambiguity surrounding choice and commitment in elective relationships during a period when we are witnessing high divorce rates and appear to be questioning traditional values of commitment. As Ray Pahl (2000) asserts in his important book about friendship, the idea that 'good friends are all you need' contains a number of consequences. It raises critical questions about responsibility and caring: practices which are formalised by legal and religious regulations in marital and kin relationships but not in looser kinds of ties. Concerned about whether an increasingly fragmented and amorphous group of individuals can sustain social needs that were once supported by the state and voluntary sector, governments and non-government agencies are now asking exactly what kinds of values and motives are binding people together into caring networks.

The ongoing withdrawal of state welfare provision in many areas of life in Western nations generates fears of a deficiency in the kinds of community networks needed to replace the state's former role in redistributing wealth and maintaining well-being. Governments and charitable associations of Western societies are also concerned that growing self-reliance and accompanying transformations in personal relationships are eroding a culture of trust, commitment and caring, leading to a crisis of responsibility. These concerns are provoking governments and charitable organisations to conduct research on changing levels of civic involvement, social trust and forms of care, which are addressed in Chapter 5. For example, the British government's first ever national strategy for carers in 1999, *Caring for Carers*, expressed concern about the kinds of factors that might be determining the extent of caring in the future:

> In particular, the growth in the number of lone parents, changes in patterns of marriage, the increase in the number of people living alone, and increased mobility among family members, may mean that people will be less likely in future to be part of the sort of relationships which can result in informal caring when someone becomes sick, disabled, vulnerable or frail.
> (Department of Health, 1999: 20)

More recently, the Salvation Army[1] conducted a study in British society of the key themes of community, individuality and responsibility. The charity identified a 'responsibility gap' resulting from a growing deficit of care for vulnerable groups including the elderly and those with physical, learning or sensory disabilities. The organisation also identified a lack of support for informal carers caring for people in need in their own homes and the critical shortage of childcare places, exacerbated by women taking

on more of the economic responsibilities for providing for their households. The report states:

> Our research shows that in contemporary British society, many
> people do not feel an obligation of care to their extended family, their
> local community or vulnerable sections of society. At the same time,
> however, they have increasingly accepted responsibility for their own
> health, financial well-being and the care of their immediate families.
> They have diminished expectations of what governments can or should
> do for them.
>
> (Henley Centre/Salvation Army, 2004:8)

The rapid rise in the number of individuals who are choosing to live
alone rather than marry is further cause for public concern. This shift in
living arrangements across Western societies including the United States,
Britain and Europe, raises questions about changing values and patterns
of living and interacting with others.[2] It is estimated that 46 per cent of
households in the UK will be made up of single occupants by 2010.[3]
These social trends have, then, generated uncertainties about how informal networks and forms of care-giving are changing in contemporary
Western society and provoked public debates about the strength of
traditional family and community networks. They fuel public fears that
we now live in an individualised society characterised by an erosion of
responsibility, morality and trust in personal relationships and everyday
transactions.

At the centre of these uncertainties are the changing social roles and
aspirations of women. By appearing to choose independence and careers
over marriage, and preferring divorce over bad marriages, the growing
demand by younger women for personal autonomy is being associated
by many commentators with a relinquishing of traditional feminine
caring roles in society. Women have therefore been placed in the spotlight
in debates about demands for equality in social and intimate ties.
However, an emphasis on flexibility, equality and mutual respect in
today's relationships obscures the hierarchical constraints of gender that
continue to shape sexual, family and kin relationships.

Broadly feminist in its perspective, the book provides a focus on
relations of gender and power for an understanding of changing social
and personal ties. I draw on debates in sociology, cultural studies, philosophy and feminist theory to address ways that traditional ideas about
sociality have been challenged by social and cultural transformations
associated with postmodernism, globalisation and changing modes of

communication. Feminist debates are used in order to examine ways that contemporary feminine and masculine identities are being expressed, regulated and negotiated though informal networks and how those networks of friendship *organise* and yet also *question* relations of gender and power. Important anxieties about changing gender relations that raise public and academic concerns about care and commitment are thereby addressed.

Friendship has, then, been marked out as a privileged type of relationship in the context of rapid social change. There are a number of points that can be made about why it is a favoured bond in our society which will be addressed in the chapters to follow. However, with regard to definitions, friendship is illusive. As Graham Allan (1996) points out, friendship is a unique tie defined *only* on the basis of the relationship that exists, rather than on the basis of a genealogical connection. In contrast to neighbours, kin or workmates, the only criterion for identifying someone as a friend is the quality of the relationship. Thus, as Allan (1996: 85) emphasises: 'The boundaries drawn around the category are not rigid; there are no clear-cut lines around who should be included and who excluded.'

The lack of widely agreed principles for measuring a friendship therefore allows the bond to be used in a highly flexible way to include family as friends and friends as family. However, there are important class, gender and ethnic differences in the organisation of friendship, as addressed in this book, demonstrating that this personal tie is deeply embedded in the social order. For example, sociological research has identified the middle classes as a group that claims more friends than the working classes. Sociability among the working classes tends to be organised around relations of kin and around local venues such as clubs and pubs (Allan, 1996). Middle-class friendships are more likely to be planned and purposeful in the sense that specific arrangements are usually made to meet friends as the main purpose of the activity. Nevertheless, despite being shaped by social structures, friendship is appealing because it is defined as a relationship between equals with little sense of hierarchy or difference in status. It is also regarded as reciprocal but without the objective of gain. Hierarchy is veiled by the fact that most friendships are made between people of similar status and position in the life-course. As Graham Allan (1996) and Rebecca Adams (Adams and Allan, 1998) assert, informal ties such as friendship need to be examined in the context of wider social structures, that is, in terms of how they facilitate and reproduce structures of power and privilege. All-male fraternities such as Masonic lodges and rotary clubs use friendship to advance economic and political interests, as described in Chapter 3. Thus, as a remarkably fluid concept, friendship can be used to refute or confirm gendered identity and the staging of heterosexual difference as explained in Chapters 3 and 4.

Postmodern associations and identities

A key theme of the book, then, is that a friendship discourse is being superimposed on a whole range of relationships which are considered to be in a state of crisis or transition. The deconstructive approaches of post-structuralism, feminism and postmodernism show that traditional markers of identity such as class, gender, age, nation and ethnicity are being questioned and loosened, giving way to new opportunities for autonomy. The self is being reconfigured by novel forms of sociation: new sexual communities and friendship networks, new urban movements, and new forms of global communication. New discourses of belonging are thereby being opened up. Some of these emergent subjectivities are mediated through new information and communication technologies.

The argument advanced in this book is that despite the presence of hierarchy in informal ties, friendship is being used as a metaphor to express people's aspirations for new, non-hierarchical personal ties. This is happening at a time when social ties are being loosened from institutions of family and kin and being disembedded from neighbourhood or traditional communities. As Gerard Delanty (2003: 144–5) states:

> Friendship may thus be seen as a flexible and deterritorial kind of community that can be mobilised easily depending on circumstances, and can exist on 'thick' as well as 'thin' levels, for friendship comes in many forms. Cutting across the private and public spheres and with its emphasis on choice, it also has the features of postmodern community.

Whether we are living in an age of postmodernity or a period of transition, of late moderntity, is a question still being disputed. Modernity represents a period from the eighteenth-century Enlightenment during which attempts were made to enforce rational order on the natural and social world, characterised by rationalism, humanism, liberalism, socialism, feminism, civilisation and progress. Postmodernity, from the late twentieth century, represents a loss of confidence in universal truth and progress (Lyotard, 1984), the erosion of tradition and social hierarchy, the collapse of distinctions between high and low culture and the dominance of social relations characterised by social fragmentation, instability and discontinuity (Harvey, 1990).

The nineteenth- and twentieth-century Western construction of 'imagined communities'[4] – and their imagined disintegration – has been a central preoccupation during the advent of late modernity and the rise of a postmodern consciousness. However, accounts of these social changes differ in terms of the effects of new social values and ideals on social consciousness. For example, David Harvey (1990) interprets postmodernism as a condition that encourages polarisation and homelessness and undermines highly cherished values. Conversely, Zygmund Bauman (1992) asserts that postmodernity discards the delusions of modernity, leading to a more tolerant and multifaceted society. The postmodern condition delivers new principles in daily life of ethical directness, tolerance and responsibility. Rather than approaching postmodernity as a social condition sharply demarcated from modernity, Bauman (1993) approaches it as a mature phase of modernity in which modernity's discourse of rationality is viewed as obsolete. The historical inevitability and moral absolutism of modern thought, which conveys authoritarianism, is now being replaced by a form of contingency which can deliver new standards of emancipation, tolerance and empowerment. Thus, traditional power relations are replaced by contingent ones. Part of the search for intrinsically non-hierarchical relationships is the intensified mistrust of all forms of authority: from teachers, to politicians, to the monarchy.

This phase and set of ideas contains positive elements of change, signalling a withering away of the kinds of surveillance and control that traditional 'community' activated. It is a change in social consciousness that coincides with the rise of new social networks in which identities are reconfigured by transformations in spatial arrangements and modes of communication. This postmodern era is characterised by a retreat of modernist ideas about social and personal relationships and the rise of a reflexive, chosen community (Lasch, 1994). Since friendship is privileged within debates about the postmodern condition, features of postmodernity that pertain to changing social and personal relationships associated with Internet, mobile phone and e-mail communication are addressed in this book. The approach is to use friendship conceptually, as a device for tracing the recent history of ideas about changing personal and social ties and for exploring emergent perspectives about modes of association and belonging. I argue that a new approach to belonging, community and social ties is needed in order to take account of new communities and forms of belonging. I also provide a cultural analysis of relevant popular media texts to illustrate some of the ways in which ideas about changing identities are being mediated through popular culture. Teenage magazines, advice manuals and the television show *Sex and the City* are examined in order to offer a rich range of examples of public responses to new identities associated with new social ties.

Outline of the book

The book is divided broadly into three sections. In the first section, Chapters 1 and 2 trace the history of ideas, both distant and recent, that resonate today by influencing or illuminating contemporary notions of friendship, community and network society. The second part, Chapters 3 and 4, examines ways in which gendered power relations and gendered identities are shaped by friendship and, importantly, how friendship is shaped and regulated by gender identities. The third section, Chapters 5 to 8, begins by critiquing the contemporary thesis of 'community decline' and identifies new communities of belonging. Chapter 6 then summarises ideas about the 'network society', and Chapter 7 provides examples of network sociality and a range of changing intimate relationships brought about by the use of the Internet, including Internet dating, virtual diasporic communities, communities of care, and other computer networks. Contemporary ideas and academic debates about changing informal ties are explored by using empirical sources ranging from statistical data to sociological research findings to identify trends and tendencies.

Chapter 1 considers historical ideas, concepts and debates about friendship, community and society from Aristotle, Scottish philosophy and classical sociology. The historical foundations of the 'decline of community' thesis and the roots of both individualisation and the modern concept of friendship are addressed. Nineteenth-century debates in classical sociology about the decline of community are then described for an understanding of the rise of the individual-centred society and the emphasis on the 'personal'. In this way, the backdrop to the current emphasis on the self and intimacy is detailed. Early twentieth-century sociological studies of personal relationships are then mapped out to show how the loss of 'community' was being both mourned and searched for in a series of community studies. By the late twentieth century, friendship was reinterpreted as a private and individual concern. Historical sources are, then, drawn on to contextualise and provide an understanding of current ideas and trends.

Chapter 2 traces changes in ideas about the self and personal relationships. It examines the contemporary, ideal 'pure relationship' proposed by Anthony Giddens (1992). The concept of the 'pure relationship' is critiqued by pointing to the lack of evidence to support this move to equality in relationships. Following Jamieson (1999), I point out the disjunction between ideas about 'pure relationship' and actual experiences of intimacy. However, I argue that the importance of the concept of the 'pure relationship' lies in the fact that it constitutes a deep *aspiration*: a desire and impulse for friendship, equality and mutual trust in sexual relationships. Uncertainties about commitment, trust and caring brought about by the transient nature of contemporary relationships are examined here. The example of 'family as friends' is explored as another example of this democratising impulse. I critique the way that *caring* has been masked within the individualisation thesis, thus concealing the gendered relations of power involved in caring for others. The unequal distribution of the responsibilities of caring between men and women remains unscrutinised, thereby confirming the subordination of women's status by the association of femininity with nurturing. Women are therefore being reproached for demanding equality in relationships, for renouncing responsibilities that they wish to be shared equally with men.

The second section of the book looks at the articulation of friendship through gender difference and, in turn, how gender differences are organised and shaped through informal relationships such as friendship. Chapter 3 charts the ways in which male solidarity in the public sphere reproduces patriarchy. Information in this area is still surprisingly limited, but the studies outlined here provide clues about how friendship networks influence the flow of information among male elites. The chapter looks at ways in which informal male networks such as politics, all-male fraternities and clubs, sports teams and peer groups in schools are used by men and boys as an expression of hegemonic masculinity and a resource to gain power in the context of politics, employment, education and leisure. Secret and male-only societies such as the Free Masons and London Clubs are examined in this context alongside other examples including the peer regulation of heterosexual masculinities in schools. Men's and women's informal ties differ in terms of the extent to which male friendship is used to gain access to power. I argue that all-male or male-dominated associations reproduce hegemonic masculinities and that they are necessarily 'collusive' by bonding against women.

Chapter 4 describes how women's same-sex friendship networks are used as a vital *resource*, but rarely as a pathway to *power* in the same way as men. It explains how female bonding is marked out and circumscribed by the idea of the feminine 'caring self'. The idealisation of female friendship as intimacy and selfless caring has, however, been questioned within feminism (Jamieson 1999). The gendered nature of the constituents of 'intimacy', 'self-disclosure' and the 'project of the self' that comprise the subject within the individualisation thesis are not acknowledged by Giddens. Thus, the link between intimacy and caring that signifies femininity is ignored, implying that equality and choice in the 'pure relationship' is a *self-interested* rather than *selfless* project.

Women's use of friendship is not only identified as a crucial support network for the care of dependents, with no equivalent informal network available to them in the public sphere. Importantly, it is also approached as a desire for freedom as expressed in single-sex groups in the context of urban leisure. But the fact that the bid for female autonomy is often articulated *through* friendship has prompted a denunciation of women's group friendships in the news and popular media. A seemingly rootless, nomadic quality to young women's lifestyles is threatening to wider society and deemed irresponsible, especially when conveyed in the image of noisy, drunken groups of young women spilling out on urban streets at night. Taking 'time out' is still regarded as the preserve of men. I argue that public criticisms of group female friendships are linked to the public fear that young, single women's independent lifestyles threaten their destinies as wives and carers. Going a step further, the notion of the 'female crowd' is examined as an uncertain yet ominous emergent category that raises questions about the gendered nature of fluid, postmodern 'elective' associations and 'liminal' communities.

In the third section of the book, Chapter 5 begins by assessing debates about the breakdown of community by examining the example of Robert Putnam's thesis of social decline. Putnam (2000) argues that the decline of social capital and civic engagement in the United States has led to a prominent weakening of social bonds. The United States, he claims, is rapidly becoming a nation of strangers. I question this approach by addressing the weakness in the concept of social capital and the culture-bound and class-bound nature of the idea of community participation and decline. I suggest that changes in people's social relationships are leading not to social disengagement, but to new forms of social connection based on movements such as political protest (for example, Greenpeace and Amnesty International), and new modes of networking based on information technology. The chapter describes new forms of belonging ignored by Putnam's thesis based on project identities among oppressed or marginalised groups such as members of the gay, lesbian, bisexual and transsexual groups. 'Queer communities', 'families of choice' and 'non-standard intimacies' exemplify the more fluid and transient forms of multiple belongings that characterise the postsocial relations of postmodern society. I examine the importance of informal networks and the building of new communities for people who have 'come out' and may have been ostracised by their families. Queer communities offer a safe place where people can explore non-normative identities. Queer identities are being narrativised and re/mediated in Internet communities and through the queering of subcultural public spaces (Bryson, 2004; Binnie and Skeggs, 2004).

Theories of social decline also tend to overlook the significance of long-distance communication as a major type of social interaction in contemporary societies because social interaction is defined narrowly in terms of direct, face-to-face interaction and locality. Thus, in Chapters 6 and 7, I look at the implications of the 'disembedding' of personal bonds in the context of computer-mediated intimacy and 'community'. Experts on city life have suggested that *networks* are replacing traditional neighbourhoods and communities as a feature of today's urban environments (Castells, 1996–98). Life is being resocialised by interactive communication technology, from the Internet to the mobile phone. Chapter 6 deals with the concept of the 'network sociality'. It explains Castell's thesis of the rise of a network society based on information technology. New notions of postsocial community are identified, based on emergent information flows, new approaches to work and new uses of the Internet. The idea of 'networked individualism' (Wellman, Quan Haase, Witte and Hampton, 2001) is addressed by showing how the Internet enhances existing personal ties and offers new forms of social engagement. The chapter describes ways in which the Internet is creating 'virtual communities' and sustaining trans-territorial diasporic networks. Tribal groups, ethnic minorities and ethnonational diasporas are being connected through new information communication technology. In this way, indigenous groups such as the Australian Aborigines are able to create 'virtual nations', to preserve their cultural heritage, and link with Native American tribes in the United States and Canada. In this way, 'network' has the potential to be empowering.

Chapter 7 examines intimacy on the Internet by charting some of the key ways that people are interacting in virtual space. It looks at chatrooms, and computer-dating agencies to identify the characteristics of computer-mediated romance, friendships and forms of social support. It addresses Castell's idea of 'real virtuality' by citing ethically dubious examples of computer games conceived from real footage of war. Mobile phone use among the young is also explored in order to identify new modes of social interaction, and the associated fears parents have in children's use of these new forms of interactive technology. Texting, the sharing of mobile phones and the exchange of credit to pay for charges are now key features of ritual gift giving that has become a tacit part of the establishment of friendship. Chapter 7 shows that frequency of face-to-face contact is no longer the dominant mode of communicating in the age of the Internet.

Internet, e-mail and mobile phones are aspects of communication technology transforming private life by resocialising it. Postsocial relations are a feature of postmodern life. However, we need to be cautious about the implications of some of these shifts in social and personal relationship. If new communication technologies are providing a new form of 'networked individualism' as a characteristic of postsocial relations in the age of the Internet, then where does it leave trust, commitment and care? The final chapter draws attention to ethical issues by exploring some of the problems thrown up by the apparent freedom and choice offered by postmodern relationships. The apparent growth in self-interested values and lack of trust signals a potential crisis of morality in Western society. The chapter looks at ways in which 'trust' is being defined and how governments are using a discourse of trust as a form of regulation by appealing to ethical issues such as social capital, health and wellbeing to signify 'good government' and combat the growing distrust in authority.

Jacque Derrida's (1997a, 1997b) work on friendship, democracy and social justice is looked at in order to explore ways of transcending the individualised and depoliticised nature of friendship. Derrida allows us to consider the possibility of relocating friendship back into the public sphere by developing the theme of unconditional hospitality and respect for the Other. Here, friendship is used as a metaphor in the search for a new ethical politics and recovery of a new kind of collective sentiment. Finally, feminist ideas about the ethics of care are then addressed in order to place responsibility for the Other at the centre of debates about new social ties.

1
Changing Ideas about Social Ties

This chapter charts the origins of the deployment of friendship in social thought as a symbol of equality in modern intimate relationships. The sense of equal partnership and of mutual regard was being invoked at a stage when friendship was being centrally idealised in an Aristotelian fashion. Importantly, through a rhetoric of equality, the concept of friendship served to conceal traditional hierarchies. This modernising, egalitarian notion of friendship depends on a society in which the central unit is no longer the community, but the individual self. This chapter therefore explores ideas about changing social ties by considering the roots of modern social thought that explained a shift from community to individual values. It looks at the tensions that emerged between views of society and the self: ideas that distinguished between a benevolent, utopian 'community' and a suspect, self-interested 'individuality'.

Current debates about the retreat from 'community' to individual self autonomy are anchored in nineteenth-century thinking. But we need to go back further than this period. The rise of the rational and conscious individual subject, which lies at the heart of the modern concept of the self is a perspective inherited from an earlier era: the philosophy of the Enlightenment of late seventeenth- and eighteenth-century Europe and North America. Friendship was a central theme of this classical philosophy, and it was during this period that Aristotelian ideas about amity were recovered by prominent moral philosophers such as Adam Smith who conceived of intimate friendship as a *modern* relationship emerging out of commercial society. Ties of friendship distinguished modern commercial society from earlier, rural associations. Intriguingly, eighteenth-century moral philosophy drew on Aristotle to place emphasis on *ideals* of friendship freed from the constraints of market exchange. By contrast, the nineteenth- and early twentieth-century social thinkers concentrated on uncovering the *structural* changes in societies which, in turn, had profound implications for social and personal relationships (Pahl, 2000).

A striking legacy of classical social thought is highlighted in this chapter: the idea that the 'progress' of modern societies provokes the erosion of traditional, kinship-based, local communities. Changes in social thinking coincided with a shift of focus to profound structural changes: of industrialisation, urbanisation, social mobility and migration. These ideas undermined the notion of the fixed and rooted nature of individuals. While traditional communities and customs were said by social scientists to be undermined during industrialisation, large-scale social organisations such as the state attracted and expanded meanings of progress and individual identity through ideas of nationhood as a key way of connecting individuals, through a sense of belonging, to an imaginary community (Anderson, 1991). Today, democracy is founded on the notion of the civic rights of the self-determining individual. This 'individualised self' was anchored less and less in a traditional community, while intimate relationships came to take on increasing significance as a key feature of modernity. Chapter 2 therefore follows this thread by examining the shift of emphasis in social theory to *intimate relationships* as a key feature of self-identity in late modernity, and the role played by ideas about friendship in this transformation. The economic, cultural and political destabilisation of traditional community values coincide with the ascendancy of intimacy, privacy and the project of the self.

This chapter shows how the nineteenth-century mourning of the decline of community, with the rise of the privatised nuclear family and more impersonal public relationships, stimulated a nostalgic search for community in early twentieth-century sociological empirical studies. The capitalistic demand for a lean, mobile workforce was inconsistent with the idea of traditional cohesion of community composed of close neighbourly ties. A mobile, private nuclear family was foregrounded by functionalist sociology in the early twentieth century, prompting a focus on sexual relationships and the intimate relationships between parents and children. At the same time, friendship was freed from family ties during this period to serve diverse and multiple goals, ranging from instrumental, to emotional, to altruistic. Both the eighteenth-century idea of friendship as *freed* from commercial concerns and the nineteenth century idea of friendship as *market-like* and *individualised* coexist today. We find, however, that they operate in distinctive contexts, and this is brought into sharp relief when examining gender differences in meanings and values about personal relationship in Chapters 3 and 4. This chapter chronicles, then, how friendship came to function as a modernising dynamic in a rapidly changing society.

The Aristotelian legacy

The concept of friendship developed by Greek philosopher, Aristotle (384–322 BC) has made an enduring impression on ethical codes governing the intersection of the social and the personal, lasting to the present day. He inspired Enlightenment approaches to friendship of the late seventeenth to eighteenth century in Europe and North America within inquiries about personal morality, decency, virtue, loyalty and trust.[1] These are all values intensely sought after and fiercely contested in today's rapidly changing world, both at a personal and global level. Aristotle identifies three kinds of friendship among propertied adult males in Athens: the first is based on utility, the second on pleasure and the third on civic virtue or welfare. The first two kinds of friendship, utility and pleasure, are transitory because they rely on a shared activity, whether it is work or leisure. The third type of friendship, civic virtue, is the kind that lasts. It allows the individual to reach a higher ideal than the self by devoting energies to improving society. This third definition is the one that endures. Aristotle focuses not only on the public sphere but also on the personal, on the self. Elevating friendship to an ideal, Aristotle (1955) defined the friend as 'another self', thereby placing this bond at the core of a person's identity. Aristotle continues to influence our ideas about male friendship as chivalrous, heroic and public. As such, his approach is remarkably contemporary and pertinent. By examining the connection between the political and the personal, he highlights the affiliation between personal bonds and civic duty.

By placing this relationship in the public sphere of civic duty, Aristotle's definition of friendship played an organising role within conceptualisations of justice and democracy in political theory. Friendship functioned as a moral force. This bond contained a virtuous quality, existing between 'men of good character' who share mutual goodwill. It was a relationship transcending obligation to be defined as a voluntary commitment. The pursuit of well-being and the quest for justice are not dislocated from one another, but rather become an extension of one another through the moral virtue of friendship. So Aristotle idealised friendship as a relationship that formed the foundation of harmony and consensus within politics. Regarding politics as the business of friends, Aristotle identified the Greek polis of Athenian democracy as an arena of like-minded men allied in citizenship by the ties of friendship. This politics evoked two concepts that are highly regarded today: equality of rights and intimacy. Accordingly, Aristotle's concept of friendship is central to the idealisation of citizens as friends and of the friend as a moral guide.

However, it is model of friendship that excludes women as friends of men or each other. The friendship ideal therefore reinforced a *gendered* notion of self-identity, sanctioning the idea of the autonomous individual male. This idea of the autonomous self is pertinent today as a taken-for-granted, established mode of masculine subjectivity (see Chapter 3). The eighteenth-century Enlightenment concept of the self was essentially a masculine idea involving a privileged individualism. Although the idealisation of friendship in classical thinking defines it as a moral code centred within politics, it dehistorisises friendship into an absolute and abstract concept of male agency, bound up with civic duty and rights in a public and political context. It authenticates male subjectivity and action by excluding women, not only rendering friendship between women an impossibility, as Sandra Lynch (2002: 101) argues, but also marginalising women's caring role in the private sphere of domesticity.

The friend has become an impossible ideal in traditional philosophical literature: a reflection of oneself. This ideal 'other self' is unthreatening, unchallenging and never a genuine other because it fails to take account of difference. It is such a fluid concept that it lends itself, at one and the same time, to an exalted like-mindedness and can operate as a reflection of one's own narcissism (Lynch, 2002: 101). Friendship's capacity to ignore *difference* allows a utopian ideal to be invoked: friends and citizens connote *equality*. Recognising its deeply narcissistic potential, Derrida (1997a) asks whether this traditional, idealised conception of friendship is really about 'believing in ourselves'. However, within discussions of morality the individual is held responsible for his or her actions. And this is reflected in current law by the holding of individuals to account. These ideas resonate within modern thought, as indicated in the enunciation of friendship in modern social thought and social practices.

Scottish moral philosophy and new codes of liberal and fraternal values

So how did scholars in the eighteenth and nineteenth centuries, whose ideas act as a backdrop to debates today, interpret the changing social and personal ties that coincided with industrialisation, urbanisation and migration? The influential Scottish moral philosophers of the eighteenth century regarded intimate friendship as a *modern* kind of relationship growing out of commercial society. Adam Smith (1759) maintained that before impersonal markets developed, all friendships tended to be based on necessity. Only in a market economy can friendship be truly valued since before this period it was inevitably tangled up with financial and welfare needs. The market that characterises industrial society frees human relations from financial objectives by separating instrumental, self-interested relationships from 'sympathetic' relationships. The ideological splitting of the public and private spheres, which became entrenched by the nineteenth century, was being augmented during this period, with the public sphere of politics and business confined to men and the domestic sphere to women. The separation of the commercial world from personal life allowed male friendship to be structured by compassion and affection rather than rational, instrumental factors. A growing ideological and physical segregation of commercial and personal life persuaded scholars to argue that commercial society liberates personal relations from the market. Impersonal markets were said to co-exist with a separate system of personal relationships based on personal affection rather than exchange or utility.

Adam Smith was influential in developing exchange theory and the idea that a market-driven view of society shaped other, non-economic aspects of life. Yet he claimed that personal relationships lie outside this commercial realm. He rejected an economistic fit between market exchange and personal relations because he believed that personal relations are difficult to define. Exchange theory for markets was not transferable to personal relationships (Silver, 1989, 1990). Commercial society was conceived as a set of economic relations that freed up rather than discouraging personal relations because such relations rested outside instrumental and calculative orientations. The possibility of acting altruistically, without self-interest invokes, for Adam Smith, a form of moral integration and tolerance of others outside of the calculations of the world of commerce. Thus, mafia-style kinship alliances, once prominent as a way of defending market transactions through the policing of blood ties, gradually declined to become a residual style of commercial negotiation.

The emergence of a new commercial society coincided, then, with a new moral approach that echoed Aristotle by emphasising benevolent social bonds framed within a new moral code of liberal and fraternal values. During this era, the idea of friendship is based on sympathy rather than necessity, in a new universalism that characterises civil society. Adam Smith (1759) believed that the strengthening of friendship ties was provoked by the economic need for social mobility in a commercial society. Importantly, however, he also argued that this leads at the same time to a fading of family ties, of loyalties and alliances formed by blood relationships and characterised by hierarchies. He claimed that the friendship-style relationships of extended family bonds are gradually weakened and, indeed, replaced by bonds of friendship. This argument is intriguing precisely because this trend is identifiable in a contemporary social context as part of a postmodern sociality, as addressed in later chapters.

As friends were increasingly perceived to be more benevolent with the increase of migration in the eighteenth century, strangers were now approached as more neutral rather than as a potential enemy. Importantly, in his valuable analysis of the Scottish philosophers of the eighteenth century, Allan Silver (1989, 1990) argues that the Scottish moral philosophers actually had a better grasp of the changes in the character and value of friendship associated with the rise of 'commercial society' than later classical nineteenth-century thinkers such as Marx and Tonnies. When compared to previous centuries where patronage and family connections functioned as hierarchical associations to secure loyalty and protection, friendships could now, in principle, be placed on an equal footing of mutual aid between 'men of good character' within networks that stretched beyond family relations. Fraternal bonds between like-minded men, exemplified more recently by the Free Masons and London Clubs as discussed in Chapter 3, were being recognised as a feature of modern industrial society. As far back as the late eighteenth century, philosophers such as Francis Hutcheson (1755) were remarking that conjugal relationships should mimic friendship as constant reciprocal relationships.

Importantly, a key theme of this book, that friendship is deployed as a key symbol of progress towards non-hierarchical relationships, originates during this period. Friendship begins to invoke equal partnership and mutual regard as an Aristotelian ideal that extends to apply to the private sphere of conjugal intimacy as well as the public sphere of politics between men. Crucially, this deployment of friendship as equality hides traditional gender, class and racial hierarchies. Thus, the extension of the idea of friendship as a model for relationships between spouses was underpinned, and therefore undermined, by the patriarchal assumption that women would defer to men in practice. The following chapters explore this theme further in the contemporary gendered context of shifting ideas about love, intimacy and self-identity before examining new modes of sociality being formed through new information technologies.

Nineteenth-century tensions
between community and individuality

Instead of focusing on patterns of relationship that constitute friendship and their impact on social cohesion and community, classical sociology's project of comprehending human relationships in the nineteenth century centred on wider social institutions that shaped or related to work and family. Although intimacy began to emerge as a detectable feature of a true relationship through the work of Simmel, informal and non-familial personal relationships were, by and large, ignored by the discipline. This impeded knowledge about friendship and about unconventional relationships that blurred the sexual/love and work/care boundaries (see Budgeon and Roseneil, 2002).

Nineteenth-century intellectual founders of the sociological tradition, including Tonnies, Marx, Durkheim, Weber and Simmel, presented the broad thesis that modernity brings with it an accelerated depersonalisation of social relationships. A key theme of much sociological work of this period was the collapse of traditional community-based relationships in industrial society and the rise of anonymous, self-interested and fragmented individuals in urban cultures that no longer represent the spirit of collective life. For example, the recovery of traditional ties could only be confronted nostalgically for Tonnies ([1887]1974). Traditional, rural, community-orientated society was being replaced by a form of anonymous, capitalist, and competitive individualism. A sense of unity, of belonging to the people of a particular locality united by ties of neighbourliness and kinship, was viewed as an experience of a homogenous premodern society, incompatible with complex modern society. Thus, the 'death of community thesis' augments a new 'self', a self-centred individual, with particular implications for changing modes of friendship and intimate, personal relationships. Despite dissenting voices, the pessimistic sense of social decline invoked in these interpretations of change fed into the 1950s and 1960s notions of 'modernity destroys community'.

Writing at the turn of the last century, Georg Simmel ([1905]1950a and b) reiterated the theme of human alienation in urban settings in his essays on the modern metropolis. He held that life is becoming increasingly impersonal in modern society, claiming that social contacts are growing more inhospitable, sporadic and fleeting. Urban life and the money economy are identified as the primary symbols of such changes. He argued that people suffer from a strong sense of homelessness: the sense of continuity and stability that once defined traditional society is drained from society. Individuals feel uprooted, powerless and unable to understand or direct their lives, reinforcing a general sense of anxiety. A feeling of cynicism towards political and moral leaders becomes a strong feature of modern society, fostering a crisis of authority. People therefore tend to withdraw from active political life into the private realm, signalling the trend towards privatisation. For Simmel, the assertion made by eighteenth-century moral philosophers, that a sense of liberation and abundant options would be offered by modern society, is deceptive.

Simmel arrived at this conclusion by examining the effects on personality of personal interaction and group dynamics in modern city life. Believing that small group communities would become increasingly significant in modern society, he explored the nature of reciprocal relations, arguing that the dyad formation constitutes the ideal relationship. As soon as a third person enters the scene, the intimacy, closeness and sense of responsibility associated with the dyad is dissolved; the relationship is transformed by the formation of an anonymous, super-individual structure which appears to exist and operate on its own (Simmel, [1901–8] 1950b: 127–8). The potential anonymity associated with large group membership was a problem for Simmel because it allows individuals to relinquish responsibility (1950b: 134). He argued that the 'objective structure' that frames the social grouping in the form of the 'collectivity' or 'community', could lead individuals to pass personal responsibility over to society (1950b:133). Instead, he believed that intimacy was an important measure of a true relationship, ensuring commitment. Simmel exemplifies the tendency during this period for wider social groups of urban society to be viewed as problematic, as alien, as anonymous and impersonal.

Simmel emphasised the lack of trust in metropolitan life and the lack of safety of this society. He pointed to a commodification of relationships resonating as an urban conflict about material gain and profit. This argument contrasts sharply with Adam Smith's earlier thinking: that commercial society is liberating, that it holds important virtues allowing for a distinction between relationships of an instrumental nature and those based on sympathy and affection. For Simmel, modern society is one in which people are more manipulative in their treatment of friends. In sharp contrast to the individualism underpinning the approaches of Giddens on self reflexivity, examined in Chapter 2, Simmel argues that self-disclosure is dangerous to the rational subject. This dichotomy between self-restraint and self-disclosure impinged on ideas about friendship and love, with love perceived as reckless and friendship as rational. Thus, for Simmel, responsible intimacy excluded the notion of the emotional, self-disclosing subject. A continuing deep tension existed, then, during this period between the privileging of rationality and the privileging of free affective expression (Lupton, 1998: 83). While the modern subject was defined by rational control over emotions and the body, it was conversely also defined by a new power of self-expression involving a yielding to one's own feelings. The traces of this dichotomy or 'dualism of approaches to the emotions' remain with us today, for example, in the form of the gendered split between a masculine instrumentalism and feminine emotionalism and the contemporary resolve to construct a new kind of sensitivity between husbands/fathers and their families.[2]

A decline in social control and rise in personal freedom were anticipated by Simmel, who foresaw the increasing possibility of developing varied personal relationships. He accurately predicted that in the future, individuals would define social encounters solely as sociability, as ends in themselves. People would be more likely to describe themselves by their personal relationships rather than by their heritage or the old community traditions of class, ethnic identity and nation. He therefore represents classical thinkers' views about the breakdown of community at the same time as identifying some of the more fluid and transient forms of multiple belongings that now characterise the postsocial relations of postmodern society which are discussed in the later chapters of this book.

At the same time, Simmel prefigures concerns about the insecurities of the postmodern age, where problems of belonging are heightened (Delanty, 2003: 131). He also expresses the contemporary tension between individualism and the social good, revealing that the dramatic shift in the relationship between freedom and equality were also central themes of nineteenth-century thinking. These concerns connect with the divergent tendencies of socialism and individualism, with socialism characterised as equality without freedom, and individualism involving uniqueness, specificity and moral loneliness. With the rise of a new individualism in modern society, which Simmel identifies as 'the individualism of difference', a societal collective is implied and aimed at unifying diverse social elements. For Simmel this implied collective is based on reciprocity, a giving in return that must apply if an individual-centred society is to survive.

Significantly, both socialist and conservative rhetorics of the nineteenth century embraced the 'death of community thesis', contrasting a past golden age with a disaffected and selfish present. European sociological theories of community were characterised, then, by a romantic anti-modernist discourse of community as something lost and irretrievable (Delanty, 2003). Yet in nineteenth-century North American political philosophy, the work of De Tocqueville (1969) provided a discourse of community as a condition that *could* be revived. In *Democracy in America*,[3] Tocqueville endeavoured to recover tradition and the organic unity of state and civil society. His work forms part of political philosophy which deploys the concept of community as a normative theory. For Tocqueville, the state and civil society are interchangeable. The state is a political embodiment of the nation that expresses a cultural or civic community, shaped by common language, customs and history. De Tocqueville considered Americans' enthusiasm for forming and joining associations to be the most distinguishing feature of society in his time. His approach connects with communitarianism which defines citizenship as participation in the community, measured by allegiance, solidarity and commitment. This discourse, which has inspired modern republicanism in the United States, focuses on the civic foundations of the polity but shares with classical sociology the concern with belonging. Comprising a normative theory of political community, the thesis embodies the communitarian ideal of bringing together a traditional conception of community and the conditions of modernity. Thus, for example, nationalism attempts to combine political unity with a nostalgic vision of a past cultural community.

Tocqueville's approach is deployed by writers such as Robert Putnam (1993b, 2000), who forms part of the civic republican tradition which is based on a mode of civic communitarianism. Putnam's thesis about the popular participation of citizenship in the United States today, which is addressed in Chapter 5, forms a neo-Tocquevillean perspective about the decline of community values and civic engagement. Putnam defines civic engagement in terms of 'social capital', calling for social responsibility to be taken up not by the state but by civil society. Thus, it is not the state that makes civil society flourish, but the civil society that produces better public institutions. Carrying a nostalgic view of community in postwar America, Putnam claims that contemporary American society is characterised by a decline of social capital: by apathy, self-interest and a lack of connection with public life.

A stress on the negative consequences of capitalist industrialisation revealed, then, a crisis of morality, communal care and solidarity within both classical sociology and political philosophy of the nineteenth and early twentieth centuries. Notwithstanding particular distinctions between different social thinkers, this broad standpoint impacts on social theory today. While modernity delivered contradictory forces of standardisation and diversity, centralisation and decentralisation, the accounts of modernity highlighted the atomised existence of the individual.

As Knorr-Cetina (2001) puts it, this individual is free yet hedonistic, active yet also disintegrated, divided yet passive. The rise of an individual-centred society means that individuals' experiences are now at the hub of the analysis of social and personal relationships. Yet the kinds of traditional community that nineteenth-century scholars yearned to recover were based mainly on obligatory ties that individuals were born into. The legacy of nineteenth-century thinking was the use of 'community' as a slogan that held together the myths and illusions of the day (Delanty, 2003). This crisis of community remains with us today in a new context of globalisation exemplified by the regional and transnational movement of people, goods and knowledges, and the rise of new modes of communication served by information communication technology. The question is whether the term 'friendship', signifying the desire for equality and flexibility in new social relationships, is being deployed in a postmodern context to transcend and deal with this sense of communal loss. The following chapters explore this theme.

Despite the obsession with community decline by social and political thinkers during the nineteenth century, the significance of Simmel's work is that he emphasised the importance of *small groups* within the processes of urbanisation. These small networks show the potential of cities to become the setting for new kinds of group affiliations embodying new encounters and experiences. Indeed, for Simmel (1955), conflict could become a stronger basis for the formation of identities among distinct group associations and social networks than just shared common values. Thus, the idea of the rise of urban *unity* as something obtainable by adapting to *diversity*, through a mix of discrete networks, was seen as something achievable. Robert Park (1952) and other members of the Chicago School viewed the city as capable of embracing diversity and leading to a flourishing multicultural space. Today, cities are celebrated as spaces of multiple 'scenes' and communities by sexually and ethnically diverse groupings (see Chapters 5 and 6).

Twentieth-century community, family and friendship

The search for community among neighbours

During the early twentieth century, there was no sociological research tradition in Western society of empirically studying the role of friendship in reproducing or contesting the class structure or the institution of marriage. Census surveys of the period typically excluded friendship. By the late twentieth century, a small number of significant studies were exploring the way that friendship maintains class position and marital status (Allan, 1979, 1989; Willmott, 1987). The classic community studies of the early twentieth century identified a pattern of privatisation. They also concluded that friends do not play an important role in community life. In a 1920s American empirical study called *Middletown* by Robert and Helen Lynd (1929), a number of families admitted they did not have friends in their neighbourhood, suggesting a lack of trust, a lack of interaction with neighbours, and an emphasis on interaction with relatives. The introduction of car use meant that people no longer had to live in the town centre to keep in touch with friends. Families and their individual members could scatter in various directions to take part in various leisure pursuits away from home and maintain long-distance friendships. As a consequence, many people saw little of their neighbours and no longer called on them as a source of friendship and social support.

Privatisation was described as a trend led by the middle classes and perceived to be spreading to the working classes. It was assumed that people were hesitant about being friendly with neighbours for fear of being dependent on one another. The Lynds's observations that neighbours no longer knew each other, and that they spent time visiting friends that lived elsewhere, fuelled the nineteenth-century mourning of a loss of community. This finding led sociologists to debate about the growth of a form of possessive individualism prompted by geographical and social mobility, and associated with social isolation. Yet, closer inspection revealed that 'community' was being defined in this study in a very narrow way, as 'local neighbourhood', favouring *physical proximity* over all other forms of contact. Physical presence was considered paramount in defining the intensity of a relationship.

Research during the early twentieth century consolidated the idea, then, that friendships were more likely to flourish if people lived close to one another, given the costs of long-distance contact (for example, Festinger, Schacter and Back, 1950). This research attention to *local* relationships led to the neglect of long-distance relationships (Adams, 1998). It reflected the sociological tradition of conceiving the individual as *embedded* in society through primary groups of family, neighbours and workmates that privileged proximity and face-to-face interaction. Within forms of social interaction, visual cues and non-verbal face-to-face communication were seen as vital. This made it all the more difficult for later writers to assert that modes of social interaction involving transport, telephone, e-mail and other computer-mediated modes of communication could be accurately conceived as genuine modes of social integration.

David Riesman, Denney and Glazer's (1951) *The Lonely Crowd* is an example of a cluster of sociological writings in the North American context that continued to interpret social change negatively. North American suburbia was identified by the sharp segregation of gender roles. An emphasis on male careerism and female home-making in 1950s suburbia was said to lead to a masculinisation of cities and feminisation of suburbs. In contrast to the *Middletown* study, however, *The Lonely Crowd* research lamented the expendability of kinship relations as a feature of social and geographical mobility prompted by the search for material gain and pursuit of success. Riesman and colleagues believed that people were unwilling to get absorbed into a community since it would be more difficult to tear themselves away when they would have to move on to follow job opportunities. This sustained the nostalgic sense of community deprivation.

The mobile nuclear family

The growing emphasis on intimacy, privacy and equality as a crucial way of defining the 'modern family' can be traced back to the 1940s and 1950s. Contrasting with the pessimistic tone of the search-for-community studies of the early twentieth century was Talcott Parson's (1949, 1951, 1966) American functionalist theory which was influential in repositioning the nuclear family at the centre of the social order. The idea of a small, agile, modern family form contrasted sharply with that of a past, multi-functional, extended family and its attendant diverse social commitments. According to Parsons, the contemporary Western nuclearised family was the most adaptable to urban society, unencumbered by social, political, religious and educational obligations. Wider kin and friends were marginal to this emotionally self-contained unit.

The decline of extended kinship networks and the promotion of the nuclear family form by governments, academics and media meant that the household became an increasingly private and emotionally intense unit during the twentieth century. Even the custom of visiting grandparents each weekend was no longer regarded as a family obligation given that they now probably lived several kilometres away. Older men and women living alone – whether grandparents, cousins or aunts and uncles – were now regarded as peripheral. Inevitably, this led to significant problems concerning the mental and physical care of the elderly and public debates about their social marginalisation. For extended kin who were marginalised from the nuclear family, friendships could now be entered into for their own sake and judged on their own terms, at least in principle. Friends were also now peripheral to the small, nuclearised family form in which intimacy was exclusively shared between a conjugal couple and its offspring. The instrumental rationalism of the husband was said to blend with the emotionalism of a nurturing, maternal woman within a *marital relationship of friendship*: a 'companionate marriage'. Friends were seen as significant only at distinctive transitional phases of life such as when a marital partner is lost or not yet found. Parsons saw peer friendship as important mainly to young people, providing psychological support only during an intermediary period of the life cycle towards adulthood. He implied that this source of psychological support is closed down as peers get absorbed into marriage arrangements (Parsons, 1964a).

Importantly, then, friendship functioned as a model relationship and a modernising impulse to cement the relationship between husband and wife. For example, Young and Wilmott (1957: 30) refer to the husband and wife as 'partners' in a 'new kind of companionship' as a sign of the rise in the wife's status and of a growing equality between the sexes. Claims were also made that intense interaction between conjugal partners can sustain a secure sense of self by shielding them from a sense of disorder beyond the home (Berger and Kellner, 1974). This turmoil beyond the privacy of the home was seen to be prompted by the fragility of a socially constructed world. But as Jamieson (1999) highlights, the gender inequalities that structured personal life were underestimated in an effort to provide more positive accounts of family life. It was no coincidence that ideas about the need for the couple to be intimate 'friends' coincided with public debates about the breakdown of family values.

Examples of friendship-style marriages were thin on the ground. Finch and Summerfield (1991: 24) point out that the nearest to a companionate ideal was to be found in the more middle-class areas of London's East End where research on social networks was conducted, in areas like Woodford where husbands were more likely to rush home from the office to be with their wives in the evening. Research on working-class areas in the North of England such as Ashton in Yorkshire, showed that among miners' families, men and women tended to lead quite separate lives with the husband's entertainment typically being outside the home (Dennis, Henriques and Slaughter, 1956). The strong contractual basis of marriage in this example, where men's duties were to deliver the wages and women's to take responsibility for the home, suggests to Finch and Summerfield that 'companionship' was largely a middle-class attribute. Huge variations in experiences of marriage existed in this period, based not only on class differences but also differences in occupational and regional cultures and differing rates of change. The mismatch between the lived experiences of heterosexual couples with lives structured by inequality, and an ideal relationship of intimacy and equality portrayed by sociologists is repeated today, as Chapter 2 addresses.

The focus on the mobile, nuclear family and the husband–wife relationship as a form of friendship also overshadowed the role that same-sex, platonic friends played. Friends constituted a crucial form of support to otherwise isolated nuclear families by replacing traditional kinship networks with personal friendship relationships. The rise of the companionate marriage as the most crucial relationship in personal life coincided with the stigmatisation of homosexuality. Devoted, expressive, romantic friendships between heterosexual adults were sexualised while same-sex romantic friendships were pathologised (see e.g., Faderman, 1981; McIntosh, 1968; Raymond, 1991; Smith-Rosenberg, 1975; Weeks, 1981).

Notwithstanding the devaluing of friendship in the early twentieth century, the heightening of *intimacy* as a form of bonding in the family – between couples, and parents and children – may have encouraged a re-evaluation of friendship (Pahl, 2000). In a generalised sense, an emphasis on self-expression and 'disclosing intimacy' was now applicable in all familial relationships. Accordingly, friendship relationships were no longer perceived to be embedded in the wider community that was perceived to be withering away. Friendship bonds were restructured into voluntary and altruistic attachments of 'disclosing intimacy', as Ray Pahl (2000) argues in his valuable work on friendship. Yet, at the same time, the early twentieth century accent on a competitive, entrepreneurial society beyond the private nuclearised family, as perceived by Parsons, encouraged personal and social relationships to be framed within a new functional standpoint based on market rationality. Market rationality was seen as the glue that bonded societies together.

As an example of this utilitarian approach, Pahl (2000: 46) refers to Dale Carnigie's book, *How to Win Friends and Influence People*. Published in 1937, this book transparently described friendship as a device for gaining economic success. Friendship was approached both as a form of self-interest and as a form of healthy living, confirmed by Carnegie's claim that 'well-connected' people live longer. So at the same time that research in the mid-twentieth century was confirming a pattern of privatisation of social and personal relationships, friendship was being proclaimed as something good for you: as a way of advancing career and personal interests. Writers of the 1960s, such as Peter Blau (1964), echoed the instrumental approach to friendship exemplified by Carnegie. Influenced by exchange theory, friendship was seen as a relationship motivated by expectations of social rewards, encouraging people to mix with others for material gain. It spawned a set of utilitarian approaches to human relationships including impression management, which emphasised potential rewards as the incentive for attachments (Pahl, 2000: 50). These approaches reveal the dominant discourses of the period: instrumental rationalism promoted the search for material gain which was viewed as social progress. It remains a dominant thread today, now evolved into a discourse on networking, as espoused in self-help manuals such as Carole Stone's book *Networking: The Art of Making Friends* (2000).

Local working-class and cultivated middle-class friendships

During the 1950s and 1960s, when a 'social imagination'[4] was being mobilised to stress the collective basis for individuals' circumstances and dispositions, a number of studies attempted to recover the presence of communities in urban slums[5] and suburbs.[6] Yet remarkably, long-distance friendships were excluded from these kinds of studies. Instead, the focus was on the creation of new local communities (Adams, 1998: 159). Within the study of suburbs, William H. Whyte (1956) highlights the significance of nearness to local relationships. He summarises ways in which 'organisational' families are separated from their previous lives. Yet how people were sustaining relationships with friends and relatives from their previous places of residence and original communities was not examined.

By the mid-twentieth century, evidence that the importance of locality was differentiated by class was provided by the British empirical research tradition, headed by the valuable work of Graham Allan (1979, 1989, 1990, 1996). It was found that friendship arises more firmly from social context among the working class than the middle classes. Community links remained as important for working-class women as men. While men met in pubs, working men's clubs or business men's clubs for support and companionship, women typically used the privatised home as a venue for socialising, drawing on kin and neighbours living nearby for help during times of great hardship. Church attendance was declining in this period, yet religious organisations were important in helping women and children. The Mother's Union and the Girls' Friendly Society provided contexts in which women could meet other women for friendship and mutual support (Davidoff, Doolittle, Fink and Holden, 1999: 219).

Research also revealed that Britain's working class placed far more emphasis on kinship ties and had little time for recurrently cultivating new friendships (Allan, 1979). Patterns of sociability among the working class were more likely to involve close contacts with small sets of longstanding friends as well as kin. These friendships tended to be enduring, often made at school. The narrow confinement of working-class patterns of friendship to specific settings was an adaptive custom according to Allan (1979, 1990), arising out of the constraints of working-class conditions. For example, the house was not designed for non-kin visitors. Working-class families had fewer material resources to draw on, in terms of finances, transport and time. Although the pattern of close contacts among the working class may be a result of material constraints, it may also have been shaped by the values of the class and period which emphasised the importance of kin and neighbourhood ties.

By contrast, among the middle classes, a custom of cultivating friendship was identifiable by the mid-twentieth century. They were found to have twice as many organisational affiliations as the working class (Goldthorpe, 1987; Hall, 1999), and twice as likely to mix with work colleagues outside work (Hall, 1999). Although the friendships of the middle classes were more likely to be wide-ranging and diverse, Pahl (2000) argues that friendship became a source of deep anxiety among the middle classes. The category of 'unsuitable' friends arises from the utilitarian, instrumental nature of the masculine-style, fraternal strand of today's friendship. On the one hand, modern friendships often signify social demands that cannot be reciprocated. On the other, friendships are curtailed by the fear of making the wrong kinds of friends that could undermine one's potential for upward social mobility.

Aspirational friendship became an important kind of middle-class association. Although the middle-class home has typically been regarded as a setting in which to entertain friends, the pressures placed on middle-class families, especially wives, became immense. Emphasising the centrality of ritual gift-giving to middle-class friendships, the dinner party has become a vital feature of reciprocity among the middle classes in which strict, yet often unspoken rules structure contemporary modes of food offering. Television programmes and magazines offering a profusion of advice and tips on the appropriate décor, table arrangements for dinner parties and etiquette, have coached the middle classes to nurture friendships in private. Both the friends and the styles of home living are selected from a mixture of wide-ranging geographical contexts. Being cosmopolitan, nomadic and well travelled gradually became hallmarks of middle-class accomplishment as people gradually learned to flirt with the bohemian style of the upper classes through exotic foreign holidays while maintaining the security of the professional job and suburban mortgage.

The pattern of locally-based, kin-centred personal relationships among the working classes and longer distance, 'disembedded' associations among the middle classes has prompted scholars to ask whether the term 'friend' may be a middle-class concept that fits neatly into the liberal ethos of a relationship characterised as freely chosen (Allan, 1979, 1989; O'Connor, 1992; Pahl, 2000). Class differences in patterns of socialising are revisited in the context of levels of participation in voluntary organisations in Chapter 6.

Most research on the social ties of diasporic communities in mid- to late-twentieth-century Western societies has been characterised by a focus on kin relationships. Kin relations have, however, been central in shaping social ties among some ethnic minorities since they tend to have extended kin living in the same household. As Allan (1996) points out, social ties among ethnic minority communities have been responsive to social and economic conditions, as well as connected with religious and moral principles of 'family' and the ordering of relationships. Through 'sponsorship', kinship and informal ties of friendship have been vital in facilitating migration to Britain and in deciding where to live, regionally (Ballard, 1994). Kin and friendship ties have constituted a crucial source of support in environments where the host communities are hostile, and where ethnic minorities have been discriminated against. The sharing of backgrounds, religions and experiences becomes an important aspect of belonging in a racist society. Being part of tight-knit networks can often ensure the provision of moral, cultural and social support as well as economic security (Warrier, 1994).

However, importantly, kinship and friendship ties among ethnic minority communities are diverse, dynamic and changing, both by responding to the economic and social conditions in which they are located, and by producing new interpretations of traditional ways of living. Among Afro-Caribbean black communities, which are characterised by matrifocal kinship relations, friendships among women are vital as a way of organising the care of dependents and balancing paid employment and childcare (Allan, 1996). This contrasts with the social ties among South Asian communities where the husbands' kin have conventionally shaped the social networks of husbands and wives. East African Sikh settlers to the United Kingdom have tended to live in nuclear household types (Bhachu, 1985). Among second-generation ethnic minorities, new identities and new interpretations of traditional customs are emerging, supported by new modes of expression through the broadening access of information communication technology on a global scale. As described in Chapter 6, new diasporic networks are being facilitated by people who are using new communication technology to promote a new sense of community and personal identity cross-nationally.

The mid-twentieth century decline of localism

The shift from territorially bound theories of social integration that privileged physical proximity, to theories of long distance or virtual interactions is a very recent one, as Rebecca Adams (1998) points out. This is despite the fact that long-distance relationships have existed since the birth of modernity with colonialism and migrating populations. Although urban sociologists did not focus specifically on friendship, they began exploring the effects of technological shifts in transport and communications during the 1970s, providing important insights into changing community relations. Melvin Webber (1973) examined the decline of localism, asserting that cities were first formed with the sole objective of lowering the costs of communication between interdependent specialists. Advances in technology then allowed people to disperse and continue to retain intimate real-time contact with business and other relationships. Loyalty to a residential community diminished and, at the same time, communities based on beliefs and interests emerged. Thereafter, social network scholars coined the term 'personal communities' to describe the shift from neighbourhood communities to 'despatialised communities', characterised by networks that cross city and national boundaries (Craven and Wellman, 1974: 78).

Later studies in the 1980s and 1990s began mapping the characteristics of long-distance relationships maintained through the use of new communication technology: the Internet and then the mobile phone. Network analysts provided research evidence that communities were not declining, but were being freed from the spatial boundaries of neighbourhood and kinship (Fischer, 1982; Wellman, 1996). From the 1980s onwards, scholars began deliberating about whether the establishment of electronic communication was leading to social integration or isolation (see, for example, Pool, 1983). From the late twentieth century, with the help of new technology, relationships were being formed and maintained on a massive scale even between individuals who have not initially met face-to-face. These shifts are addressed in Chapters 5 to 7.

Conclusion

This chapter has examined the diffusion of the thesis of community decline by classical thinkers of the nineteenth century who distinguished a golden age of social cohesion from an alienating and self-interested present. Premodern societies tend to be viewed as harmonious and cohesive, as absent of conflict or social change, while modern societies from the industrial period onwards are characterised by power, diversity and change. This disaffected present-day was firmly set in the urban context where social change was most rapid. Thus, an in-built nostalgia influenced the very roots of classical theory's classifications of, and approaches to modernity. 'Community' became an idealisation, a symptom of a myth about the malaise of social unity that continues to influence ideas about society today (Rundell, 2001: 25).

The Aristotelian concept of friendship based on codes and cultures of honour and affection are surprisingly contemporary features whose roots nonetheless lie within the moral codes of a former era based on slavery and patriarchy. Importantly, though, the neglect of friendship in nineteenth- and twentieth-century views of changing social and personal relationships through the focus on self, family and community allowed the classical Greek concept of friendship, as honour and chivalry, to be preserved as a crucial trace within current modes of thinking about friendship. Friendship has been preserved as a spiritual ideal above a sea of instrumental rationalism. And, importantly, this idealisation of friendship has been scarcely scrutinised or challenged. It has therefore been a highly malleable concept deployed liberally to signify the assertion of individual selfhood; the desire for fluid, non-hierarchical relationships, the desire to belong, to be well connected, and to trust and be trusted. There is, then, an extraordinary mismatch in modern society between an ideal and the complex and muddled everyday reality of friendship. These desires, associated with self-reliance and personal choice, coincide with the shift from ascribed to elective relationships, leading to problems of commitment and trust in transient relationships today. This is the subject matter of the next chapter.

2
Freedom and Choice in Personal Relationships

Following accelerated social and geographical mobility in nineteenth- and twentieth-century Western societies, loosening kinship and neighbourhood ties coincided with aspirations towards a new kind of intimacy. As a result, changes in social relationships in late modernity have been characterised by two apparently contradictory trends. On the one hand, today's emphasis on love and sexual intimacy involves the privileging of intense personal, sexual bonds over other kinds of social ties. On the other hand, this intensity of personal bonds coincides with an accent on more fluid, loose, transitory relationships corresponding to a more mobile lifestyle. New forms of household arrangements, moving populations, rising divorce rates and modes of interaction mediated by new media technologies, led to the re-evaluation of the model relationship. Dilemmas thrown up by the apparent freedom and choice of personal relationships in contemporary Western society are the subject matter of this chapter. By tracing how personal bonds are being characterised in contemporary Western society, this chapter considers ways in which friendship is being exploited as a model for the majority of intimate sexual and familial relationships, both heterosexual and homosexual. It pinpoints key *aspirations* that exploit the concept of friendship in the pursuit of freedom, choice and equality in modern relationships.

From the mid-twentieth century, popular and academic discourses were advocating a form of intimacy in heterosexual relationships based on equality and trust. The 'companionate marriage' exemplifies the appeal of a sexual relationship based on friendship, as espoused in the early and mid-twentieth century by sociologists such as Young and Willmott (1957) in the UK and Parsons (1964a and b) in the United States, with the objective of bonding the conjugal partnership, as described in Chapter 1. By the 1990s, this strand of thinking was being further advanced by scholars such as Giddens (1992) and Beck (1992; Beck and Beck-Gernsheim 1996). Giddens postulated the 'pure relationship': a bond based on equality and a form of mutual self-disclosure. Attributes of friendship – expressed as companionship, equality and disclosure – came to occupy centre stage within reappraisals of sexual love. Echoing the version of friendship used by the eighteenth-century philosophers of the Scottish Enlightenment as a modern, progressive relationship, friendship is expropriated in today's Western society as a modernising factor to sanction long-term sexual relationships. Importantly, then, the ideals and values of friendship have been deployed to endorse modern sexual love.

The individual-centred society

By the mid-twentieth century, a number of sociologists were bemoaning the passing of traditional forms of social solidarity and the rise of more individualised modes of sociality characterised by corporate connectedness and networking. The individual was now viewed as an isolated unit forced to search for solace within privatised spheres of life (Berger, Berger and Kellner, 1973; MacFarlane, 1978). The time-honoured values of care and guardianship once promised by 'traditional community' were overtaken by explanations of society based on instrumental and expressive individualism. The breakdown of traditional kin and community ties provoked by industrialisation and urbanisation compelled individuals to become self-reliant, not only materially but also emotionally. In this new scenario, the centre of the universe was no longer the family and community but, rather, the individual. Traditional community was superseded by a stress on individual self-reliance and *personal* welfare, signalling new modes of personal relationships and an individual-centred imagination (Knorr-Cetina, 2001).

Late twentieth-century debates about changing forms of sociality encompassed both negative and positive elements. The modern stress on the individual self was interpreted pessimistically by Christopher Lasch (1979), who highlighted the problem of de-collectivisation as an immediate response to industrialisation and modernisation. The individual of industrialised, technological society was conceived as an uprooted, confused and amorphous self, contrasting sharply with the stability of past traditional society. In traditional communities, people grew up and died in the same place, had fixed identities, worked with the same people throughout their lives and were circumscribed by rigid social hierarchies. Lasch's (1979) pessimistic reading of individual agency is marked by anxieties about the shortcomings of the individual and the kind of society producing it. He observed the rise of narcissism, characterised by self-love and self-indulgence and expressed by an increasing reluctance of individuals to share with one another. Under these conditions, the individual becomes intensely self-absorbed and restless with no moral universe in which to anchor his or her identity. Lasch (1995) therefore made an appeal for a return to the merits of community, family and religion.

The conditions of intimacy

In contrast to Lasch, the approaches of Anthony Giddens and Ulrich Beck offer a more optimistic analysis of the shaping of the identity of the modern individual. Giddens and Beck contend that although an ideology of individualism tested the legitimacy of traditional notions of solidarity in late modernity, people's lives came to be less constrained by tradition and increasingly subject to individual choice (Giddens, 1990, 1991; Beck and Beck-Gernsheim, 1995, 1996). With urban social ties no longer bound together by tradition alone, a new form of collectivity emerged based on reciprocal individualisation, accenting self-identity and mutual relations. This process of 'individualisation' calls attention to the element of choice in social and personal relationships for Beck (1997, 1998; Beck-Gernsheim, 2002) and involves transformations in the sphere of intimacy according to Giddens (1990, 1991, 1992).

Giddens (1992) argues that intimacy is being reconfigured by a series of global shifts in late modernity involving communication, technology, relationships and identities. Globalisation transforms local and personal contexts of social experience with local actions being increasingly influenced by distant institutions and events. This set of changes coincides with the rise of more democratic forms of knowledge, prompted by the collapse of traditional forms of authority. New forms of transportation and communication of information and entertainment lead to a 'disembedding' of time and space within social practices on a global scale, according to Giddens (1990). This process of disembedding allows the removal of social relations from local contexts of interaction, such as neighbourhoods and local communities, and gives rise to new forms of sociability. Through new technologies such as broadcasting and interactive media, communities drawn from local space that once had a strong sense of identity are now saturated with information about events taking place beyond their locality. New kinds of social interaction mediated by mobile phone, e-mail and Internet, are therefore leading to new identities and virtual communities, as discussed in Chapters 5, 6 and 7. The rise of mass communications fosters increased reflexivity, allowing institutions and individuals to collect and store large amounts of information. Individuals can therefore become more self-reliant by incorporating expert systems in their lives, according to Giddens (1991).

In premodern societies, a person's identity was fixed from birth by kinship, gender, religion and social status. Today, a person's activities and actions can be facilitated and monitored by regularly accessing knowledge from sources like the Internet. As part of these changes, then, the self and self-identity are being liberated from the rules and regulations of past, traditional forms of authority such as parents, the local priest or the teacher. Today, self-identity is no longer preset, but instead perceived as a reflexive project for which the individual is responsible as the author of his or her life. It is now recognised as a process, something continually reproduced as part of an individual's reflexive actions in relation to his or her biography. A stable sense of the unified self is fostered through a feeling of biographical continuity, and is conveyed to others by maintaining a unique but evolving narrative about oneself (Giddens, 1991: 54). Life therefore constitutes a series of decisions in which we attempt to uphold a 'narrative of the self'. Choices must be continually made by the individual in order to produce a consistent self-narrative, and this consistency is anchored within intimacy. As a result, social and personal relationships become more self-governing. The erosion of traditional authority means that individuals must actively choose their sexual partners rather than rely on traditional family and community alliances.

These shifts provoke radical changes in heterosexual practices and family life. Love has become a central part of the rise of individualism and the most important way of finding meaning in life (Beck and Beck-Gernsheim, 1995). Selfishness and conceit are dangers inherent in individualisation which can be counteracted by the ideology of love and the rise of the emotional self (Lupton, 1998). The unified, rational self of modernity is challenged by the search for love: affection, sensitivity and passion. The emotional self was once regarded as an exclusively feminine condition, characterised by the aspired sensation of intimacy and delicacy of feeling. In today's expert-driven self-help literature, being in touch with one's feelings has become a positively valued form of self-fulfilment for all. Yet, paradoxically, this emphasis on love as a key to the construction of self comes at a time when love has turn out to be more fragile, more uncertain and more vulnerable to annulment. The unique emphasis on intimacy becomes increasingly attractive during an era of rising insecurity triggered by rising divorce rates. This insecurity also provokes the desire for an intensification of the bonds between parents and children, prompted by the search for a permanent bond of affection with ones' offspring, according to Beck and Beck-Gernsheim (1995).

Giddens places less emphasis on affection for ones' children, asserting the centrality of sex and romantic love to the modern intimate relationship and to self-identity. For Giddens (1992), romantic love holds a privileged position within the project of the self. This sexual bond is characterised as a 'pure relationship', exemplified by the qualities of mutual disclosure and equality. He claims that men and women are now developing relationships characterised by 'confluent love', an emotional and sexual equality linked to a 'plastic sexuality'. Sexuality is no longer bound by the needs of reproduction. This is a more responsive kind of sexuality that acts as a 'communicative code', a medium of self-realisation and an expression of intimacy (Giddens, 1991: 164). The fact that each person is equal under the law undermines the legitimacy of patriarchal relations. Gay and lesbian relationships, according to Giddens, are pioneering this new kind of 'pure relationship', by reinventing the parameters of relationships and transcending conformist patterns of heterosexual behaviour.

The shift in emphasis from social to private relations can, then, be described in terms of a set of dualisms that characterised debates about the very nature of society between the nineteenth and twenty-first centuries: an accent on 'traditional community' gives way to that of 'intimacy', and an emphasis on 'solidarity' is superseded by 'personal love' (Jamieson, 1998). However, the uncertainty generated by the weakening of traditional bonds of family and local community places an enormous burden on the individual. Intimate relations of trust take on more and more significance in recovering the sense of ontological security once provided by the extended family. According to Giddens (1992: 58), the individual forms a self-identity in the context of the pure relationship. He argues that rather than relying on external factors for its existence, this new, democratic kind of relationship is entered into voluntarily and is contingent on delivering satisfaction to both parties. It is a contract between two equal individuals which can be ended when one or both partners wish to leave. This new relationship is distinctive because it is no longer constrained by normative systems. It is, rather, safeguarded by the continuous monitoring of the intimate bond by both parties. With sex no longer yoked to marriage-like arrangements, diversity in styles of personal life can develop. Couples are able to negotiate their own rules of sexual conduct. So relationships become potentially more mutually satisfying yet also much more fragile.

The 'pure relationship' as friendship

Under the present-day conditions of choosing our own destinies, the modern attributes of friendship are introduced into sexual relationships as a crucial aspect of the management of anxiety. Trust in others and mutual disclosure becomes an important psychological condition for ontological security. While the appeal of friendship is surpassed by that of sexual love under late modernity, at the same time, sexual intimacy increasingly comes to resemble friendship. The deployment of the qualities of friendship allows Giddens's claim for a type of intimacy based on gender equality to be charged with optimism. Lovers become best friends in a reawakening of the motives of the companionate marriage: friendship becomes the model for sexual love. As part of this shift towards egalitarian relationships, a culture of emotions is underscored by mutual disclosure with a person's feelings, sentiments, affections, passions and moods exposed, inspected and pored over as indicators of a better person. Structured by the objective of 'finding oneself' through romantic relationships, sexual intimacy becomes a crucial form of self-discovery. Like friends, lovers usually require markers of intimacy such as sharing information viewed as special to the bond: sharing secrets, giving advice and so on. The stability of this new 'pure relationship' depends on this set of disclosing practices. Indeed, the telling and sharing of secrets becomes a strategy of loyalty (Pahl, 2000). In this insecure environment, friendship between lovers comes to have profound meaning as a support mechanism and nurturing system for the inner self.

Although intense intimate relationships can be non-sexual, today's preoccupation with the body and sexual pleasure is central to the construction of the self and the pure relationship, ensuring the priority given to sex within the intimate relationship. Resonating with Aristotle's perspective, friendship is now conceptualised as an ideal relationship, emphasising attributes regarded as egalitarian: respect, mutual disclosure and companionship. It is an association entered into voluntarily. Thus, late modernity brings with it a new kind of sexual bond which, drawing on the ideal of friendship, is no longer defined by 'family' ties, but entered into for its own sake in a framework of mutual benefit or well-being. It can, like friendship, be ended any time that one or both parties believe the relationship is no longer beneficial, and it is not necessarily linked to reproduction. This tradition is emulated within marriage with the loosening of past elaborate ceremonies of union between wedding couples. Today, less formal and more casual companion-like conduct predominates. Without legal supports or formal rituals to indicate whether we have been admitted to a particular plane of intimacy, confiding becomes a powerful signal to the sexual partner that the opportunity to move the relationship to a level of greater closeness is being offered (Reis and Shaver, 1988). Thus, despite the fact that few friendships necessarily involve mutual understanding and many entail unequal relations of power (Allan, 1989), the concept of friendship in the 'pure relationship' signifies the yearning for equality and choice in long-term sexual relationships.

Freedom and choice

The freedom of choice and contingencies of modern life involve an increased risk of isolation and meaninglessness (Bauman, 1996: 50f). Individuals are forced to rely on their own resources in constructing new forms of togetherness since individuals can no longer fall back on traditional collectivities to create a coherent life course and identity. While the breakdown of traditional forms of power and control are potentially liberating for Bauman, the stress on choice and agency across contemporary Western societies also entails negative effects. This is shown by the burden placed on individuals to succeed in all aspects of their lives. The idea that we have abundant freedom and opportunity to tackle almost anything confers shame on us if we fail to reach the heights we aspire to. If individuals fail in aspects of their lives, whether in education, work or love, the discourse of individualisation implies that they can only blame themselves rather than the structures of inequality operating in wider society.

Moreover, important uncertainties about how to initiate and form relationships, and about how to handle commitment and caring, are raised by Giddens's emphasis on the voluntary nature of intimacy in late modernity. 'Speed dating' may be taken as an example of the dilemmas of initiating relationships. In an age where matchmaking between families has been dismantled by the dominant ideology of individual freedom and choice in marriage and sexual partners, and where psychologists tell us we don't know how to date anymore, 'speed dating can be identified as a fun and efficient way of 'going about things'.[1] Beginning as a New York craze, speed dating entered the dating game at the turn of the millennium as a popular and fun activity for busy, professional singletons.

Featured on the American television serial, *Sex and the City* which delved into the lives of 'thirty-something' women for whom dating is a perennial issue, speed dating 'promises to help you find love – faster'.[2] Three minutes is considered long enough 'to appeal to or to alienate someone'. Its growth and popularity exemplifies not only the dilemmas of the 'cash rich and time poor' as a key feature of modern urban culture, but also the atomised nature of interaction in urban environments. It can be interpreted as a fun activity, yet also as a sign of a profoundly fragmented and superficial society, exacerbated by a 'long-hours' culture and lack of meaningful contexts for young people to meet beyond the frantic urban club scene.

Troubled by the social implications of this kind of vulgar interpretation of freedom and choice in personal relationships, scholars such as American anthropologist Walter Williams (1992: 193) ask whether people can 'live comfortably with the uncertainty of not knowing how long their partnership will last'. Williams goes on to say: 'These are questions that terrify many, and people are pulled between their desires for the adventure of love and the security of a long-term relationship.' In cultures where male–female intimacy is constrained by arranged marriages with no concept of dating, individuals are shocked by Anglophone patterns of sexual relationships, as Williams (1992: 193) points out in his discussion of traditional Javanese society. He states:

> While they admire the material wealth of the United States, Indonesians often wonder 'why Americans seem so intent on making themselves miserable'. After watching American movies together, I noticed how often they expressed puzzlement about the way Americans experience so much stress by falling in and out of love. 'Why', they asked me, 'do Americans experience such fragile personal relationships?' One Indonesian spoke for many when he told me that he had the impression that 'Americans don't seem to have a hold on anything. They don't seem committed – to their relationships, their friends, or to anything else.' It is obvious to them that Western romanticism and traditional forms of family life are not working for many Americans.

Non-emotional, arranged marriages in traditional cultures such as in Java, are sealed at wedding ceremonies where the emphasis of the event is on economic and social obligations of the couple. 'Love' or other expressions of emotion are not made. Interestingly, the lack of intimacy in Javanese arranged marriages are supplemented by same-sex friendships that meet individuals' emotional needs (Williams, 1992). Williams goes on to argue that the American nuclear family is increasingly unable to cope with the stresses of modern living. He claims that 'progressive voices' in the United States have been unable to create an ideal model of an alternative future beyond the patriarchal nuclear family.

'Re-inventing the self'

The dominant discourse of emotional self disclosure in love and marriage is, then, pleasurable yet precarious: it can instil bonding through trust yet it still involves the risk of potential rejection. A 'do-it-yourself' biography becomes, then, a risk biography, a state of permanent endangerment (Beck and Beck-Gernsheim, 1996: 25). For Giddens, the rise of systems of professional advice offered to help individuals face the 'ontological insecurities' of modern life is a key feature of post-traditional societies. Personal sexual relationships can therefore often become intensely self-centred, systematically excluding sympathy for others. However, Giddens makes selective use of psychological theory, emphasising aspects that accentuate equality and democratisation, and underplaying explanations that draw attention to the conflicts and inequalities of relationships (Jamieson, 1999).

Nevertheless, this expert-led, self-therapy explanation is a compelling aspect of Giddens's theory of reflexive modernisation, and reflected in popular discourse on self-help. While the sense of self and the regulation of personal behaviour traditionally emanated from the social institutions of the family, religion and education, today we have medical counselling, forms of personality management, and self-help books and manuals that counsel individuals on self-improvement. Evaluating and using these forms of expert knowledge apparently helps us assess our own intimate relationships, allowing individuals to act reflexively. For example, under a section on health tips in the March 2004 issue of *OK! Magazine* that reports the gossip and rumour about the lives of celebrities, a book called *Reinvent Yourself* by Fiona Harrold is advertised. The accompanying comment is:

> It's never too late to make changes to make things happen, according to life coach Fiona Harrold. In her book Reinvent Yourself (£4.99, Piatkus), she explains the seven steps that will help you achieve your life-goals. Says Fiona: 'Truly successful reinvention comes from digging deep into yourself and pulling out old beliefs and attitudes that restrict you from fulfilling your potential, and being the person you feel you genuinely are.'
>
> (*OK! Magazine*, March 2000, p. 124).

The front cover of the book shown in the column has the following caption written beneath the title: '7 STEPS TO A FRESH NEW YOU'. Confusingly, a 'new you' can be re-invented by searching for the 'genuine' you. Strip away the layers, and you find an authentic self, which is imaginary yet real, contrived yet natural. But it's nice to know that a life coach can smooth away the confusion and help us fulfil our potential. However, expert help not only comes in the form of a life coach, it also comes in the form of a whole range of beauty products to pamper the body as well as the mind. The advertisements dotted throughout the magazine emphasise expert help, indulgent care, with words like 'deepness', 'freshness', 'newness' and 'naturalness' to appeal to the readers: 'expert care' for blonde hair in the form of 'Perfect blonde'; 'indulgent care' offered by Nivea visage facial masks; 'deep' emphasised in 'Cool Water Deep' fragrance for men; 'freshness' offered by Maybelline 'EverFresh' makeup; 'newness' and 'naturalness' offered by 'colour so natural only you know it's new "nice'n easy" ' hair colour. Re-invention of the self involves revitalising or reordering the body image.

Waves of celebrities photographed throughout *OK! Magazine* instruct us on how good we can look (but also how bad we can look when caught off guard), and the kind of lifestyle we can aspire to if we take good care of ourselves. They offer us little homilies that we can learn from. Actress Zoe Lucker from British TV show, *Footballers' Wives* (ITV) offers an insight into the show's success: 'I think viewers love watching all these people who have so much money but who are desperately unhappy. It's nice to realise there's more to life than money' (p. 72). In response to the question, 'how does it feel to be touted as the next big thing?', after her meteoric rise to stardom in a string of Hollywood films, Keira Knightley remarks: 'I think it is a business that's here today, gone tomorrow. You never know what tomorrow's going to hold' (p. 42). The Ashley Pearson column that boasts delivery of 'the juiciest gossip' in Hollywood, states: 'Britney Spears is finally talking about her spur-of-the-moment marriage, and says her concert tour is helping her find herself: "This whole show is like me doing therapy in front of the whole world" ' (p. 87). The 'expert' advice is aimed at affirming individuals' right and obligation to make a strong commitment to themselves. The idea is that before you can commit to others, you must learn to love yourself by 'getting in touch' with your 'feelings'. It validates subjectivity thinking over social thinking by emphasising sociality as something that flows from, and is secondary to, self-commitment (Knorr-Cetina, 2001: 524).

Expert advice is now even packaged into holidays abroad where we can learn the skills needed to communicate effectively with ourselves and our partner. A one-week cruise on a Love Boat in the Mediterranean[3] is designed for couples who are set a series of special tasks in learning how to relate to one another. An Italian cookery course in Tuscany aimed at premarital or young marital couples apparently helps them improve their relationships by encouraging equal opportunity activities through the sharing of time together. The kitchen is transformed from a conveyor belt of food production to a relaxing and intimate space in which the couple share in the pleasures of food preparation over a glass of wine at the end of a busy day.[4] Within the new therapy literature and training, then, friendship is increasingly being called upon as a metaphor to validate sexual and kin relationships. The growth in advice from therapists, sexologists and psychologists is apparent. For Giddens, this rise in expert systems is a positive trend that strengthens a coherent, autonomous self.

A critique of the 'pure relationship'

The democratic relationship, with its accent on emotional disclosure, is an alluring idea. However, radical shifts towards equality in heterosexual relationships are yet to be substantiated. Since empirical evidence about people's personal lives is inherently difficult to gather, it is not easy to confirm or refute Giddens's generalised account about intimacy, as Lynne Jamieson (1999) points out. Drawing on the evidence that does exist though, she highlights a weakness in Giddens's argument: that there is a wide gap between cultural ideals and the structural inequalities of personal relationships not acknowledged by Giddens. Thus, the rhetoric of the 'pure relationship' colludes with the therapeutic discourse to conceal gender inequality.

Equality and the mutual exploration of each other's self-identities, as an attribute of the pure relationship, are exaggerated. Jamieson (1999) cites contrary empirical evidence about young people's sexual values and identities and their initial sexual relationships which indicate that mutual pleasure, emotional intimacy and equality do not characterise the heterosexual relationships of the young (Holland, Ramazanoglu and Sharpe, 1994, 1998). This is confirmed by research on teenage sexual morality, discussed in Chapter 3. In my own collaborative research, we found that teenage sexual identities are collectively policed through homophobic and misogynistic bullying (Chambers, Tincknell and J. Van Loon, 2004a). And research about older heterosexual couples suggests that men complain of lack of sex while women complain of lack of intimacy (Duncombe and Marsden, 1996). Research evidence also indicates that intimacy and self-disclosure can be difficult to obtain if festering discontents exist between couples about inequalities in divisions of domestic labour and childcare. Importantly, couples often use a number of strategies to conceal or overlook inequalities within domestic divisions of labour regarding child care, housework and control over money in order to protect the relationship (Brannen and Moss, 1991; Pahl, 1989). Relationships are often construed as equal by couples through drawing on the idea of corresponding responsibilities and duties such as housework being considered equivalent to a husband's income. Acts of *practical* love and care may be more important than intense mutual disclosure, according to Jamieson.

By taking for granted the positive value of self-disclosure in therapy, Giddens disregards studies that explore the negative aspects of our reliance on experts, as Jamieson (1999) points out. Feminist work on gender and power in personal relationships suggests that a therapeutic discourse produces gender stereotypes that perpetuate the systematic subordination of women, for example in the sphere of mental disorder and domestic violence (Busfield, 1996; Dobash and Dobash, 1992). For Lasch, this emphasis on the individual and self-help is precisely what leads to the narcissistic personality. He viewed the negative characteristics of this trend as symptomatic of social disintegration, arguing that 'As the world takes on a more and more menacing appearance, life becomes a never-ending search for health and well being through exercise, dieting, drugs, spiritual regimens of various kinds, psychic self-help and psychiatry' (Lasch, 1979: 140). Bauman (1990) also considers self-disclosure to be destructive of relationships, being concerned by the intensity with which we are provoked into mutual confession.

Countering Giddens's view of self-disclosure as a creative process leading to ontological security and trust in others, Foucault asserts that therapy functions as a mechanism of regulation and control. For Foucault (1977), the explosion in 'experts', who assist us in making choices and taking charge of our lives, are forms of regulation leading to self-absorption. Expert influences are concentrated on the self in order to motivate individuals to behave in socially sanctioned ways. As Nikolas Rose (1990) claims, we live under an appealing delusion that our lives are a personal matter. But our intimate feelings, desires and relationships are shaped by this new breed of 'engineers of the soul', who play a central part in the administration of individuals whether in the family, at work or in the conduct of ourselves. A range of 'technologies of subjectivity' have been developed wherein political power has come to depend on expert techniques to shape and enhance the psychological (mental and emotional) capacities of citizens. These techniques depend on day-to-day surveillance as part of the regulation of the self. By advising us on how to manage our relationships, our children and our lives, therapists and counsellors gently cajole us into new ways of feeling, thinking and performing. Our subjectivities have become the object of new forms of knowledge and the target of new forms of power (Rose, 1990). Exaggerating the extent of the manifestation of the 'pure' democratic relationship, Giddens also disregards the interconnections between public and private spheres of society. Changing patterns and expectations of marriage and partnership have shifted the emphasis from marriage as an *institution* to marriage as a *relationship*. But as David Morgan (1996) contends, the move from 'institution' to 'relationship' in the twentieth-century public story of the family is misleading. Gender inequality criss-crosses the public and private sphere: through the division of labour in the home, gender segregation in the labour market, and unequal gender distributions of wealth and income. Jamieson (1999: 482) states that: 'There is no weighing of either theoretical or empirical states of play by Giddens and the *Transformations of Intimacy* seems strangely cut off from the interrelationships of structure and action.' These concerns are revisited in Chapters 3 and 4 in relation to gender identities and differences in personal relationships.

Notwithstanding these weaknesses of empirical evidence and gender blindness in Giddens's concept of the 'pure relationship', the importance of his theory is that this kind of bond is upheld in today's Western societies as a vital aspiration, as an ideal. Given its promise of equality, it is one sought particularly by women. This aspiration is endlessly probed and pondered over in popular media discourses, exemplified by teenage and women's magazines, Hollywood romance films and situation comedies such as *Friends* and *Sex and the City* (see Chapter 4).

Family as friends?

Tensions between the desire for personal autonomy and the security of family belonging are implied by the increasing popularity of the terms 'family as friends' and 'friends as family'. A number of key trends, leading to more complex and diffuse family links, have led to the widespread linking of the word 'friends' with 'family'. In addition, the tie between parents and children is now conferred more sentiment than that between children and extended kin than in the past, offering credence to the bonds of the modern nuclearised family (Davidoff, Doolittle, Fink and Holden, 1999). Indeed, from the 1970s, efforts at making friends with children – characterised as a 'disclosing intimacy' – were part of the shift towards child-centred family households with children coming to play a fundamental role in emotional life (Beck and Beck-Gernsheim, 1995; Jamieson, 1987, 1998). Individuals are now expecting to experience friendship-like bonds with family members. At the same time, friends are gradually becoming more important to those who have low levels of contact with their family, prompted by the prevalence of divorce and separation, and the devaluation of extended kinship bonds. Significantly, empirical evidence suggests that friendship's attributes of equality and mutual disclosure serve to modernise or renovate contemporary family relationships.

So are friends becoming *more* important than family and wider kin during late modernity, or are family and friendship somehow converging, in terms of expectations and behaviour? In an important recent empirical study of family and friendship in the United Kingdom, Pahl and Spencer (2001) interviewed a wide range of individuals and families about the role of friendship in family life. They found evidence that friends are taking over some of the functions of family, with friends now more important in support networks than in the past. A blurring of the categories of family and friends is being experienced with individuals becoming more selective in choosing the kin with whom they socialise and keep obligations. Following previous studies in which choice has been identified as a crucial factor in distinguishing between family and friends (Finch and Mason, 1993), Pahl and Spencer found that friends are viewed as *chosen* while family are defined as *ascribed*. Importantly, however, a blurring of the relationships of kin and friends was also identified. This pattern was exemplified by a criss-crossing of both friendship and family roles and by the language respondents used.

'Kin' and 'friendship' were terms used interchangeably yet with differing meanings. On the one hand, when the term 'friend' was used to describe family relationships, such as a family member viewed as 'like a friend', the association was treated as something positive and valued. And likewise, when a friend was considered as kin, the comparison was positive and indicated the strength of the tie. On the other hand, when a friendship was regarded as a 'duty' then the term 'family' was introduced as a pejorative term if described as 'family-like'. The boundaries between family and friends are, then, becoming more permeable but 'friendship' is clearly being used to authenticate family relationships that are cherished, to signify the worth and appeal of the bond. Its absence signifies negative bonds bound by a sense of obligation.

Pahl and Spencer found that the use of the term 'family as friend' covered all kinds of family members except grandparents. Family members were seen as analogous with friends if the relationship was perceived as chosen rather than a duty, or if there were strong emotional bonds. Importantly, members of family were also viewed as friends if the relationship involved *disclosure*. The role of confidant is so significant that it acts as a determinant of the quality of friendliness of the relationship. Friends were regarded as 'family' if the relationships had been tested by difficulties and sustained by a joint commitment to the continuation of the friendship or if the friend had provided emotional or other support over time. Friends were also viewed as family if the pair had known each other since they were children or if the friend was considered 'one of the family' by being invited to family events.

Confiding is a form of exchange that has a high level of suffusion between family and friends, according to Pahl and Spencer. Individuals confided in family, friends and sexual partner. Parents were seldom chosen as confidants for fear of upsetting them or of being judged. This suggests that friends predominate as confidants. Regarding gender differences, it was confirmed that women tend to have more confidantes than men, and middle-class men have more confidants than working-class men. This supports earlier evidence that working-class men rely more on their wives for emotional support (Willmott, 1989; Wellman, 1992). As discussed in Chapter 3, research about male friendships implies that men tend to rely on women rather than other men for emotional support, and heterosexual men are much more dependent on their partner for such support. Importantly, Pahl and Spencer (2001) found that friendship has overtaken family for psychological affirmation because friendships are *chosen* rather than *ascribed* relationships. This endorses my interpretation of Giddens's pure relationship, that choice and equality are highly valued attributes *aspired to* in intimate relationships though not necessarily achieved. The elective nature of relationships is now increasingly being privileged over compulsory relationships.

It seems, then, that the value of friendship is being enhanced as extended kin recedes in importance and that kin relationships are only treated as equal to friendships when relatives *become friends* in a trusting and rewarding relationship. Is friendship therefore overshadowing kin as a more dominant relationship? As Jamieson (1998: 74) asks: 'are good friends all you need?' Not quite. She argues, crucially, that the historical shift from 'community' to 'intimacy' encouraged us to perceive kin and friendship as similar relationships, that kin and friends together 'are seen as potentially constitutive of a community of people bound by shared sentiments' (Jamieson, 1998: 74). She stresses the important distinction between these two kinds of relationships. Mothers' continuing dependence on their male partners during the stage that children are growing up need to be taken into consideration in accounts of changing personal relationships in families with children. And the growing emphasis on friendship in family relationships deceptively conceals power and conflict. It encourages a blurring of the distinction between structural relations of power and the subjective experiences of desires and aspirations.

By addressing subjective experiences and aspirations about familial and friendship relationships, Pahl and Spencer's findings establish that 'friend-like relationships' have come to represent the most *sought after* type of relationship (Pahl and Spencer, 1997). These friend-like relationship types function to enhance kin ties rather than replace them. Despite the fluid nature of the concept of friendship, its deployment as a metaphor for family cohesion indicates that Western societies have a strong idea of the meanings and parameters of friendship as a modern and aspired relationship.

Conclusion

During late modernity, more informal networks based on non-hierarchical relationships are being sought, offering individuals the potential to reinvent narratives of self. These new living arrangements are prompting academic speculation that individuals are becoming self-reliant and self-reflexive and that social ties are becoming more intimate, private and personal, yet fluid and transient. Emphasising the reflexive nature and active agency of individuals, Giddens (1992) identifies family and friends as sites for the democratisation of intimate relationships. He argues that modern confluent relationships now promote companionship and friendship, emphasising choice and compatibility over commitment, and leading to a critical tension between commitment and choice.

These new kinds of living arrangements and ideas of self are increasingly relying on friendship as a metaphor, as a way of moving beyond traditional nuclear family forms and exploring individual identity. We find that in this climate of change, the symbol of friendship is being exploited to proclaim the modernising features of sexual love and marriage, as a democratic relationship. The concept of friendship signifies important aspirations. The confiding nature of friendship upholds a new project of the self in an era when 'self' identity, rather than family or community identity, becomes a primary ingredient of society. Accordingly, in late modernity, the affirmative features of friendship – companionship, equality and mutual disclosure – have been reconfigured within academic and popular discourse to validate heterosexual intimacy as a crucial component of self-identity.

However, a key weakness in the idea of the 'pure relationship', and its association with friendship, is the presumption of equality. While the egalitarian attribute of friendship functions to modernise *ideas* about sexual love and wider kin relationships, the ideal of friendship veils gender inequalities in intimacy. There is plenty of evidence to support Giddens' claim for a rise in expert systems in late modernity, exemplified by the popularity of psychotherapy and self-help discourses. Yet there is scarce evidence to support the claim that the democratic 'pure relationship' has been achieved, as Jamieson (1999) points out.

Notwithstanding these flaws in the idea of the 'pure relationship', I have argued in this chapter that the use of the notion of friendship and equality in today's intimate relationships is symptomatic of important aspirations towards equality and mutual understanding, especially by women. This feminine desire for a more balanced and equal partnership with lovers and husbands is explored in Chapter 4.

3

Hegemonic Masculine
Identities and Male Bonds

The next two chapters enquire into ways that heterosexuality, gender and power are organised and articulated through friendship and wider social relations. This chapter begins by reviewing past and present debates about heterosexual male friendship. Male friendship has traditionally been articulated as a social and cultural resource through group memberships and networks. Traditional forms of male networking are explored in this chapter through the example of secret and male-only societies and clubs such as the Free Masons. Personal and formal single-sex relationships are, for men, a form of capital (Bourdieu, 1983a). I then address wider friendship bonds between men that perpetuate and cement hegemonic masculinities and examine challenges to those bonds. I argue that masculine friendship is circumscribed by discourses of fraternity and dependent on expressing difference from, and opposition to, femininity. Transformations in personal relationships that challenge or transcend heterodominant forms of bonding through gay and lesbian identities and social ties are addressed in Chapter 5, as new forms of belonging within queer communities and 'families of choice'.

By drawing attention to the complexity and contingency of gender identities and relations, I argue that gendered subjectivities are constructed through power and difference, and articulated through friendship and personal bonds. Friendship is a key social tie at the core of the management of gendered normality. But how does this work, given that neither gender nor friendship is a fixed category? Gender is so fluid and troubling that it needs to be regulated by perpetually regenerating notions of 'normal' gendered identities and practices: that is, normal femininity and normal masculinity (Butler, 1990). Friendship in Western societies is part of the social, cultural and moral regulation of gender identities, For example, as discussed in Chapter 1, friendship within classical thinking is regulated by being signified as an inherently masculine virtue: as bravery, loyalty, and civic duty.[1] Forming part of the legacy of the Old Testament and Greek philosophy, a romanticised image of male camaraderie was contingent on the claim that women were incapable of having true friendships. Following Aristotle, male friendship was located exclusively in public life from which women were banned. Masculine friendship is, then, placed in opposition to feminine ties by being idealised in terms of social worth and set apart in terms of physical space.

In these two chapters, I explore how gendered identities are managed by friendship and how friendship is managed by 'intelligible genders'. For Judith Butler (1990: 17), intelligible genders are identities that organise consistent interactions and uphold stability within sex, gender, sexual practices and aspirations. Hegemonic heterosexual masculinities are made intelligible, based on sexual and gender difference. This chapter looks at how these differences are played out through heterosexual, single-sex personal associations and friendships. These male-only associations privilege and validate heterosexual masculinity as a range of identities defined in relation and opposition to Others which include femininity, gay and non-hegemonic masculine identities (Connell, 1995).

Changing approaches to male friendship

Key shifts in identities and social institutions such as the family and employment have led to a questioning of the privileged status of heterosexual, white masculine identities (Connell, 1989). These transformations include the weakening of the nuclear family through rising divorce rates; the decline of the so-called male breadwinner status; the public acknowledgement and complexity of fathers' desires to maintain strong relationships with their children after divorce; anti-racism and an awareness of multicultural politics; and the destabilisation of heteronormativity by the rise of a dynamic gay and lesbian movement. The ascendancy of the 'emotional self' in late modernity, with its emphasis on self-disclosure, coincides with the questioning of traditional masculine identities.

Conflicting perspectives on male personal relationships illustrate the dilemmas thrown up by these wider social changes and by the shift from 'friendship' as a symbol of *civic duty* to that of *intimacy*. Explorations of male friendship from the 1980s were accompanied by the rise of masculinity studies and a 'crisis of masculinity' discourse in gender and women's studies (see, for example, Connell, 1987; Segal, 1990). This field of research began by problematising men's friendships, defining 'friendship' not as heroism or public responsibility, but as the more modern relationship of emotional bonding exemplified in Chapter 2. With the emergence of 'intimacy' as a dominant discourse that organised relationships, women's practices and expressions of friendship became a model against which men were unfavourably compared and found lacking (Seidler, 1992). This viewpoint provides an inadequate analysis of male friendship yet it has dominated recent literature on gender-based distinctions in personal relationships, reinforcing the contention that women have 'deeper' friendships than men. For example, Victor Seidler (1992: 17) contrasts a golden past, in which authentic male friendships were 'passionate' and 'involved', with a problematic present in which men's relationships with other men are apparently shallow and superficial. For example, in the book, *Men and Friendship* (1983), Stuart Miller argues that men's friendships today are 'generally characterised by thinness, insincerity and even chronic wariness' (1983: p. xi). This interpretation relies on an idealisation of the classical role of friendship and a bemoaning of men's inability to emulate women in treating friendship as intimate disclosure.

Research on men's friendships in the 1980s and 1990s followed this view, suggesting that the reluctance to express personal vulnerabilities led Western, middle-class men to interact less intimately, and that their exchanges are characterised as superficial and emotionally distant rather than expressive and open (Harvey, 1999; Pease, 2002; Reis and Shaver, 1988; Sherrod, 1987). Men apparently seek companionship rather than intimacy, and commitment rather than disclosure (Sherrod, 1987: 221). Male intimacy was perceived as equivalent to emotional humiliation and therefore incompatible with masculine self-control (Helgeson, Shaver and Dyer, 1987). More recently, Andrew Singleton (2003: 131) argues that 'the behaviours that might characterise intimate male-to-male relationships are at odds with culturally dominant "hegemonic" forms of masculinity and the way this masculinity is expected to be performed'. Evidence also suggests that men are more likely to disclose to women rather than other men (Derlega, Winstead, Wang and Hunter, 1985; Hacker, 1981; Pahl and Spencer, 2001; Rubin,1983). For example, an in-depth study of 200 men and women in the United States in the 1980s showed that two-thirds of the men were unable to name a close friend (Rubin, 1983). Of those who could, the friend was most likely to be a woman. By contrast, three-quarters of the women in the research could easily mention one, two or more close friends, who were nearly always women. Married as well as single women named other women as their best friends. A more recent study in Britain, by Pahl and Spencer

(2001), found that women tended to have more confidantes than men, middle-class men had more confidants than working-class men, and that men do not act as confidants to women. Other contributors to debates about male same-sex bonds went to some lengths to avoid the 'male friendship as impoverished' label. Scott Swain (1989) argued that it is misleading to measure men's friendships against a standard set by women's intimate relationships in the way that Rubin (1983, 1985) does. Swain (1989: 71) asserted that men's friendships are characterised by a 'covert' and 'active' style of intimacy and should not be subsumed under feminine models of intimacy. Barry Wellman (1992) suggests that friendship should be more broadly defined to prove that men's friendships do flourish as intensely as women's. Yet to define friendship narrowly as emotionally supportive companionship is misleading, he argues, because men do not engage primarily in that kind of bonding.

Similarly, Giddens (1992: 126) signals a new definition of friendship in late modernity based on the qualities of the 'pure relationship', arguing that men's same-sex relationships lie *outside friendship*. He confirms that men's relationships are 'fraternal' because they involve bonds that arise from sharing an exclusive male experience. In contrast to the characteristics of the pure relationship, then, fraternity remains a system of bonding marked out as an exclusive male domain. The upsurge of interest in 'male bonding', within the rise of masculinity studies during the 1980s and early 1990s, led to contradictory claims. Efforts were made to recuperate an authentic form of male friendship, yet also to set male friendship apart as distinctive and unique. Conversely, efforts were also made to include male friendship as part of a new, intimate form of interaction.

While some scholars wonder whether today's concept of friendship is relevant for men at all or else talk in terms of a privileged male experience, others remind us that the issue of power is obscured by such approaches and needs to be recentred, arguing that men's same-sex relationships are indicative of economic and political survival. For example, Michael Messner (1992, 2004) asserts that in addition to studying the meaning and value of friendships for men, we should ask the question: 'How do these male friendship patterns fit into an overall system of power?' (1992: 217). Does power and privilege continue to structure men's relationships?

Male bonding and gender differentiation

Important changes in approaches to masculine identities and expressions of gender difference have contributed to a re-evaluation of male authority within relationships between men, and between men and women. Gender identities are no longer theorised simply as 'roles' learned through socialisation. Masculine and feminine identity formations are now being conceptualised as relational, as constructed variously in opposition to one another through social interaction. Drawing on post-structural theories and 'queer' paradigms, gender has recently been approached as something reproduced through recurring performances that present the idea of a predetermined, natural and unchanging gender (Butler, 1990). Important research in studies of gender and education, which I shall return to below, show that through modes of domination and subordination, hegemonic masculinities are delineated by men and boys in relation to and against an Other (Davies and Harre, 1991; Haywood, 1996; Jackson, 2002; Mac an Ghaill, 1994; Mills, 2001; Renolds, 2004; Salisbury and Jackson, 1996: Skelton, 2001). The fixing of friendship as a *gendered* category relies on this positioning of hegemonic masculinities in relation to, and against, an inferior and marginalised Other. Friendship is a personal association used to support hegemonic masculinities by *staging* sexual difference. It constitutes a site for the organisation of gendered identity by establishing a relational framework for performing gender difference. Thus, men and women tend to bond *against each other* by sustaining friendship relationships in contradistinction to one another. This even occurs among young people who struggle to negotiate alternative gendered identities (Frosh, Phoenix and Pattman, 2002; Paetcher, 1998; Renolds, 2004).

The public sphere of politics and work is defined as an inherently masculine articulation of friendship, by being contrasted with a subordinated feminine form of bonding, a type of association conceived as private and domestic. Today, a residue of the Aristotelian discourse of virtuous, exclusively male friendship prevails in popular cultural narratives such as Hollywood movie epics from *Ben Hur* (1959) to the *Lord of The Rings* trilogy (2002, 2003, 2004). Intimating a persistent differentiation of male and female friendships along the public/private axis, Hollywood epics, comics and computer games address boys and men by celebrating *public*, action-led and goal-oriented representations of personal relationships. This contrasts with representations of female friendship in the domestic medium of television drama as private, domestic and intimate. Exemplified by British soap operas such as *Coronation Street* and *EastEnders*, the focus on the domestic realm in soaps highlights the increasing value placed on the female friendship as nurturing, and deployed to cement neighbourhoods, extended kin and communities. Thus, the public/private dichotomy continues to influence contemporary ideas about masculine and feminine friendships at a symbolic level. Distinctions in popular media narrativisations of personal relationships often convey the vestiges of the power and privilege that symbols of male friendship have traditionally been founded on, and reveal aspirations to reproduce them.

The privileged space of male fraternities, particularly white, middle class fraternities is being progressively challenged by women's and non-white men's entrance into the public spheres of education, employment and politics. As borne out by research in linguistics (see Cameron and Kulick, 2003), Daphne Spain (1992: 72) states: 'Talking in private about private issues (as women do) does not have the same potential for social power that acting in public on public issues (as men do) has for social power.' Furthermore, the investment of heterosexual male bonding with power against the Other is now being contested by gay men as well as women. At the same time, the emphasis on agency in recent studies highlights the active role played by the individual in constructing a gendered and sexed identity. While the homosexual potential of men's intimacy is policed by peers, from the 1970s onwards the gay liberation movement challenged conventional power relations not only between men and women, but also between men and men. And this, in turn, affected the way friendships were organised between men (Nardi, 1992: 4). Nevertheless, homosexual relationships continue to be policed, not just in non-urban, non-Western and poor regions of Third World countries but in many male-dominated associations across First and Third World cultures through homophobic responses of violence or verbal bullying.

As Eve Kosofsky Sedgewick (1985: 83–96) argues, when associations between men are not organised by virtue and civic duty, problems emerge in managing the parameters of intense 'homosocial' bonds between men, especially in areas where such bonding is crucial for the efficient organisation of the team. The accent on sex as a key to identity in late modernity causes trouble in regulating the 'platonic', that is, the 'spiritual' and 'non-physical' boundaries of same-sex friendships. A sexualisation of society heightens attention to the body, sensual pleasure and sexual performance in relationships. It implies that beyond blood ties, erotic discourse organises personal bonds (Seidman, 1991). Male identities depend on intense bonding in male-defined institutions such as sport, the military, politics, and employment environments from heavy industries to the top management positions of multinational corporations. The marginalisation of masculinities that inhabit non-hegemonic positions is, then, a crucial social mechanism that regulates heterosexual masculine bonding, as detailed in the following examples.

Traditional forms of public male solidarity

Informal public power

Male bonding against an Other, as a way of securing and reproducing power, has traditionally operated both overtly and covertly through men-only political and business networks, and also in more highly regulated clubs and associations such as the Free Masons and the Rotary Club. These social networks have advanced men's political and business interests as a key feature of informal masculine power (Starr, 1987). Opportunities for men to socialise in public spaces defined, both formally and informally, as exclusively *male* spaces are fewer in number today than in past centuries in Western societies yet are still abundant. Clubs pubs, taverns, college fraternities in the United States, lodges housing Elks' and Freemasons' meetings are all types of large gatherings of men that ensure that male friendships are more impersonal than women's intimate relationships: by being less dyadic and by emphasising collectivities connoting solidarity *against* the 'other sex' and often other ethnic groups of men. Confirming Max Weber (1978: 907) and Georg Simmel (1950a and b: 364) who identified men's houses and clubs as zones of power from which women were excluded; white middle-class men's experiences with other men continue to be *spatially* structured by power and privilege. These men-only organisations show how crucial friendship is in reproducing and regulating patriarchy through hegemonic masculinity.

Until recently, when social integration was enforced by law, clubs like Cosmos and Metropolitan in Washington DC were viewed as contemporary versions of ceremonial huts (Feinberg, 1988; Pressley, 1988). As well as excluding women, these clubs have excluded groups of men based on race, ethnicity and religion. Men's friendships were instrumental in promoting power among white men in business and politics. When the courts banned the exclusive male memberships of these clubs, they acknowledged that all-male associations give men a socio-economic advantage. Male friendships socialise men into a masculinised public domain that works to marginalise or exclude women. This kind of male networking is rendered opaque because it works in a myriad of interlocking ways that cut across business links, across work/leisure relationships, across family networks, and across classes and ethnic groupings, as examples below reveal.

Male fraternities and clubs

A study of all-male fraternal organisations such as the Masons and Odd Fellows in nineteenth-century North America shows that the rise of male organisations met a specific need during a period of rapid social change and instability (Clawson, 1989). Fraternal orders of the period operated as a form of defence for a manhood that was under threat, rather than purely as a rite of passage to manhood. But what, exactly, was being threatened? Artisanal manhood was being eroded by three key changes: industrial capitalism, the emergence of feminine values and a cultural critique of masculinity. Male-only fraternal spaces encouraged solidarity among men and separation from women to bolster masculine power (Clawson, 1989: 41). Male spaces, lodges and orders involving a culture of male ritual were primarily aimed at networking and would not have been used for developing intimate relationships in the way that women's relationships were (Hansen, 1992).

The Freemasons are a famous and fascinating example of an all-male fraternal organisation. This association is regularly reproached for being a secret society of men who take solemn oaths to further their own interests, extend obligations and favours to Masonic brothers, and who recognise one another by secret signs such as a handshake. British Freemasonry is mainly composed of middle-class businessmen and members of the police force. By contrast, in France, Italy and Latin America, they are revolutionary left-wing organisations in response to the historical needs to resist fascism. This global men's association has exercised a profound influence on political and public life, and contributed to the systematic marginalisation of women from politics and business. In nineteenth- and twentieth-century Britain, many leading military commanders, members of the royal family and politicians were Freemasons. Sir Winston Churchill joined at the age of 26 in 1901, but resigned in 1912 due to pressures of work (Ridley, 1999). In France women were admitted to Masonic lodges from the beginning of the eighteenth century. However, women's lodges and mixed lodges failed to become established. In Britain, the conditions that excluded women were strongly worded in the early twentieth century during a period when Freemasonry was under threat from the rise of Fascism and when women were demanding equal rights with men. The existence of women's and mixed lodges in Europe caused alarm in Britain. Even today, the Freemason attitude towards women is fixed, as rather quaintly described in texts about the fraternity such as the following:

> The Freemasons' attitude toward women seems extraordinarily out of date. They are outstandingly kind to their wives and to their female employees, who are far less likely to encounter harassment or disrespect from Freemasons than from many employers or higher business

executives. But the Freemasons not merely exclude women from their own ranks but also refuse to have any dealings with any other society that accepts women.

(Ridley, 1999: 277)

Such organisations are not violating the Sex Discrimination Act in the United Kingdom, which allows members of private clubs to exclude individuals because of their sex. At a time when women are playing more prominent roles in business, the professions and commerce, there are strong calls for the restraint of Freemasonry in Western democracies. For example, in Switzerland in 1937, nearly one-third of the population voted in a referendum in favour of a constitutional amendment to curb the power of the Freemasons. In the United Kingdom, members of parliament continue to demand that members of organisations and professions be compelled by law to disclose Freemasonry membership. The Unlawful Societies Act was passed in the United Kingdom in 1799 to destroy the Radicals and the Trade Unions, but left the middle-class Freemasons intact. The Act was repealed under Prime Minister Harold Wilson's government in 1967 in recognition of the blatant discrimination against other kinds of political organisations. In 1997, Freemasons were forced to register with the Justice of Peace, demonstrating the continuing ambivalence expressed about Freemasonry in a Western democracy. Not surprisingly, the membership of most fraternal societies has declined in recent times. Male-only societies run counter to the general demand for equality between men and women. Moreover, transparency is being demanded in many walks of life, thereby calling into question the secrecy that binds fraternities together.

The gentlemen's clubs of London are another example of all-male spaces that have played a central role in the social and political history of the nation for the last 300 years. Unique though they are to London, equivalents exist in urban metropolises globally. The history of the London clubs represents a social history of English upper-class men. Many of the earlier clubs of St James's Street and Pall Mall were politically based, having roots in the coffee houses of the eighteenth century (Lejeune and Lewis, 1979). While gaming and gossip were key amusements, politics became a crucial aspect of gentlemen's clubs: Brooks was identified with the Whigs, and White's linked to the Tories. Today, the Carlton remains as a stronghold of the Tory Party. Membership of such clubs were once a matter of hereditary privilege, but a number of new clubs emerged in the nineteenth century to meet the demands of the burgeoning middle classes. Few non-political clubs allowed active Socialists to join, with the attitude that 'Socialists, like women, are not, on the whole, clubbable' (Lejeune and Lewis, 1979: 14). In the late nineteenth century there were more than 200 male clubs in London. Today there are still around 30 major clubs and, and a number of specialised clubs and dining clubs.

The most famous political club, the Carlton, was formed in 1832 mainly as a rallying point for opponents of the Reform Bill.[2] And, until the end of the century, it undertook many of the functions now carried out by the Conservative Central Office. Disraeli's first action after joining the Tory Party in 1837 was to arrange to be elected to the Carlton. Two of the most renowned political events to take place at the Carlton were the meetings held in 1911 when Bonar Law[3] was elected leader of the Conservative Party, and in 1922 when a decision was taken to stop supporting Lloyd George and the Coalition Government. In the 1970s, officers of all Conservative constituency associations throughout Britain were invited to become associate Members and Harold Macmillan became chairman of the Carlton at the age of 83. The British political hierarchy was therefore being formed, confirmed and reproduced within the context of these crucial sites of male fraternity.

At the other end of the class spectrum, Working men's clubs were designed as male enclaves until the mid-twentieth century. Women were only allowed in this designated male space if escorted by a man. Today, working men's clubs are run as family organisations, with women as well as men taking responsibility for club affairs and, tellingly, those events geared to 'family entertainment' (moving away from the usual exclusion of women and children). British working men's clubs became the key centres of the social life and leisure landscape of many towns. Yet the Working Men's Club and Institute Union continues to have a 100-year-old rule that women cannot be associate members, preventing them from visiting other working men's clubs without being signed in as a guest, and banning them from standing for election to the local branch committee or national executive. A number of attempts have been made to change this situation. In 2003, the secretary of Bishopthorpe Social Club, near York, lost her complaint of sex discrimination against the CIU, because she was denied associate membership but won leave to appeal. A two-thirds majority was required at an annual conference to drop the longstanding rule which was not obtained. The CIU maintains that this is not in breach of the Sex Discrimination Act because private member's clubs are excluded from the legislation. Significantly, single-sex clubs and clubs with fewer than 25 members are not obliged to conform to the Sex Discrimination Act.

However, many of Britain's male-dominated sporting clubs have been forced for financial reasons to allow women to join. The Marylebone Cricket Club (MCC) resolved to admit women in the late 1990s because the Sports Council withheld a £4.5 million Lottery grant for excluding women. Two major companies refused to sign sponsorship deals with the MCC over the same issue. Similarly, the Leander Rowing Club, Britain's oldest rowing club that has provided the bulk of the United Kingdom's international teams, dropped its 179-year-old ban on women being members in 1997. It did so only after being offered a £1.5 million National Lottery grant on condition that women be accepted on the same terms as men, to comply with the Sport's Council's open membership policy.

Public male communities

The perpetuation of male clubs may not simply be a continuation of tradition. When Daphne Spain (1992) looked more closely at the division between men's formal and informal power in other cultures, she found that men's control of public affairs was not simply associated with male solidarity, as predicted. Instead, she discovered that greater male solidarity was connected with greater female participation in public activities, suggesting that greater male solidarity may be something that emerges *in reaction to* women's increased participation in public life. Men's demands for all-male alliances may become more intense when women's activities threaten the definition of public events as masculine. 'Men's friendships, then, reproduce, often in the privacy of ceremonial huts, privileges perceived as lost to women in the public sphere' (Spain, 1992: 68). This coincides with the assertion that the separation of the spheres was something consciously imposed on society to confine women to the domestic sphere and banish them from education, professions and politics rather than something that gradually evolved (Davidoff and Hall, 1994). Contemporary forms of male bonding expressed, for example, in the recent rise of 'laddism' as a mode of masculinity adopted by schoolboys and adult men in British urban spaces and popular culture[4] may be related, then, to the challenges to hegemonic masculinities being made by women's growing autonomy.

Men's friendships in Western cultures are no longer unequivocally located in the public sphere, now traversing both public and domestic domains. However, by linking personal associations with the context of business, politics and public services, hegemonic masculinity is preserved. The 'old-boy networks' of the British upper classes, based on links formed in public school such as Eton and Harrow and old universities such as Oxford and Cambridge, remain important forms of solidarity that perpetuate an elite class. Sports teams and leisure pursuits continue to be crucial cultural contexts for fostering male friendships, operating as a privileged realm of male solidarity that relies on opposition to women as Other. Male privilege is reproduced by linking masculinity with power and the public sphere in pubs, at race tracks, on street corners and beaches, at men's clubs, in gangs, fraternities and informal networks. Together with home and work contexts, these places are referred to as 'the third place' in men's lives, characterised as 'parochial' settings rather than private or public (Oldenburg, 1999). Members are made up of fluid networks of men from similar social 'backgrounds'. 'Public communities' are formed around these third places, so although they are designed for enjoyment, they are highly productive in supporting the context of work through networking.

Race, class and masculine bonding

In sharp contrast to the enclaves of white male power discussed above, Clyde Franklin (1992) explored the expressions of masculinity in the early 1990s among working-class and upwardly mobile African-Americans in relation to their friendship networks. Research on black men's friendships is limited, but Franklin uncovers some important variations of race and class. He found that working-class friendships for African-American men could often be intense, affectionate and self-disclosing. This is partly because of a shared ideology characterised by affection, intimate talks, nurturance and holism. Greeting and responses such as 'yo, bro', 'hey, home' are powerful utterances which 'are more than greetings and responses; they are political statements, connoting survival, togetherness, and commonality' within a shared oppression and victimisation. As one interviewee stated:

> When I talk with my friends, they know what I'm saying, you know ... the feelings, what I'm talking about, what I like, don't like. White guys can't do that ... and bourgie black guys either.
>
> (Quoted in Franklin II, 1992: 206)

For upwardly mobile black men, a loss of male–male friendships was experienced in terms of numbers and quality because they participated in those mainstream social and economic institutions that discourage same-sex friendships among men (Franklin II, 1992: 203). They are likely to have internalised the same stigmas, such as homophobia, independence, pursuit of power that define traditional versions of white masculinity: resulting in non-self-disclosure, competitiveness and confidence. Many upwardly mobile black men claimed to have little time to cultivate deep relationships and some questioned whether 'it is necessary for there to be deep relationships between men' (Franklin II, 1992: 210). Thus, for working-class black men, race can often be the variable that organises and structures men's friendships, whereas for upwardly mobile black men, it is more likely to be class. This implies that as black men become increasingly socialised into white male professional cultures, they internalise a white Western Anglophone masculine ideology of detached non-intimacy.

Peer regulation of male heterosexual identities

This section looks at ways in which peer regulation is used to establish heterosexual masculine identity from an early age by drawing examples from the contexts of sport and school. I examine how hegemonic masculinity is reproduced through peer pressures among boys and men by bonding against feminine and gay identities, as well as by resisting regulation and control by teachers. Classic studies of the subcultures of male sports reveal that sport provides a vital context for men's friendships and in sustaining gendered and sexual difference. In the field of gender and education, a number of studies in primary and secondary schools indicate that heterosexual masculine identities are performative and entail an investment in homophobic and misogynistic verbal bullying.

The policing of heterosexual masculine identities in school

A British study of young teenagers' collective sexual values and attitudes to sex education in schools that I conducted collaboratively with colleagues shows that male bonding against women starts at an early age (Chambers, Van Loon and Tinknell, 2004b and c). In interviews with boys and girls between the ages of 12 and 14 in single-sex groups, we uncovered the strong pressure placed on boys to declare and perform a heterosexual masculine identity. This was articulated through the sexual bullying of both girls and other boys who failed to conform to a dominant heterosexual masculinity. For both boys and girls, the collusive nature of the teenager's everyday sex talk was a central part of an articulation of a collective sexual morality in single-sex groups. This collective sexual morality produced and regulated gendered identities. We discovered that two forms of sexist harassment, homophobic bullying of boys and misogynistic bullying of girls, converged to reinforce a dominant heterosexual masculinity.

Performed by boys from around the age of 14 and over, bullying took the form of a ritual humiliation through sex talk by the hostile policing of girls' and each others' sexual identities. It was an important avenue for cultivating boys' rank among all-male groups. In contrast to the girls, the boys in our focus groups enacted heterosexual masculinity as physically and verbally intimidating towards others by being attention-seeking and disruptive. This is echoed in other studies of male behaviour in schools. Nayak and Kehily (1996: 218) argue that verbal abuse acts as a demand for attention as a feature of hegemonic masculine identity and could be a reason for the intensity and boldness of male sex talk as a performative style. We found that in all school types[5] that contained male pupils aspects of hegemonic heterosexual masculinities associated with misogynistic and homophobic bullying cut across class differences. It also cut across ethnic differences in the schools that contained a predominance of Asian pupils. Actively positioning themselves in opposition to all expressions of femininity, boys viewed girls as a main focus of disdain unless boys were regarded as 'gay'. Girls' sexual agency was policed and condemned by boys by their investment in the virgin/slut dichotomy, with no equivalent distinctions used against boys. A consensus of sexual amorality operated among the boys' groups which contrasted with that of the girls. For example, in a discussion about responsibility, pregnancy and contraception, pregnancy was identified by the boys as a risk that boys were not responsible for.

It seems likely, in mixed ethnic groups, that boys' disdain for girls may be an important way of managing ethnic and other differences between the boys in order to gain group consensus against a 'common enemy'. The boys' sex talk was attached to a shared culture of 'laddishness' which developed by age 14 in the private school and earlier, by age 12, in the inner-city comprehensives. It was not only founded on scorn for girls but also for themselves and their own bodies, exposing their own anxiety about sex. The terms of abuse used by boys in sex talk form part of discursive resources that boys draw on to consolidate masculine subjectivities as shown in other studies (Haywood and Mac An Ghaill, 2000; Wood, 1984). Gay identity was taboo: it had to be exclaimed loudly and often, through verbal teasing. Evidence elsewhere suggests that this generates fears among boys that they may be gay if they feel affection for one another (Haywood and Mac An Ghaill, 2000). We found that between the ages of 12 and 14, male victims of homophobic bullying were rarely targeted for being suspected of being homosexual as such, but because they deviated from some other physical, behavioural or attitudinal norm such as being overweight, shy, thin or 'nerdy'. When asked if they used the term 'gay', Year 9 boys at a large comprehensive school conveyed that they used it as a general term of abuse:

Year 9 boy: Yeah
Yeah
Call people 'gay' but you get …
Yeah we always call people gay and they're not even gay.
Interviewer: What about boys you think are gay, Are really gay?
Year 9 boy: I'd beat them up.

This kind of study shows, then, that the performative aspect of the boys' expressions of macho sexual confidence is a central feature of homosocial bonding. As Debbie Epstein (1997: 167) states: 'For men, the avoidance of stigmatisation and the production of acceptable masculinities seem to depend, at least in part, on harassing women and other men.' These school-based studies of young people indicate that heterosexual masculinity is constructed and validated by ridiculing femininity and homosexuality simultaneously through abusive terms directed at all women and homosexual men. Male peer groups police individual members' intimacy with women by conferring high status on men who are sexually active but, also, by condemning as effeminate those who form intimate relationships with women (Messner, 1992). While sexual objectification may allow men to cope with the fear of emotional closeness with women, men must conceal from their friends any intimate relationships they may eventually form with women. As Messner points out in the context of sport, under these circumstances, the possibility of confiding in other men about their experiences of intimacy with women is ruled out.

Male friendships in sport

Michael Messner's (1992, 2004) classic study of friendship, intimacy and sexuality among sports men in the 1980s found that sex talk about women works to bond men together in the sporting context: it disconnects sex from male intimacy and disconnects intimacy from sex with women (Lyman, 1987: 151). The tendency for young men to talk about their sexual exploits with women is a crucial form of male bonding that marks men out as heterosexual. It acts as a declaration of men's emotional self-control. Against a fear of commitment with women, swapping stories and jokes about women and about one another confirms the lack of any need for intimacy.

Messner confirmed that men who participate in both professional and amateur sports, from athletics to baseball, tend to speak with reverence about the depth of friendship with team-mates. As one of his interviewees said:

> I'd say that most of my meaningful relationships have started through sports and have been maintained through sports. There's nothing so strong, to form that bond, as sports. Just like in war, too – there are no closer friends than guys who are in the same foxhole together trying to stay alive. You know, hardship breeds friendship, breeds intense familiarity ... You have to commonly endure something together – sweat together, bleed together, cry together. Sport provides that.
>
> (Messner, 1992: 218)

This romantic representation of friendship as something formed in 'adversity' and fashioned out of 'enduring hardship' is a common feature of male same-sex bonding. War, politics and sport offer men a context for mutual respect, closeness and deep affection between men, echoing the Aristotelian idealisation of male friendship.

While friendships forged in sporting battles are likely to be among the most intimate bonds men experience with one another, they are shot with ambiguity. Sport offers an opportunity for cross-racial contact between men, yet friendships among team members often perpetuates racism against black men with a myriad of social, cultural and familial pressures that deters any cross-racial friendships from developing beyond the sporting context. So sport offers men an opportunity to be in each other's company yet, at the same time, an emotional distance from one another must be maintained by organising around an inherently competitive activity. Nevertheless, Scott Swain's (1989) concept of 'covert intimacy', referred to by Messner, describes a deep affection between men in contrast to the verbal intimacy common to women's friendships. It is a form of affection expressed precisely through shared activity in the sense that 'actions speaks louder than words'. This appeal to a more authentic, 'deeper' male friendship is a common set of desires among men.

Given that sporting men interact regularly in a context in which their bodies are on display, Messner (1992) also inquired into the ways in which the potentially erotic bond is policed among sportsmen. Potential sexual bonds between men are neutralised through overt homophobia, enacted by 'the displacement of the erotic toward women as objects of sexually aggressive talk and practice in the male peer group' (Messner, 1992: 227). This kind of male bonding in opposition to women and non-normative masculinities resonates with our findings above and several other studies of masculinities in school settings (see Frosh, Phoenix and Pattman, 2002; Jackson, 2002; Mills, 2001; Renold, 2001; Salisbury and Jackson, 1996; Skelton, 2001). The insulting labels directed at boys who challenge conformist masculinity are a central form of peer regulation and a major aspect of forming a gendered and sexed collective identity.

A study of male friendship among young American white sportsmen by Steven Harvey (1999) confirms that gender segregation was not just about women but also men who failed to display traditional hegemonic characteristics of aggression, domination and loud banter. Male bonding was closely linked to the establishment of a team hierarchy. The mutual exchange during activities functioned to establish boundaries between hegemonic and non-hegemonic players. The interplay between athletes and the establishment of physical and emotional dominance ensured the marginalisation of non-hegemonic players. Non-athletes were often described as 'dirtbags', 'brainiacs', or 'dirties'. The wider celebration of athletic participation in the form of public rallies and homecomings confirmed the feelings of being of higher status than other men. As well as the array of nicknames, a family discourse was invoked by comparing the team to a family and team-mates to brothers, thereby solidifying their group identity and separating themselves from outsiders. A fear of being perceived as homosexual led many of the men to place great emphasis on less intimate forms of bonding and prevented the players from forming intimate relationships. Harvey states that, consistent with research on male friendship of the 1980s, male friendships remain largely dependent on the external experience rather than the sharing of intimate emotions: 'it is difficult to say that men's friendships do indeed represent meaningful, intimate relationships. Rather, through their mutual experiences in sport, the male relationship develops a deep connection that is based not on shared interpersonal communication, but on shared emotional experiences' (1999: 102).

The tendency for heterosexual male friendships to be regulated by sexist and homophobic discourses indicates that male friendship and male-gendered identity remains dependent on asserting power over, and despising, women and gay men. Attempts to police intimacy with women and prove manhood through sexual conquests is, of course, highly oppressive for straight as well as gay men and women.

Alternative masculinities and male bonding

A language of change being expressed by certain academics such as Singleton (2003) and Beynon (2002) suggests that Western societies have reached a stage when new masculine identities, with a more nurturing and feminised sensitivity, are now possible without reprisal.

A wide body of academic and popular wisdom suggests that men would benefit from more rewarding relationships if they were more open and intimate with one another and with women (Biddulph, 1995; Clare, 2001; Connell, 2000; Segal 1990; Whitehead, 2002). Some studies have indicated that many boys and men choose not to foster masculinities through hegemonic discourses and practices in attempts to transcend normative heterosexual masculinities, stressing the multiplicity of masculinities that both intersect and vie with one another in school and adult settings (Gilbert and Gilbert, 1998; Haywood, 1996; Mac an Ghaill, 1994; Martino, 1999). Studies have shown that alternative masculinities are nevertheless invested with power, usually relying on the inferiorisation of women or some other social group, with high emotional costs incurred by boys who stray from the hegemonic norms. Importantly, middle-class male youth are among those who have the personal resources and cultural capital to perform alternative identities.

In a year-long ethnographic study, Emma Renolds (2004) examined the extent to which 10- and 11-year-old white working-class and middle-class boys perform and experience masculinity in non-hegemonic ways in primary school. She reports that boys face real penalties when they cross the gender divide. By contrast, Renolds found that 'hegemonic boys' are able to flirt with other masculinities without penalty, that is, without being insultingly positioned as Other, as a reflexive position. A small minority of boys actively and recurrently positioned themselves in other, non-hegemonic masculinities. As a consequence, they experienced habitual bullying and violence yet their experiences did not fit neatly into the categories of oppression or celebratory liberation. The working-class boys in the group experienced the most difficulties in maintaining this subject position. Significantly, it was white, middle class high-achievers who were most able to continue to invest in alternative masculinities. They found that the pedagogic space was the one that they could most comfortably occupy to sustain their difference – more accessible to high- than low-achievers. Yet they were simultaneously subverting and reinforcing hegemonic masculinities by distancing themselves from all things feminine and female or 'girlie'. Nevertheless, two-thirds of the boys openly expressed their discontent over the pressures of hegemonic masculinity and the impossibility of being able to achieve it.

In an Australian study of dedicated men's groups and relationship change, Andrew Singleton (2003) found that group involvement enabled members to transcend traditional masculine modes of relating and forming intimate relationships. They were able to develop trusting relationships with one another. Men's groups that encourage the performance of intimacy cover a number of areas including the exploration of men's spirituality, the campaigning of men's rights', antipatriarchal consciousness-raising and anger management (Flood, 1998; Pease, 2000). Singleton's research on Christian men's groups indicates that group involvement allowed participants to achieve more intimacy in everyday relationships, but that the changes were not motivated by a commitment to challenging traditional codes of masculine behaviour. As Singleton (2003: 144) states: 'Their comments suggest that the men are not refiguring their masculine subjectivities or practices across a range of contexts. Rather, they came into a place in which openness was encouraged and, for the most part, they "did intimacy" with other men for the time of their involvement in the group.' He discovered that middle-class men require a legitimating context, such as a religious involvement, in order to achieve any intimacy. This legitimating context is something that most men don't usually have access to.

As mentioned in Chapter 2, expert advice on self-improvement has become ever more popular in the West in relation to the rise of the project of the self; exemplified by an explosion of popular media self-help books and magazine articles. Yet there the vast majority of this literature on emotional relationships is explicitly or implicitly addressed to women, not men. In contrast, popular magazines aimed at men reinforce an image of amoral, laddish same-sex solidarity organised around consumption. In collaborative research I conducted on teenage and men's magazines in Britain, we found that men's periodicals, such as *Loaded, FHM, Esquire, GQ* and *Nuts*, rely on an ironic register to convey the powerful signifier of sexual hedonism (Tincknell, Chambers, Van Loon and Hudson, 2003). These texts collude with the idea that men relate principally to objects, including women, as sexual objects. In a typical issue of *Loaded* magazine, articles range from interviews with male actors; short jokey, flirtatious interviews with young female actresses or pop stars who are usually photographed lying down and pouting; computer sex ('shagging online with the aid of gadgets'); and an article about matchmaking for singletons in Ireland, which contains the caption: 'With all those gorgeous sex-starved Irish fillies on the hunt for non-stop call-me-Daddy action, how could I loose?'[6]

Discussions in men's magazines about men's personal relationships are framed within sporting activities and machines – guns, motorbikes and cars – the kinds of objects and activities that conventionally bond men together or mark them out as masculine (see Tincknell, Chambers, Van Loon and Hudson, 2003). Moral irresponsibility, hedonism, and a discourse of laddism are mobilised in the representation of a raw and 'natural' masculinity that attempts to recover an authentic pre-1980s pre-SNAG (sensitive new age guy). In stark contrast to the Aristotelian notion of 'men of good virtue' shown in Hollywood epics such as *Ben Hur* and the *Lord of the Rings* trilogy, amorality characterises many of today's popular cultural representations of men's personal relationships. Within a backlash against feminism, the adolescent behaviour of men has been legitimised by the emergence, in less epic contexts of television drama and magazines, of the 'lad' who has replaced the 1980s 'new man' that was largely invented by advertising (see, for example, Faduli, 1993). The 'lad' portrayed in television comedies, newspapers and men's magazines is an image of amoral 'self-centred, male identified, leering' young men obsessed by sport but has a charming boyish vulnerability and retrieves patriarchy by using irony to affirm the sexual objectification of women (Whelehan, 2000: 5).

By contrast, we find that women's glossy magazines are marked by discourses of moral responsibility. From teenage magazines such as *Bliss*, *Sugar*, *J17*, and *19* to women's magazines such as *Elle* and *Cosmopolitan*, the emphasis is on women purchasing commodities in order to secure meaningful relationships with men as a mark of femininity, by improving and 'pampering' the body. Articles such as 'How I found my sexual confidence' focus on 'being in a long-term relationship', and 'how to act natural when he fancies you' (*19*, July 2000). While these girls' and women's magazines are characterised by a preoccupation with how to 'do' relationships with boys and men – how to begin, sustain and end relationships with them – men's magazines contain no serious advice on how to 'do' relationships with women. Managing intimate, romantic, sexual relationships with the opposite sex is defined as women's work. Popular discourses about the self in both men's and women's magazines share one thing in common: an insistence that our identities are determined by our sexuality.

Significantly, then, the abundance of expert advice available on intimate relationships is rarely addressed to individual men or boys. And this is also confirmed by the address used in sex education lessons in schools, which employs a discourse of morality and responsibility that speaks for girls, not boys (Chambers, Tincknell and Van Loon, 2004b and c; Francis and Skelton, 2001). The dominant discourse of emotions asserted by Giddens, discussed in Chapter 2, is a feminised discourse that speaks largely to a female audience. One of the most noteworthy aspects of research findings on changing masculine identities, then, is the way that heterosexual male identities have apparently excluded themselves from the emotional discourses of self-disclosure defined by Giddens (1992) as part of the contemporary project of the self. Hegemonic masculinity requires a strong sense of agency in the sense that 'doing' dominant masculinity requires constant self- and other-monitoring. By contrast, the 'project of the self' turns out to be a feminine venture because it relies on a discourse of disclosure that remains alien to, or at least highly problematic, for hegemonic masculinity.

Conclusion

This chapter demonstrates that a key feature of men's personal relationships is the use of friendship for personal gain, group alliances and the reproduction of dominant heterosexual masculinity. Through established and multiple networks of male fraternity that reproduce male power in the institutional contexts of business, politics and sports, men can use informal networks to access power. Heterosexual men's privileged position in the social structure encourages the formation of same-sex bonds, but they are the kind of bonds that limit the degree to which the self is revealed in them (Nardi, 1992). Male bonds fix gender difference through the peer regulation of hegemonic heterosexual masculinities at a very young age by marking out femininity and gay identities as inferior.

While traditional relationships between heterosexual men are 'collusive' by bonding against women and marginalised male identities, men's status and well-being tends to be bolstered by women's supporting role both in the public sphere (secretaries, nurses, waitresses, office cleaners) and through women's physical care-taking role in the domestic realm. Men often turn more to women for emotional talk. However, the unstable nature of heterosexual relationships which coincides with women's increasing autonomy, the desire for a democratisation of relationships, and the rise of sexual politics and sexual movements such as Lesbian and Gay Pride has led to a re-examination of the privileged position of hegemonic masculinities (see Chapter 5). Heterosexual men's relationships with one another have entered a period of review. The challenges being made by the articulation of alternative masculinities indicates current and future possibilities for dismantling men-only public spaces as privileged spaces against othered identities. Some of these challenges are addressed in the next chapter.

4
Feminine Identities and Female Bonds

This chapter enquires into ways that heterosexual feminine identities are articulated and negotiated through friendship and conversely, how ideas about female friendship are shaped by discourses of femininity. Among young and middle-aged urban, single and partnered women, conventional intimate dyads are gradually being supplanted by a new set of social dynamics characterised by *group* friendships. Women at leisure are now highly visible in single-sex groups in public metropolitan settings across Western societies: in pubs, clubs, cafes and bars. These public spaces have recently become important sites where young women are making claims for self-autonomy. Significantly, these trends are also being marked out by the media as anomalous and disturbing. Emergent forms of *group* female bonding among single career women are signifying women's entrance into public space, a space once reserved for men. However, women unaccompanied by men in leisure contexts are being represented in various popular media representations as troubling. This chapter provides an analysis of British news reports of working-class single women who are condemned, in Western nations such as the United Kingdom, for binge drinking. It then provides a case study of the way shows like *Sex and the City* represent the friendships of 30-something singleton women as amoral, self-absorbed and needy. The idea of the 'female crowd' is then explored in order to trace the ambiguous relationship women have with postmodern associations of 'elective' associations and 'liminal' communities.

Before exploring significations of changing modes of friendship among young heterosexual women, the chapter begins by providing an overview of the patterns of bonding among women with families. It outlines the key constraints of family and employment commitments that women usually face, and how discourses of femininity have shaped attitudes to women's friendships. In this chapter I identify two interrelated aspects of femininity that regulate all women's relationships: nurturing and respectable womanhood. The nurturing, caring self, and the physical manifestation and conduct of respectable womanhood are gendered characteristics by which individual women are routinely judged as wanting. In their bid for independence, women continue to experience a number of social and cultural pressures to conform to particular feminine roles structured by an ethos of caring for others. The chapter shows that women's bid for gender equality in employment and in personal relationships is kept in check by allusion to women's *potential* as wives and mothers. With there being no male equivalent to this restraint, it explains why the forging of same-sex friendships by women in the context of urban leisure is often viewed as a defiance of feminine decorum.

The most obvious differences between men's and women's friendships concern the extent to which friendship is used as a resource to gain access to power, whether economic, social or cultural. While women's friendship networks are used as a vital resource, women are rarely able to use same-sex friendship as a pathway to *power* as men do. The category of 'woman' is not invested with authority. Indeed, women's status is conventionally dependent on and *authorised by men*. In Western societies until the mid-twentieth century, feminine decorum was contingent on marriage or being chaperoned by a male relative in public. In many parts of the world, unaccompanied women are illegitimate subjects and their mobility continues to be curtailed. For instance, in Saudi Arabia women are banned from driving motor vehicles. Through endorsement by fathers, husbands, and male employers, women have habitually been obliged to secure their status through relationships with men (Raymond, 1986).

As mentioned in Chapter 3, by approaching friendship as a form of civic duty within classical thinking, women were excluded from public affairs and thereby denied citizenship. In more recent times in Western societies, employed women are often unofficially and illegally barred from employment networks that offer access to information that can enhance promotion. While 'unaccompanied women' are less and less likely to be denied service in public venues such as private clubs in the context of leisure, they are still being marked out as 'Other', as the previous chapter indicates.

Female friendship and the nurturing self

The emphasis on intimacy, affection and empathy in academic and formal discussions of women's friendships is underpinned by a feminine discourse of *nurturing*. The idea of the 'caring self' has been established as a feminine norm which regulates women's identities. It remains a powerful signifier of female bonding by constituting the criteria by which women's everyday lives are judged, whether or not they have children. Public and official discourses of the early twentieth century – religious, medical, educational and academic – maintained gender difference through family roles by categorising women as 'nurturers'. In sociology, the functionalist model of the family categorised women as specialists in emotionally supportive relations (Parsons, 1959). And, despite appeals to female nurturing as 'natural' and biologically determined, the production of the feminine caring subject required careful training and was institutionalised through school and college courses in Western societies. In Britain, women were trained during this period in domestic practices such as cooking, hygiene, needlework and home crafts in the school curriculum for girls. Training courses and employment were also available to young women in health care, social care, nursing and primary school teaching. Mirroring the activities of housework and childcare, the gender segregation of the workplace asserts a feminisation of cleaning and caring.

So the production of a feminine caring self was actively institutionalised and regulated in the early twentieth century through state categorisation, and educational investment. School and college courses that trained women to become caring subjects ensured that intimacy, compassion and service to others were signified as key ingredients of a feminine identity (Skeggs, 2002). Low-paid caring jobs were an avenue to respectability for working-class women, while middle-class women would undertake the same work as full-time housewives or pay working-class women as housekeepers and child carers. The institutionalisation of the feminised caring self as a subordinated category made its mark most forcefully on working-class women. To paraphrase Beverley Skeggs (2002: 61), the experience of 'cleaning toilets and bottoms', which was signified as degrading work, is construed as a form of responsibility that provides respectability for women, especially working-class women.

Academic studies of girls' friendships in the late twentieth century showed how this nurturing discourse was internalised in women's everyday lives as fundamental to their identities and relationships with one another. Valerie Hey's (1988) ethnographic analysis of 13- and 14-year-old girls' associations in school and home settings revealed that girls develop homosocial alliances and draw boundaries that are connected in a complex way to their experiences of the nurturing aspect of the mother/daughter bond. Girls brought up by a female care-giver place great importance on intimacy and compassion. This works positively, according to Hey, by permitting girls to be nurturing towards one another. But it also works negatively by producing oppressive exclusionary, monogamous relationships. However, Hey also argues that the tight-knit friendship groups of girls' subcultures have the potential to be subversive: to destabilise the public dominance of boys/teachers/adults in schools, and even undermine heterosociality and heterosexuality. Importantly, like boys, girls use friendship to *resist* surveillance and control by those who claim power over them: teachers, parents and boys. In this way, the institutionalisation of the feminised caring self as a subordinated category can be challenged.

The cultural emphasis on women's 'natural' nurturing role as wives and mothers justifies the responsibility placed on women to cement domestic ties among kin and the wider community. Willmott's (1987) study of social and personal relationships in North London in the 1980s shows that women took on the burden of maintaining friendships on *behalf* of their husbands and family as well as for themselves. From taking charge of the catering at men's sports events to taking time off work when children are ill, women are nominated the emotional and physical caretakers of men's and children's needs (Aitchison, 2003). Friendships among all ages and groups of women are judged by these familial values, whether they are single or married. Thus, the feminine discourse of a 'caring self' circumscribes women's friendships and wider networks.

The culture of female friendship, with its accent on intimacy and altruism, was celebrated by radical feminism as a feature of the women's movement in the 1970s and early 1980s (Faderman, 1981; Raymond, 1986). This was during a time when the family was identified as a site of oppression and women were called to draw on friendship as a key resource to combat the isolation, domestic violence and stress of family life. Comparisons between male and female friendships in the 1980s led to a feminist idealisation of the intimacy, selfless and nurturing aspect of female friendships (O'Connor, 1992). Echoing Simmel (1971) who highlighted the importance of *sociable interaction*, O'Connor refutes the categorisation of female friendships as a relationship founded on intimacy and empathy.

The idealisation of female friendship as intimacy and selfless caring was questioned by feminist scholarship from the late 1980s, and early 1990s, by highlighting the structured subordination of all carers, both paid and unpaid. 'Prior to this, it had almost become unthinkable that friendships between women could be defined in other terms' (O'Connor, 1992: 63). At the same time as this questioning began, the thesis of individualisation, with its emphasis on intimacy in elective relationships, gained currency in social theory as symptomatic of wider social transformations characterising late modernity. A feminised, intimate and caring subject was deployed by Giddens (1992) as a model for the late modern self, as outlined in Chapter 2. Yet, paradoxically, the gendered implications of the ingredients of 'intimacy', 'self-disclosure' comprising the 'project of the self' were unacknowledged. The connection between intimacy and caring that signified femininity was concealed by reconfiguring 'intimacy' within the pure relationship as a *self-interested* rather than a *selfless* project. Caring was ignored in the equation, thereby avoiding a critique of the relations of power that structure the care of husbands, children and the elderly as feminine and subordinated. By failing to identify caring as a responsibility of wider society as a whole, including of men, this implied that women were shirking *their* caring responsibilities in their quest for self-fulfilment.

By the 1990s women's friendships were being characterised in both positive and negative terms. Intense intimate bonds were recognised as a beneficial way for women to secure a sense of ontological well-being. Yet women were often represented in academic research and popular discourses as self-interested, two-faced, gossipy, neurotic and at a juvenile phase in the progression towards normal psychosexual development (Hey, 1997; O'Connor, 1992; Raymond, 1986). This negative response was fuelled by a heterodominant view that intense single-sex friendship relationships are illegitimate: that is, that they constitute only intermediary stages in the movement towards heterosexual contentment (Duck, 1983). The feminisation of friendship as 'nurturing'/ 'intimacy' is, then, an unstable signifier that must be continually regulated and normalised through a heterosexual discourse. It can either connote sexual subversion through the threat of lesbianism or can be recuperated and contained through heteronormative conformity to signify a caring, feminine self that is distinguishable from public and civil hegemonic masculine bonds.

Support networks among women with families

Recent surveys indicate that women generally have higher levels of civic engagement or 'social capital'[1] than men.[2] Social responsibility falls on the shoulders of women in the form of voluntarism: charity work, parents associations and the kinds of collective values that, according to Robert Putnam (2000), sustain civic society. But for working-class women with families and children, friendships are often a vital means of domestic survival rather than a way of enhancing either community, political or work ties. The conventional link between femininity and nurturing means that women with male partners and children tend to bear the emotional work of home life. Whether in small rural settlements or large urban districts, mothers typically shoulder the burden of ferrying young children to and from school. In doing so, they form crucial all-female networks through contacts generated around school and after-school children's clubs and sports activities. A British survey conducted by the health insurance company BUPA in 2002 shows that in 80 per cent of cases, mothers take time off work to care for their children when they are sick. Fifty per cent spend their lunch breaks dealing with child-related issues.[3] The availability of support services and networks – such as childcare, nearby relatives and partners – is crucial in determining the kinds of associations mothers make. In Britain and North America, the lack of affordable childcare restricts the friendship networks of women in poorer families.

Thus, for women with young children social support, in the form of kinship and friendship, is essential to the smooth-running of family life. British government statistics show that women are likely to be able to call on a greater number of people for help in a crisis, than men.[4] They are, therefore, more likely to speak to and know their neighbours, and are regarded as more neighbourly and more likely to trust neighbours than men. However, men are more likely to have a better perception of a local area, and are more likely to feel safe walking alone after dark in their local area than women, indicating women's feelings of vulnerability in public spaces when on their own. The British General Household Survey of 2000/1 reports that 31 per cent of women said they never went out on their own after dark compared with 8 per cent of men, signifying the ambivalent relationship women have to public spaces. Married women's contacts have traditionally been private and local rather than public in nature, and tended to be with other women, confirming a privatisation of friendships. For married women, the home has traditionally been a crucial site of friendship formation in neighbourhood communities (O'Connor, 1990; Pahl and Spencer, 2001; Wellman, 1992).

Important class differences in women's friendships have been identified in studies of personal relationships. Middle-class married women tend to rely on friendship networks more heavily than relatives (Allan, 1990, 1996; Harrison, 1998; O'Connor, 1987; Oliker, 1989; Wellman, 1992). Working-class women often draw on kin, especially their mothers, for moral and practical support since they tend to live nearer their families of origin. Middle-class wives are more likely to have moved away from communities of origin and seek attachments and security among friends. In a study of married middle-class women's friendships, Kareen Harrison (1998) found that women with dependent children who worked either full or part time encountered several barriers to developing personal relationships beyond the domestic sphere. But they did not find it difficult to maintain their *close* female friendships. This group of women developed strategies of resistance, allowing them to develop close, intimate friendships and larger group friendships. These women felt a sense of entitlement to having fun, making choices and expressing opinions, allowing the women a sense of validation and self-esteem that they rarely found in other aspects of their lives. Harrison's research challenges the idea that women's friendships are unimportant and secondary to marital relationships.

A lack of research on ethnic differences in friendship patterns makes it difficult to generalise about ethnic diversity in friendship networks among married women in Western societies. It seems likely that among some ethnic minorities such as the Chinese and South Asian diasporas in the United Kingdom, women's personal relationships are influenced by extended kinship networks and strong ties, especially in urban areas where ethnic minority communities live in close proximity (see Afshar, 2002; Baxter and Raw, 2002; Westwood, 2002). However, second- and third-generation members of ethnic minority communities develop lifestyles and friendship networks that share features of the host communities with increasing reliance on friendship networks, as people moved away from their families of origin to find work. Research on young black British women suggests that a specific form of black femininity among young black women is characterised by a relative autonomy between the sexes (Mirza, 2002). This indicates the importance of female kin and friendship ties between women in child care and care of the elderly. Studies of Internet use by various ethnic groups are discussed in Chapter 6. They indicate that the technology is being used to foster a sense of community and personal identity among indigenous ethnic minorities, ethnonational diasporas and virtual 'nations' but gender distinctions and power relations between men and women in this transterritorial mode of communication have yet to be documented.

Employed women and networks of power

Over the last three decades, research findings have shown that women's friendships are structured not only by class and life-cycle phase but also by their employment and other commitments: whether they are in full-time or part-time paid employment, or whether they are full-time housewives, students or have returned to college (Adkins, 1995; Hakim, 2004; McCall, 2001; O'Connor, 1992; Suitor, 1987). Feminists have long recognised the value for women of collaboration and networking between women, with studies of workplace networking confirming that friendship and forms of networking in the workplace are vital (Andrew and Montagie, 1998; Green, Hebron and Woodward, 1990; Griffin, 1985; McCarthy, 2004; Sharpe, 1984). Yet despite three decades of equal opportunity legislation in the United Kingdom for example, women continue to be in a minority in top jobs, with unequal pay and promotion prospects evident at all levels. A new form of informal male bonding is reinforcing the glass ceiling, according to a study called *Girlfriends in High Places* (McCarthy, 2004) by the UK think-tank, Demos.[5] Since women's friendships have traditionally been located in the private sphere, women have been unable to draw on them as a resource to transform existing power structures, in the way that work-based male friendships do. Studies reveal the continuing under-representation of women in networks of power in the public sphere: in the context of economic, social and legal power. This restricts women's potential to participate in democratising employment and wider social structures (O'Connor, 1992: 20; Hakim, 2004).

Despite rising numbers of women in the workforce, they are far less independent than men, since they still earn 70 per cent of men's earnings in Western nations such as the United States and United Kingdom.[6] The causes of this pay gap include occupational segregation, where women are concentrated in a narrow range of low-paid jobs (for example, cleaning, catering and caring); the impact of caring responsibilities on women in the labour market, including the ability of women to work full time or overtime; and pay discrimination where employers reward women employees unfairly (McCall, 2001).[7] A study in 2004 by the research company, *Top Pay*, reported that 70 per cent of non-executive directors admitted they had been recruited through 'personal networks' (McCarthy, 2004). A report of women in British public life published in the same year by the Equal Opportunity Commission, entitled *Sex and Power: Who Runs Britain*,[8] demonstrates that women make up only 7 per cent of the senior judiciary, 7 per cent of senior police officers, 9 per cent of top business leaders and 9 per cent of national newspaper editors. Julie Mellor, Chair of the EOC states:

> Women are still often prevented from getting to the top because they take on more caring responsibilities than men. Until every organisation accepts that they can't capitalise on the talent available without

taking account of people's caring roles, the profile of the people who run Britain will not change. Institutions also need to examine their recruitment and selection procedures to check that they are rigorous, fair and transparent. There's no place for an old boys' network in modern Britain.[9]

Informal male-dominated networks function to exclude women from top jobs, thus perpetuating the glass ceiling. This pattern is confirmed in areas such as journalism (Chambers, Steiner and Fleming, 2004). Studies of informal networks of male academics in science, engineering and technology demonstrate that networks are regularly the source of important information about promotions, job opportunities and about research projects (Tysome, 2003). This information gives members of networks an advantage in preparing bids for research funding. With certain subject areas such as science and technology dominated by men, women who enter these fields seldom make it to senior posts.[10] According to The East Midlands Local Academic Women's Network (EMLAWN), female scientists in the United Kingdom are repeatedly held back in their careers because they do not have access to inside information about forthcoming research projects. Women working their way up the career ladder frequently find themselves shut out from such information groups (Tysome, 2003). The gender imbalance in certain science, engineering and technology subject areas can be a lonely experience for women. It can induce feelings of isolation with few opportunities available to women to share their knowledge in a way that men often take for granted. EMLAWN has therefore launched a website aimed at helping women scientists[11] by providing them with more information and outlining the various skills and strategies needed to pursue research funding successfully.

In *Girlfriends in High Places*, McCarthy (2004) argues that efforts to confront gender inequality tend to focus on *formal* barriers to women's progression, but fail to deal with the *informal* processes and relationships that disadvantage women in the work context. Exclusion from powerful male networks is identified as a key factor, with male fraternities and 'old boy networks' that rely on school and university ties still operating in many organisations. McCarthy sites a number of reasons why women are excluded from men's informal networks of power: after-hours drinking is prohibited to women with childcare responsibilities. The sexual politics of the office also makes it difficult for women to be included in professional relationships with men. Nonetheless, women's professional networks can foster the kind of confidence-building support that men offer one another in male-only informal networks.

Yet efforts to help women workers by adopting strategies such as flexible work schedules can exacerbate the situation by encouraging them to miss out on social occasions. Combining a family with a career continues to be treated as a 'women's problem', rather than a joint responsibility to be shared between both spouses. McCarthy (2004) recommends that the government and employers set up and support women's networks to improve women's representation in the workplace. However, she also acknowledges that the push to get women to network more effectively places the onus on women to change, rather than men and male dominated organisations. Chapter 6 addresses the rise of the phenomenon of 'network sociality', which has implications for women.

Network sociality, which is detailed in Chapter 6, is the expression of a new set of informational work relations founded on an exchange of data, on 'catching up' and on ephemeral yet intense encounters (Wittel, 2001). This network sociality is based on Castells's (1996) idea of a 'network society' and is said to be displacing community-based sociality. Important questions about the gendered nature of these newly emerging work ties need to be pursued to understand how far women are likely to be disadvantaged through exclusion from new modes of networking. How people are developing, sustaining and living though these new work ties needs to be examined.

Representations of female singletons' group leisure

Having identified how women's personal ties both shape and are shaped by work and domestic gender disadvantages, in this section two case studies of women's group friendships identify emergent trends by referring to popular media texts. Two distinctive types of women who engage in group friendships have been identified by the media as problem groups. Single working-class women in their early twenties and middle class 30-something career women have prompted a moral panic about the emergence of a feminised, hedonistic and amoral individualism. These women are perceived as having relinquished their nurturing responsibilities and thereby undermining family values.

'Girls behaving badly'

Turning, first, to young working-class women, a rise in the number of social risks such as excessive alcohol consumption, teenage pregnancies, and sexually transmitted diseases is prompting public anxieties about their presence and behaviour in city centres at night. The rise of small and large groups of women out together enjoying themselves in metropolitan spaces at night, drinking, clubbing and eating in single-sex groups is a recent trend that challenges the discourse of intimacy and nurturing in past approaches to women's personal relationships. At hen parties, bar nights and clubs, young women appear to be flaunting the fact that they are having fun without the company of men. This pattern of entertainment exhibits women's new-found confidence yet generates public anxiety about single-sex groups of women. Binge drinking, which is rising rapidly among women in Western nations such as the United States and the United Kingdom, is being used as a trigger for a moral panic about women's growing occupation of public space in single-sex groups.[12] Today's news media representations of a *'Girls Gone Wild'*[13] or female 'raunch culture',[14] of young women classified as 'chavs', 'slappers' and 'fat slags'[15] indicate a public indignation in response to women's bid for pleasure as part of a growing independence and freedom (Whelehan, 2000). The news media revulsion towards groups of young women who drink alcohol together in public is framed by an androcentric discourse of female relationships. Public outrage is compounded by women seeking out casual sexual encounters with men, which is exemplified by the rise of 'raunch culture' or porn culture among young American college women who are referred to as 'female chauvinist pigs' (Levy, 2005).

While alcohol consumption among young women is rising, it remains lower than that of young men. In England, for example, 28 per cent of young women and 39 per cent of young men are classified by the government as 'binge drinkers', referring to high alcohol consumption in one day. The British government's concern about binge drinking prompted an Alcohol Harm Reduction Strategy for England in 2004.[16] The report confirms that binge drinkers under the age of 25 are more likely to be men, even though women's drinking has risen over the last decade. It also states that men are more likely to commit violence under the influence of alcohol: 'Men in particular are more likely both to be a victim of violence and to commit violent offences.'[17] Yet young women are the group being singled out as the major problem as their alcohol consumption rises.

Newspaper reports in the United Kingdom regularly expose young women's public misdeeds while out at night, exemplified by headlines such as 'WHAT WAS YOUR KID UP TO LAST NIGHT: As Britain is rocked by booze epidemic, we expose shameful scenes' in *The People*.[18] The article goes on to a subheading and following description: 'OUT FOR THE COUNT: A Lad tries to help young girl as she lies paralytic in the gutter with knickers on show ... .' The report chastises young women – labelled as 'girls' or a 'gaggle of women'- for binge drinking, dressing scantily, tempting lads into bars, being slumped by club doors and violently sick in public. In 'WHY GIRLS DRINK THEMSELVES STUPID', Christen Pears[19] produces an indignant piece in the *Northern Echo* of 'scantily-clad' young women 'meandering' in streets in 'various states of drunkenness, stopping off at each of the many bars along the way'. The report admits that men remain the biggest consumers of alcohol, but the fact that young women are following suit is viewed as scandalous.

Headed, 'MY NIGHT OF BOOZE AND PUB CRAWLS', a report in the *Evening Standard* on binge drinking and brawling among young women in Richmond begins: 'It is the stout girl with the peroxide crop who initiates the incendiary chant: "Fight!. Fight! Fight!", she roars drunkenly, to a percussion of outsize metal jewellery rattling at chunky wrists.'[20] The fascination with and sexualisation of single women's bodies and clothing is part of a voyeuristic denigration of young women in the context of leisure. Descriptions of vomiting in the gutter and scuffles breaking out fuel a moral unease about young independent women. This kind of behaviour is not traditionally associated with femininity. Young women are apparently replicating the kinds of behaviour normally associated with the 'exuberance' of male youth. An amorality more comfortably associated with youthful masculinity is apparently being duplicated by young women, who are signified as a menacing group: profoundly disreputable and sexually deviant.

The classification of women into respectable and non-respectable is central to the regulation of women's identities and moral judgements about women's appearance. Working-class women's relationships to femininity have typically been associated with vulgarity. The working class woman's body is signified as coarse, unruly, in excess (Rowe, 1995). Femininity is distanced from the vulgar, pathological, the tasteless and the sexual. The Western representation of femininity as a middle-class sign of respectable womanhood was well established by the twentieth century and was confirmed through appearance and conduct. It allowed middle-class women to separate themselves from dangerous, disruptive sexual women such as prostitutes, working-class women and potentially dangerous black women. As Beverley Skeggs (2002) points out, working-class women, both black and white, are positioned *against* respectable femininity as sexual: as a deviant form of sexuality.

For example, Skeggs (2002) describes the forging of group friendship by working-class young women through collective sessions of preparing to go out on a Saturday night. They spend hours putting on makeup, listening to music and dressing up before joining the town's nightlife. She illustrates, evocatively, how this female camaraderie makes an impact in public social spaces:

> The final product from these Friday or Saturday night sessions, which were a regular occurrence, may look like femininity, but in the production of it, raucousness, rudeness, outrageousness and challenge to femininity occur. They may have the physical appearance of femininity but their performance, their conduct, is definitely not feminine. In becoming physically feminine their look contradicts their performance. When they spill into the pub and the club a lasting pleasure can ensue, based on secret jokes and camaraderie. They have constructed themselves collectively and display their localised competences. For many men it seemed there was nothing more intimidating than this loud, laughing, together group of women. They *appear* as terrifying. They were claiming their right to their pleasure and social space.
>
> (Skeggs, 2002: 105)

Skeggs emphasises that working-class women overtly perform femininity as a kind of masquerade in which, 'The putting on of femininity is experienced as a form of camaraderie' (Skeggs, 2002: 106). Feeling good about one's appearance is essential to the women's confidence in negotiating public space. It is a public performance that has to be externally validated.

A key concern in many of today's news reports is the risk women face in having unprotected sex, and getting pregnant if they are drunk. However, a rise in representations of wild, uncontrollable, vulgar young women in the popular media from the 1990s is also indicative of a renewed attack on contemporary female experiences as Emelda Whelehan (2000) argues. With women's independence, 'greater equality' and the 'raunch culture' sited as reasons for the rise in women's binge drinking, the implication is that they should have their new found freedom curtailed. This view is linked to the discourse of a crisis in family values: a public fear of crumbling moral values among independent young women. The self-regulating autonomy of the 'modern girl' of the 1950s and 1960s (Johnson, 1993) has apparently collapsed.

The female crowd: an anomaly

While public spaces were once considered to be dangerous places *for* single women or women out on their own, these spaces are now considered endangered *by* women in large or noisy groups. The impression given by news reports of female binge drinking is of groups of women invading public space once reserved for men. The female crowd may well be an emergent form of association for women at leisure. Yet the idea barely seems to exist. The linking of the words 'women' and 'crowd' is anomalous. Nonetheless, the term is intriguing because it draws attention to the changing gendered nature of spatial relations and its importance for female bonds. As Elizabeth Wilson (1992) points out, in the nineteenth century the 'crowd' was invested with female characteristics associated with criminals and minorities, despite women's absence or minority presence in crowds. The 'masses' in expanding industrial cities were portrayed in feminine terms as 'hysterical', and associated with instability and sexuality. Women have, then, been strongly associated with the 'disorder' of urban life. Wilson acknowledges the dangers of the city for women but she also emphasises the pleasures and emancipatory potential of urban life, insisting on women's right to the carnival, passion, and even the risks of the city.

This treatment of more-than-two-women-together as a menace to society stretches back to Greek methodology: the Furies, Harpies, the Sirens and the Graeae. These are hordes of female monsters often associated with death, fate and the execution of divine ordeals on the human race. The emphasis is on aggressive, uncontrollable and menacing groups of independent women. They signify the chaotic and hysterical mess, yet also the *threat*, of the feminine. They are necessarily hideous in appearance and sexually lure men to a bad end. The villainy, plurality and excess of femininity is set in opposition to the virtuous, singular male protagonist who serves to educate boys into ideas of the heroic, stable and unified masculine self.

Having published a joint article about the film, *Full Monty*,[21] I attended a performance of the famous American male strip show, *The Chippendales*, at the Royal Concert Hall in Nottingham in 2002 (purely for research purposes, of course). I was struck, not so much by the complete absence of men in the audience at this event, but at the way in which that absence had fleetingly but forcefully transformed the imposing public space of a concert hall into a feminised space: a female crowd! Despite being staged at the Royal Concert Hall, there was nothing regal about this event. On the stage, the Chippendales were appositely provocative and sexually outrageous. In response, the all-female spectators matched the outrageousness in a whirl of excitement and excess: every few minutes a great roar came from the crowd as they stood up, fists thumping the air, chanting at the male performers to take their 'kit off'.

During the interval, hundreds of women of all ages, from teenagers to senior citizens stood chatting, drinking and smoking in the bars, along the corridors, on the landings and balconies of the concert hall. Women monopolised the men's as well as the women's washrooms since, off-stage, the only men in sight were bouncers. The atmosphere was peculiarly exhilarating. The bizarre feeling of crowd euphoria familiar to spectators of popular male and mixed sports, lingered as we left the building. After the performance ended, a throng of women of all ages spilled out on to the streets. For a brief moment, the centre of the city was transformed into a temporary *feminine space* as hundreds of women chattered loudly while criss-crossing the streets beyond the venue. This experience was striking in as much as it was both exceptional, yet confined to such a narrow sphere of frivolous leisure associated with an objectification and eroticisation of the male body. The sense of exhilaration in response to a feminine conquest of a public space was not only short-lived but apparently trivial, without potential. While the assertion of women's pleasure is significant, the hilarity depended on the *interruption* and reversal of the conventional objectification of women's bodies and the traditional male domination of public space in sport and leisure.

This momentary illusion of collectivity mirrors the kinds of passionate gatherings that men are accustomed to as audiences of male sports matches, addressed by Maffesoli's term, neotribalism. Maffesoli (1996) takes on board the contradictory social trends of a disappearance of traditional collectivities and the attractiveness of social gatherings characterised as fleeting, fluid and occasional. By neo-tribalism, Maffesoli (1996) means intense, sporadic social connections that take place in a society lacking in strong values of social integration. It signifies a transitory unity of people in 'emotional communities' in one-off events such as arts festivals, football matches, concerts, shows and cinemas. These spaces are often profoundly masculinised. Women enter them on men's terms. Women's participation in neo-tribal public events such as football may be indicative of some of the successes in the battle to occupy public space; it cannot be viewed as an occupation of that space. It is a profoundly contingent, provisional, non-politicised occupation of space. Maffesoli suggests that postmodern community is exemplified by informal friendship networks that have no moral purpose or project, referring only to the relations of sociability themselves. Crowds as theatre audiences, at football matches and pop concerts, and as travellers on commuter trains are temporary, liminal communities that characterise the postmodern condition. Women's tentative access into these liminal, 'elective communities' signifies their entrance into new social ties characterised by temporary associations rather than strong symbolic bonds. However, the non-binding nature of these associations implies a self-gratifying irresponsibility ill-suited to the conventional feminine subject. Discussions of 'postmodern community' disregard issues of care, loyalty and commitment, thereby generally excluding women from their domain. To be invited into these tribal, fragmented and fleeting communities, women must transcend their nurturing roles. The claiming of public space by lesbian and bisexual women has a very vital history but the important historical need for secrecy from husbands, fathers and brothers means that lesbian spaces have been less exhibitionistic than gay men's occupation of public space (see Chapter 5). While liminal communities offer women the potential of transgression, they do so at the cost of labelling them self-interested – a charge far less likely to be levelled at men.

Amoral urban spinsters

The single person household is now one of the most rapidly rising household types in Western nations such as the United States, Britain and other European countries (Chandler, Williams, Maconachie et al., 2004; Heath and Cleaver, 2003).[22] Yet despite the dramatic rise in the number of single people delaying marriage and living alone, the female singleton continues to be portrayed as a deviant status. In her research on working-class women's experiences of femininity, Skeggs (2002) found that to be without a man is viewed as inadequate and undesirable by many working-class cultures. For working-class women, with less economic and cultural capital available to them, 'couple culture' makes it difficult to occupy public space and for them to feel as valid as married women. She states that 'the feeling of inadequacy testifies to the power and pervasiveness of heterosexuality' (2002: 114). This places pressure on many women to invest in men, not just for economic reasons but, crucially, as a form of cultural validation. Going out in all-female groups is therefore a vital way of being able to subvert this social pressure. Among urban, middle-class career women, high cultural capital allows singlehood to be negotiated more positively as a new identity through higher income and a network of friendships. However, public images of the middle-class female singleton betray deep public anxieties about her independence and apparent preference for female friendship. Spinsterhood remains a deviant spectacle.

The category of 30-something middle-class women is being marked out as a problem for being too aspirational, career-oriented and fun-loving. She is resented either for being too ambitious to marry and raise a family or for daring to combine marriage and children with a career, thereby neglecting both. The delay in marriage and fall in the birth rate, the rise in a singleton population and in cohabitation, and the escalating success of girls in secondary education compared to boys[23] are all social trends marking out girls and young women as assertive, aspirational, high-achievers who have a thirst for well-paid professional careers and group female friendship. The media disapproval of these groups of women is indicative of the serious challenges facing women as a whole in their attempts to transcend traditional dependence on men for their status.

The humour in situation comedies and films such as *Bridget Jones Diary*, and *Sex and the City* serves to illuminate shifting anxieties about the moral principles associated with romance, sex, marriage, work and friendship.[24] Comedy acts as a powerful device for investigating the moral uncertainties concerning women's increasing sexual and eco-nomic independence, as 'bearers of a new world'.[25] *Sex and the City*[26] centred on the group dynamics of narcissistic, professional and affluent, 30-something heterosexual singletons in search of sexual partners. First released in 1998, it was one of the first TV shows to provide a forum that venerates heterosexual women's *group* friendships as a context for exploring female sexual desires. In fact, integrity is about sticking to your friends, not your sexual partner who is, invariably, suspect. The hot gossip about sex is the glue that binds the characters of Carrie, Samantha, Miranda and Charlotte together. While the sexual partners are both demanding and lacking, the friends are the judge, jury, confidantes and counsellors. The boyfriends come and go, but the friendships stay.

In *Sex and the City*, the humour functions to perpetuate prejudices against the single woman, portraying her as both aggressor and victim. The contradiction of envy and scorn works by the humour feeding on public anxieties about a post-traditional, individualised urban society. The female body, narcissism, unrequited love, insecurity and confession are sites of ironic humour and moral ambiguity in female singleton sitcom, preserving powerful ideas about the disorderliness of being 'without a man'. The pleasure-seeking, postmodern singleton female subject is rendered profoundly *amoral* by the depiction of these single women's bodies, actions and anxieties as commodified self-gratification and fetish (Akass and McCabe, 2004: 179). The protagonists' agency is fated by their lack of self-confidence and their faith in consumerism. Indeed, *consumer culture* replaces the *ethical self* as an ideal, as Jane Arthurs (2003: 93) points out. In this way, the humour conveys a particular, materialistic version of femininity, a market-led postfeminism focused on consumption and 'style' (Whelehan, 2000). The consumption of fashion and men signifies over-indulgence and hedonism which, in turn, signifies feminine excess. Paradoxically, while the gossip between these single women is typically set in trendy Manhattan eating places, the protagonists are so slim that food barely passes their lips. Excess and self-denial go hand in hand. By rendering the female singleton amoral and irresponsible for choosing friendship over family, women's apparent freedom and choice comes to stand for the public sense of social decline.

A crucial theme of *Sex and the City*, like all Chick fiction, is unrequited love as the punishment for female independence. This is played out through the use of familiar constructs that define the ideal woman so as to highlight the grotesqueness of feminine singlehood. The conventional romance fairy-tale narrative is scrutinised and pored over in *Sex and the City*. While exploring the dilemmas of being unmarried, the protagonists frequently draw the conclusion that being single is preferable to faking happiness with a man, as exemplified in the episode, 'They Shoot Single People Don't They?'[27] (Arthurs, 2003). The fantasies of heterosexual romance, the search for Prince Charming, and perfect motherhood are explored in the show, but friendship and consumption are either chosen or offered as the favoured refuge. Despite the intermittent celebration of single status, and despite their smartness and apparent confidence, the moral outrageousness of the brazenly expressed sexual desire of these women is disarmed by the ironic treatment of singlehood as an unremitting dilemma: as a marginal status.

The voluntary nature of personal relationships, discussed in Chapter 2, raises important issues about the vulnerability of commitment and emotional security which get played out in female singleton narratives. Through ironic humour, audiences are alerted to the pitfalls of modern-day spinsterhood in *Sex and the City*. By exposing the *vulnerability* associated with the freedom of being able to choose one's own relationships, these women become victims. This unruly subject is dogged by superficial relationships characterised by short-lived romances, one-night stands and the fear of emotional rejection. *Sex and the City*'s satirical humour invites audiences to laugh at the retribution delivered to smug, self-satisfied single women who seem to 'have it all', who appear to be succeeding in a man's world at a man's game.

Popular media narratives such as *Sex and the City* allow the exploration of anxieties associated with today's ephemeral relationship. Urban societies' negative interpretations of rising individualism, exemplified by Christopher Lasch (1979), are projected on to the new social groups who emerge, apparently confidently, from the late modern system of fragmented social ties. The single woman is identified, in citing individualism and rampant narcissism, as the cause of social decay. Her demand for equality in intimate relationships allows the humour to confirm an assertive dimension to the character of the female singleton: she is pushy, needy and dissatisfied with the men she dates. The narrative ensures that she gets her comeuppance later. By symbolising the wider moral panic about feminine individualism, this over-confident woman is rendered hilarious. Treated as a threat to the moral fabric of society, scornful humour allows an exploration and then sets up a denunciation of women's independence. Sardonic humour exploits the central role self-disclosure plays in the management of the modern feminine self: a person's 'feelings' are exposed and pored over to portray a disorderly female subject.

Ironic humour appears to render the confessional discourse of Chick comedy both subversive *and* conformist. These singletons apparently undermine dominant discourse by using their friendships to talk about topics deemed taboo by a patriarchal discourse. Menstruation, menopause, single parenting, blow jobs, premature ejaculation, male impotence and homosexuality are all commented on with relish. But the radical bid for autonomy is derailed by the protagonists' excessive emotional vulnerability and the reminder that singlehood is *spinsterhood*. The assumption among Carrie and her friends is that the singleton is a profoundly marginalised category. The confessional mode allows the neediness of the women to eclipse the pleasure and wisdom of their status. It undermines the protagonists' power by confirming the status of unmarried woman as lack, as UN-something. The single woman thereby experiences spectacular humiliation in searching for alternative self-fulfilment.

As one critic, Stacey D'Erasmo states:

> The new single girl, tottering on her Manolo Blahniks from misadventure to misadventure, embodies in her very slender form the argument that not only is feminism over. It also failed: look how unhappy the 'liberated' woman is! Men don't want to marry her![28]

The image of victim works, then, through the confessional, centred on the independent woman's failure to find romance and form a family of her own. It works by disregarding or trivialising the wider set of social conflicts affecting the roles of women in late modernity: the conflict between women's employment and economic independence, and women's assigned nurturing role, making them responsible for the caring of society's young and elderly. The confessional constitutes a site of struggle in exploring women's identities but satirical humour evokes the isolation conveyed by *lack of family ties* to render a fun-loving, independent singleton a vulnerable, self-absorbed, amoral subject. To underline this desolation, Sarah Jessica Parker, who plays Carrie, is depicted in the media as 'a wanton, desperate woman roaming the streets of New York' (Rudolph, 1998: 13). Accordingly, the female singleton is sidelined, failing to reach the status of heroine, of champion for a new feminism or even a new, woman-centred ontology. The patriarchal fantasies confirming traditional family values remain intact. Yet personal vulnerability guarantees the intensity of the women's friendships. Ultimately, however, these stray singletons' dependence on one another is treated as a substitute for family life.

Although an enormous amount of caring is celebrated in *Sex and the City* in the form of friendship, such compassion is invalidated for being a social bond that exists outside the traditional nuclear family. Ironic humour works to regulate and discipline the female singleton, who is reined back under patriarchal control within sitcom narrative resolutions. As a morality tale, female singleton humour warns us that despite being a growing category, the female singleton remains a subordinated subject: a spinster.

Conclusion

This chapter shows how women use personal networks as an essential resource yet, unlike men, find it much more difficult to use them to access power. It emphasises that women's personal relationships are judged by a discourse of feminine respectability and nurturing which attempts to regulate feminine identities. Women have higher levels of social capital yet their responsibility for the emotional and physical care of children and husbands makes them vital domestic exchanges. In the context of employment, male networking tends to exclude women from information that could further their careers. However, a significant rise in the status and identity of independent single women is spearheading the emergence of new group friendships among both working-class and middle-class women in the context of urban leisure. Group friendships are offering single women – young working-class and older middle-class career women – an avenue for pleasure and hedonism as a reward for work, a right that men take for granted. These associations are, however, being signified as vulgar, unruly and disreputable by the media, by their association with binge drinking and other excesses.

The association of female leisure with sexuality in today's popular culture has triggered concerns about the contradiction between single women's demands for pleasure and women's potential familial roles as wives and mothers. Middle-class women's friendships are being represented in sitcoms such as *Sex and the City* as self-indulgent, irresponsible and atomised. A contemporary symbol of individualistic and narcissistic femininity is constructed and perceived as a threat to family values: the amoral, self-indulgent, arrogant and assertive singleton bent on hedonistic pleasure. Before celebrating new forms of group friendship among women, and their visibility in urban spaces at night as a postmodern fluidity of feminine relations, we are reminded that women's same-sex friendships are sharply regulated by ideologies of respectability.

5
The Decline and Rise of 'Community'

Concerns about the erosion of community continue to resonate today in debates about changing social ties among academics, governments and charity organisations.[1] The privileging of individual self-reliance coupled with the decline in nineteenth-century principles and structures of community and welfare has triggered public anxieties about a rising tide of selfishness and mistrust. One of the most influential contributors to the thesis of community breakdown is Robert Putnam (2000), who claims that American society is beleaguered by a decline in community values. He argues that societies that have better organised cooperation and civic cohesion also have better government, schools, economic growth, health and well-being. But the mechanisms that underlie these connections are imprecise.

As an advocate of a civic form of communitarianism, Putnam deploys the concept of 'social capital' to support his claim for decline in community values. The term 'social capital', which is linked to the language of civil society, is defined by Putnam as 'features of social organisation such as trusts, norms and networks that can improve the efficiency of society by facilitating coordinated actions' (Putnam, Leonardi and Nanetti, 1993b). Thus, for Putnam, a decline in social capital coincides with a decline in community values. I argue in this chapter that Putnam's thesis is an example of an unconvincing and pessimistic view of changing social ties. His conceptualisation of community is nostalgic and culture-bound. The emphasis on social values conceals forms of social deprivation. The working classes are thereby regarded as lacking in the communication skills and forms of contact needed for community networking. Moreover, Putnam privileges traditional social ties such as family and neighbourhood, thereby neglecting the new identities and new social ties associated with them.

In contrast to Putnam's thesis of social fragmentation, a number of postmodern thinkers are exploring the openness and fluidity of social ties. The deconstructive approaches of post-structuralism, feminism, queer theory and postcolonialism show how the traditional pointers of identity such as class, gender, age, nation and ethnicity are being questioned and loosened, providing new opportunities for individual autonomy. By recognising the self as socially constructed, identity and belonging can no longer be taken for granted. The self is being reconfigured by new forms of sociation: new sexual communities and friendship networks, new urban movements, and new forms of global communication facilitated by new technologies. Theorists of network sociality, such as Castells, suggest that new technology is presenting us with exciting and innovative ways of communicating by delivering new kinds of interaction and community networking. This chapter critically assesses Putnam's thesis of social disintegration. I argue that emergent forms of social cohesion such as queer communities and friends as family are examples of new forms of belonging. The next chapter follows this theme of new forms of communication and belonging in further detail by examining claims, made by writers such as Castells, of new forms of postsocial relations, characterised by intense but ephemeral online communication rather than or in addition to face-to-face communication.

The collapse of community?

Putnam (2000) argues that a sense of social disengagement and civic malaise is permeating American society despite high levels of material satisfaction. Although his book, *Bowling Alone*, is subtitled: 'the collapse and revival of American community', Putnam focuses in far more detail on the theme of collapse. The decline of bowling leagues is used as a metaphor for wider social atomisation. The general changes in postwar American social and political life are interpreted as a manifestation of a long-term decline in American civic involvement, originating in the 1960s. These changes coincide with a decline in citizens' participation in community life and good government. It is a situation that leads to psychological alienation, according to Putnam.

The popular appeal of this thesis of community collapse in the United States reveals a growing sense of anxiety about social seclusion and the drift towards privatised life among the American news media, intellectuals and government. A decline in rates of participation in civic, leisure and sociable activities from churches and unions to bowling alleys and clubrooms seem to support Putnam's argument about a widespread cultural, political and moral degeneration. This decline in social cohesion is characterised by a disintegration of 'social capital': networks of interaction that allow collective action, democratic participation and community. 'Social capital' is a term deployed to signify those forms of social organisation – including networks, norms of reciprocity and social trustworthiness – that enhance cooperation between individuals for mutual benefit. Falling rates of involvement in local community activities are of concern because they correlate with declining safety and rising crime, deteriorating child well-being, weakening economic efficiency and noticeable decline in public health. 'Weakened social capital is manifest in the things that have vanished almost unnoticed – neighbourhood parties and get-togethers with friends, the unreflective kindness of strangers, the shared pursuit of the public good rather than a solitary quest for private goods' (Putnam, 2000: 403). The growth of the welfare state, suburbanisation, divorce, women's entrance into the workforce and changing family structures are among those factors identified by Putnam that might explain the apparent breakdown of civic culture in the Unites States.

Putnam asserts that this unremitting civic decline is having alarming consequences for the predicament of health, education, happiness, family welfare, security, culture, economic prosperity and political institutions. The lack of social engagement is viewed as a sign of deep-seated alienation from social activity. He decries individualism, materialism, and privatised retreat as beliefs and values that undermine social capital. A number of changing social habits exemplify these shifts including the decline in families eating together and decline of face-to-face interaction caused by Internet use. Putnam clearly privileges local, face-to-face, family-based and neighbourhood ties. He concludes that the decline in social capital in the United States has been so dramatic that it may endanger the effective functioning of political democracy. Influenced by de Tocqueville's organic unity of state and civil society, Putnam asserts that social responsibility should rest with civil society rather than the welfare state since the effectiveness of the state depends on the unity of civil society.

The concept of social capital used by Putnam can be divided into two types: network capital and participatory capital (Wellman, Quan Haase, Witte and Hampton, 2001: 437). Network capital is made up of relations with friends, neighbours, relatives, and workmates who provide important companionship, emotional support, goods and services, information, and a sense of belonging. Participatory capital refers to individuals' involvement in politics and voluntary organisations that give opportunities for individuals to form bonds, create joint accomplishments and gather together, and articulate their demands and desires. Societies that produce rich, dense networks and cultures of association which are *voluntary* rather than government *initiated* are identified as rich in social capital. This is because public policies can then connect with the networks of civic engagement and be anchored within organic communities. Putnam (1993b) refers to Southern Italy as a model for understanding the complexities of the United States. He stresses that in regions like southern Italy, public policies have a track record of failing because traditions of cross-community associations and cultures of social trust are traditionally weak.

Importantly, 'social capital' has become a fashionable concept in the formation of policy in Western governments. This is despite it being a difficult concept to quantify, there being no single measure or index of it. For example, factors such as trust in other people, changing values and changing norms of behaviour are all subjective and intangible. Most studies of these social issues tend to look at a range of indicators rather than a single one. Despite such problems, the concept of 'social capital' is widely used by governments to assess the ways that social connectedness may contribute to a range of beneficial economic and social outcomes, such as growth in Gross Domestic Production (GDP), efficient functioning of labour markets, high educational attainment, lower levels of crime, better health and more efficient institutions of government.[2]

Significantly, Putnam does not view humans as naturally associative. He follows rational choice theory, presupposing that individuals are self-interested and wish to maximise their well-being by connecting with others as a form of personal investment. For Putnam, participation in voluntary associations enhances public mindedness and the confidence to participate in public affairs. The problem is that people fail to take advantage of the benefits of cooperation because they no longer trust one another. In circumstances where cooperation is difficult, social capital provides a mechanism for mutual benefit to overcome the inherent selfishness and competitiveness of the individual.

The enthusiasm for forming and joining associations, which de Tocqueville considered to be the most distinguishing characteristic of nineteenth-century American society, is now diminishing according to Putnam. In the last 25 years, the average membership of voluntary organisations has shrunk to a tenth of the size of membership in the previous 25 years (Putnam, 2000: 49). The centralisation of voluntary organisations and professionally staffed advocacy organisations, by shifting the headquarters to Washington, has resulted in less regular contact with members at grass-roots levels. People make payments, receive services and are no longer engaged in the day-to-day activities. Long-running organisations such as Rotary Clubs and the American Association of Retired Persons no longer facilitate social networks of involvement and reciprocity. They represent a monetary rather than a social relationship. Nonetheless, this monetary connection is vital. Although American society is often characterised by a reluctance to pay taxes, the philanthropic nature of Americans is demonstrated by 180 billion dollars a year given by Americans to charities and other good causes.[3]

Supporting public anxieties that individualisation is caused by women's growing bid for independence, Putnam argues that women's increased participation in the workforce contributes to the decline in participatory capital and therefore to community collapse. However, since social responsibility is mainly borne by women in the form of charity work, parents associations and religious activities, women have been consistently recorded as having higher levels of social capital than men, as shown for example by the *General Household Survey* (2000/1), mentioned in Chapter 4. Putnam identifies women as a problem group precisely because they have traditionally shouldered the burden of binding communities together as *invisible* carers (Sevenhuijsen, 1998). The rise in female employment is linked to a decrease in former levels of civic participation among married women. Rather than proposing that men share in women's caring activities, he expresses disapproval of women for following men in the trend towards personal pursuits, careers and consumption at the expense of collective values. Given that early twentieth-century women's organisations tended to be geared to home-makers, and that women's paid employment has risen dramatically, it is hardly surprising that women's homemaking organisations have declined significantly across Western nations. For example, in the United Kingdom, membership of the National Federation of Women's Institute fell by 46 per cent between 1972 and 2002,[4] coinciding with the increased participation of women in the workforce. But Putnam (2000: 194–202) stresses that there has been a simultaneous decline in participation by both employed and unemployed women. A further obstacle to the formation and continuation of social capital for Putnam is television. First, it competes for scarce time, with each additional hour of television viewing accounting for about a 10 per cent reduction in levels of civic activism. Second, Putman claims that television viewing has psychological effects that impede social participation. It privatises leisure time and encourages laziness and passivity.

Putnam also asserts that civic decline is taking place on a generational basis. The younger generation born from the 1950s onwards, known as

'Gen-Xers', are identified as the social group least likely to participate in those political, religious, social civic activities which characterised American society up to the early 1960s. The civic-minded generation who were born before the 1950s showed a keen sense of community spirit, forged by World War II and its repercussions. According to Putnam, they demonstrated a stronger concern for the public good, higher commitment to civic obligations, and a stronger sense of community and engagement in politics by attending public meetings or rallies, engaging in voluntary work, and by interacting with friends and neighbours. For Putnam, then, the decline in civic participation begins in the mid-1960s. He claims that the younger generation who came of age in that period have more privatised lifestyles, are more passive and less philanthropic, are less socially engaged and more likely to be estranged from the political system.

The culture-bound nature of social capital

How well does Putnam's thesis travel? If we compare his analysis of change in social relationships in the Unites States with social trends in the United Kingdom, a different set of social patterns emerges, suggesting that Putnam's argument about the decline of social connectedness in the Unites States is, at best, culture-bound and not a general trend that all Western democracies need to address. For instance, England's Health Education Authority Report is critical of Putnam's approach. The report found little evidence in England of the atomised self-absorbed individualism identified by Putnam (Campbell, Wood and Kelly, 1999). In fact, it argues that the media preoccupation with 'loss of community' is a 'moral panic', stressing that the sociability of personal communities is, nowadays, characterised as *informal*. The Health Education Authority report regarded Putnam's conceptualisation of a cohesive community as essentialist, arguing that it 'bore a greater resemblance to people's romanticised reconstructions of an idealised past than to people's accounts of the complex, fragmented and rapidly changing face of contemporary community life – characterised by high levels of mobility, instability and plurality' (Campbell, Wood and Kelly, 1999: 156). The authors concluded that his conceptualisation needed to be reworked. Yet, worryingly, governments continue to use the concept widely without the qualifications that these criticisms point to.

Government data collected on indicators of social capital in the United Kingdom are related to five main areas: civic engagement, neighbourliness, social networks, social support, and people's perceptions of their local area. Importantly, while membership of women's homemaking associations such as the Women's Institute has declined, reflecting key changes in women's patterns of work, the membership of cross-gender associations such as environmental organisations has quadrupled since 1971. In the United Kingdom, the National Trust had three million members in 2002, more than ten times the number in 1971 (*Social Trends*, 33, 2003: 19). This increase is higher than that of the 5 per cent growth in population over the same period. Other survey data in Britain shows a similar picture. The National Council for Voluntary Organisations found a significant increase in new voluntary organisations and in voluntary work since the 1970s, and a growth in new forms of sporting organisations.[5] The levels of associational membership, number of charities and donations in Britain were as high in the 1990s as they were in 1959 according to evidence from local and national studies (Hall, 1999).

Moreover, in contrast with Putnam's thesis, levels of informal sociability have risen in the United Kingdom according to time-budget studies, with an increase in out of home leisure which expands people's scope for sociability (Hall, 1999). This data contradicts the notion of more home-based or privatised forms of leisure taking hold in the postwar years. In fact, all levels of community involvement have remained buoyant in Britain. Remarkably, even television viewing of an average of two and a half hours a day has not stopped people from maintaining levels of sociability and community participation reflecting those typical of the 1950s. So television viewing does not inevitably reduce levels of social interaction in the community. Instead, it seems to have replaced an equivalent media activity: radio listening.

People's perceptions of local neighbourhoods indicate the strength of community spirit and neighbourliness. For example, the British Crime Survey conducted since 1984 which monitors the neighbourhood trust, has found a consistent drop in the number of people agreeing that people 'help each other out'.[6] This indicates a possible decline in community cohesion, but since 1996 the proportion of neighbourhoods where people are perceived to 'help each other' has risen slowly to 36 per cent by 2000. Assumptions of social decline need to be understood in the context of increasing independence since individuals become more selective about whom they mix with and call on for help. It seems likely that are relying more on chosen friends than on local neighbours and kin. This is implied by the rise in people choosing friends as family, discussed in Chapter 2.

Many of the indicators used to signify social capital have statistically significant relationships with people's demographic characteristics such as age, gender and class. For example, age has a major bearing on 'neighbourliness' which is indicated by the number of times people speak to their neighbours and the number of people they know in their area. The proportion of individuals who say they know many people in their neighbourhood increases with age. Almost three-fifths of those aged 70 and over in the United Kingdom in 2000/1 said they know many people in their neighbourhood, compared with just over one-third of those aged 16–29.[7] More women (48 per cent) know people in their neighbourhood than men (43 per cent), confirming women's responsibilities, especially married women, as caretakers of the community and of domesticity as discussed in Chapter 4. Young adults aged 16–29 are the least neighbourly and least likely to be civically engaged.[8] They have lower levels of reciprocity, defined as swapping favours with neighbours. And they are likely to trust fewer neighbours and less likely to speak to them. Trust in neighbours rises steadily with age. Seventy-five per cent of people aged 70 and above trust most or many of their neighbours compared with 39 per cent of those aged 16–29.[9] These social patterns may be indicative of either life-course differences or of social changes over time.

However, young adults have more active social networks and are more likely to telephone, e-mail and meet friends more frequently than older adults, according to British government data in *Social Trends* (2003).[10] Indeed, adults aged 30 and over are more likely to be involved in their local communities; are more likely to be involved in local organisations; be better informed about local affairs and feel more civically engaged than younger adults. Evidence suggests that young people rely more on friends in a nomadic way, by transcending the kinds of social networks shaped by geographically bounded communities (see Chapter 8).[11] This is significant because although it may be a product of youth, it may also indicate a new trend where people may be relying less and less on contacts made through proximity, and increasingly on non-local, travel, phone and Internet-initiated interaction.

Significantly, individuals who are divorced or separated have the lowest levels of social support, with 72 per cent having three or more people to turn to.[12] This group is also the least likely to enjoy living in their local area. Single people are less likely to be civically engaged and be less neighbourly than other groups. At first glance, it is tempting to think that single people are the archetypal social group suffering from Putnam's social disintegration, that they are being marginalised in some way by the wider community. If this were so, it would be noteworthy, given the sharp rise in single-person households (see, for example,

Chandler, Williams, M., Maconachie et al., 2004; Heath and Cleaver, 2003).[13] However, single people share many characteristics with young people, as they are more likely to have satisfactory friendship networks, indicating that non-face-to-face communication is a vital feature of networking among singletons. Moreover, marital status is strongly related to age, for example 75 per cent of single men and women are aged between 16 and 34, while 84 per cent of married people are aged 35 or above.[14] High proportions of lone-parent households are likely to have both satisfactory friendship and relative networks, probably because they necessarily depend on networks. Non-kin related households, such as people in flat-shares, are the least likely to know, trust and speak to neighbours and low proportions also reported satisfactory networks with kin (*Social Trends*, 2003). However, as addressed later, many such people are forming new kinds of social ties originating from new kinds of identities and forms of networking.

Class and social capital

Social capital relates to the value in social networks and social trust. So factors concerning how well connected individuals are, and how much they trust others are endowed with value. Social networks are about power, as shown in Chapter 3 in relation to the privileges of male networks. Government data bears this out, showing that educational level and class influence social capital.[15] With regard to social class, we find that level of education, employment status and income are closely related. The middle classes are twice as likely to have organisational affiliations as the working classes, and professionals are three times more likely to take part in voluntary endeavours than manual workers. Education increases the propensity for an individual to engage in community affairs. High educational level is positively related to civic engagement, social trust, neighbourliness and social support, and the way people perceive their local area (*Social Trends*, 2003). Those with qualifications are more likely to have a better perception of local neighbourhood and more likely to feel safe walking alone after dark in local area. Well educated people have higher socioeconomic resources and can afford to live in safer areas.[16] Yet people with higher incomes are also likely to have the poorest networks of relatives. The working class have the highest networks of relatives (*Social Trends*, 2003: 23). The only group that the working classes have higher contact with than their middle-class counterparts is relatives. This reflects the fact that working-class kin networks tend to live closer together and are less geographically and socially mobile.

The level of deprivation in an area impacts on indicators of social capital as shown by government reports such as the 2001 Home Office Citizenship Survey in the United Kingdom (Attwood, Singh, Prime et al., 2001). People living in least deprived areas tend to experience much higher participation in civic and social activities, and in both formal and informal volunteering, than those who lived in more deprived areas. Social capital and networking informally beyond kin are, then, privileged everyday practices that cannot be taken for granted. The lack of engagement by the working class is disturbing. They have fewer, more informal friendship networks than their middle-class counterparts. The use of 'social capital' as a measure of participation in civic society reveals that the working class are excluded from civic society when measured by Putnam's model (Hall, 1999). This indicates that social capital favours middle-class modes of networking and is unlikely to constitute a mechanism for redistributing wealth or mitigating the kinds of social conditions that lead to social exclusion.

The lack of social capital among the British working classes coincided with the decline in Trade Union membership, working-class solidarity and heavy industry during the Tory government of the 1980s. These changes corresponded with the decrease in working men's clubs and other social networks that characterised such communities. Associational memberships among the working class lowered during the same period that they were dramatically rising among the middle classes. This suggests that the levels of social capital available to the working class in Britain are not only low but also extremely fragile in the current social climate (Hall, 1999). Nevertheless, it is significant that the working classes are more likely to engage in forms of sociability that lie outside the definition of 'social capital'. As mentioned, their networks entail contacts with kin and small groups of friends that are closely connected to one another. These are often long-standing associations such as school friends. By contrast, social networks among the middle classes tend to be more diverse, wide-ranging, fragmented and ephemeral.

This suggests that, as well as being culture-bound, the concept of social capital favours middle-class lifestyles. Putnam calls for a return to a golden era of civic participation in postwar America where social capital corresponded with 'middle-class sensibilities' and symbolised a mode of 'democracy' (Boggs, 2001: 295). Notwithstanding the importance of modes of social capital such as voluntary associations, something more radical is required to tackle the problem of social deprivation in poor neighbourhoods. Improvements in employment, education, health and housing, developed and implemented at local community-based levels are needed. This is revealed by government reports that have uncovered the causes of chronic poverty in certain neighbourhoods. For example, the British government report on a national strategy for neighbourhood renewal (Social Exclusion Unit, 1998) found that over the last generation, the poorest neighbourhoods have declined even further in terms of crime, economic and labour market activity. The report admitted that past government policies have contributed to poverty with poor housing design impacting on weakening communities and rendering neighbourhoods less safe. Policies on housing allocation, rents and benefits have led to the concentration of the poor and unemployed together in neighbourhoods where few have jobs.

The decline of democratic citizenship?

Of importance to civic democracy is the decline in democratic citizenship which can be measured in the form of falls in election voting. Putnam argues that the decline in social connectedness coincides with depoliticisation: a lowered interest in political affairs by post-World War II generations and declining electoral participation in the Unites States. Over the past ten years, political involvement measured by registered electorate voting has, indeed, been declining in Western nations. For example, the turnout for the 2001 British national election was 59 per cent, the lowest in Britain in the postwar period. A similar pattern is observable in other OECD countries that have no penalty attached to non-voting in parliamentary elections: in Japan the turn-out was 59 per cent in 2000; in the Unites States it was 46.6 per cent in 2000, and in Canada it was 54.6 per cent in 2000.[17] So Putnam is right when he argues that participatory capital has waned. Some research findings indicate that this is due to voter apathy and distrust of politicians.[18] But Putnam does not explore these reasons in any depth.

Putnam privileges a version of public life based on an account of community that ignores significant popular movements of the 1960s and 1970s. The very generation implicated by Putnam as exemplifying civic decline, has been centrally involved in the emergence of a new era of civic involvement and political activism through the Civil Rights movement, the anti-Vietnam War movement, the rise of the social movements of feminism, gay rights and the environmental movement, and the growth of various community groups. As Boggs (2001: 283) states, this period 'contrast(s) sharply with the quiet, bland, conservative national consensus of the Eisenhower fifties'. Tens of millions of people took part in large-scale movements for social change from the 1960s, which drove radical changes in social policy and transformed the political landscape through grass-roots protest. Putnam discards these movements as counter-trends that all but disappeared in the 1980s and 1990s. Large-scale social movements were fuelled by distrust and cynicism in response not only to Watergate but also the rise of the political election circuses now common in the United States and copied by other Western nations. Previous levels of civic participation may well have been exceeded during this period, as Boggs asserts. This was a period that witnessed the sharp rise in centralised economic and government power characterised by a growth of corporate power.

The dwindling public trust in the US government in the 1980s and the consequent depoliticisation process was provoked by these national and global shifts. Private corporations dominated the public sphere through deregulation and privatisation, which corresponded with globalisation and the embedding of media culture (Boggs, 2001: 288). The anti-World Trade Organisation protests that began in late 1999, followed by the transnational anti-war protests against the war in Iraq in 2003, bear witness to the kinds of political responses which by-pass elections. Given successive British governments' collusion in the American government's concentration of power, it comes as no surprise that Britain is beleaguered by related voting problems. The issue of political trust is revisited in the final chapter in relation to responsibility and care.

Beyond social capital

Despite the enormous amount of empirical evidence in *Bowling Alone*, Putnam's analysis is misleading. His definition of social capital is analogous to other discourses of social cohesion, social exclusion and community: the measuring of social conditions against the distinctive norm of a stable but mythical social order (Walters, 2002). The thesis is founded on a conservative definition of 'community'. He advocates selective kinds of participation: traditional community activities representative of a largely middle and upper-middle class and older generation who joined the celebrated Rotary or Elks clubs, churches, choirs, reading groups, sports leagues and dinner parties. Boggs (2001: 284) observes:

> The older voluntary organisations Putnam cherishes went into decline precisely because they lost their *raison d'etre* as their goals became outdated, mostly reflective of a small-town America that itself was in the process of vanishing.

Indeed, many of the dwindling activities that Putnam identifies as having the potential to build social capital are scarcely relevant to 'social capital' itself. Putnam (2000: 338) claims, but fails to establish a causal link between individual political empowerment and participation in these voluntary groups. These kinds of clubs, leagues and groups existed in America and Europe alongside the authoritarian movements, parties and governments demonstrated by fascism and communism in the same way that gangs, cults, self-help groups, militias and 'identity politics' movements do today (Boggs, 2001: 285). Putnam favours relations of close geographical proximity associated with participation in recreational, social, service-oriented or political endeavours. Yet he is measuring old forms of community and participation while ignoring new forms of communication and organisation that now bring people together through new communication technologies (Wellman, Quan Haase, Witte and Hampton, 2001). Putnam's assertion of community decline is founded on a version of community that privileges family, neighbourhood and face-to-face interactions over long-distance and 'virtual' communication. However, neither 'family' nor 'community' are adequately defined by Putnam. The vagueness of these concepts allows them to be invested with enormous emotional significance without discussion of issues of power and conflict: that is, how power operates through these traditional associations to regulate social identities and practices.

Within the social capital discourse, 'community' functions as a profoundly utopian concept. It implies spontaneous negotiation between free, but socially embedded family members. Importantly, family bonds and neighbourhood networks are structured by hierarchy and authority: by gender, sexuality, class, race, ethnicity, religion, age and physical ability. Social bonds that belong to the past are recuperated by Putnam and reassembled as somehow truer, more authentic bonds. As Richard Reeves puts it, Putnam 'is suffering from a kind of Neighbourhood Watch nostalgia. He ends up worshipping a world in which men did boring jobs while women baked cookies at home' (Reeves, 2001). The assumption is that individuals only thrive in a stable, settled group with values of association preferred to values of independence, mobility and change. This nostalgic thesis articulates a vision of lost *Gemeinschaft* (Stewart, 2002). Government organisations continue to cling to local definitions of community, but as the following discussion and chapter show, they need to embrace new identities and new forms of networking.

New forms of belonging: queer communities, friendship and families of choice

No longer bound by blood ties or traditional community networks, emergent forms of sociation ignored in Putnam's thesis, are being approached as part of identity politics and the emergence of postmodern communities. Through oppression or marginalisation, groups have come together to celebrate their uniqueness and contest their inferior position in society. Some of these resistance identities are project identities that create a vision of a better society such as the environmental movement, feminism, sexual politics and black civil rights. In Western nations, groups of individuals have come together in a number of protest movements including the anti-capitalist movement, and the anti-war movement, as well as environmental movements. These are supported by non-government organisation groups such as Greenpeace, Friends of the Earth and Amnesty International, and Lesbian and Gay Pride. In the following two chapters, network society and Internet communities are explored as examples of postmodern communities. Here, 'families of choice' and 'queer communities' are addressed as examples of emergent social ties anchored within friendship support networks. At odds with Putnam's thesis of social decline, these new associations confirm that social participation is alive and well and being experienced in new configurations.

New patterns of living are being invented by non-heterosexual[19] men and women, particularly those freed from dependence on the ideology of the family and conventional heterosexual gender roles of female nurturing and male 'breadwinner'. The relaxation of social taboos surrounding lesbian, gay, bisexual, transsexual and queer lifestyles are exemplified by the recent establishment of civil unions in certain Western nations such as the United Kingdom in 2005. Prospects of living in openly non-heterosexual relationships are, then, being opened up. These new living arrangements encompass both temporary and permanent forms. Importantly, they are increasingly drawing on *friendship* and *community* as metaphors and practices to signal opposition to, or a movement beyond, traditional nuclear family forms and old community associations. The construction of a politics of difference is therefore central to gay identity politics as part of the subversion of the fixed familial and community identities of Putnam's lost society.

Queer community

Significant shifts in the mid-twentieth century, including the gay and lesbian movement and feminism, gave rise to the affirmation of sexual identity and distinctive sexual communities in the 1970s (Weeks, 1995) and post-identity queer politics in the 1980s (Weeks, Heaphy and Donovan, 2001). Relations of friendship are crucial to stigmatised groups such as those who come out as gay, lesbian or bisexual. 'Coming out' is a process of new identity formation that brings about key changes in communication with existing personal networks and involves a renegotiation of closeness and distance with existing family and friends. For white, Western middle-class individuals, the process can be distressing. For others, such as working-class, Muslim and other marginalised groups, the double subordination of sexual and ethnic minority status can lead to a traumatic set of circumstances. The process of coming out causes changes in relationship arrangements including the vital need to build or rebuild personal community. A British documentary film, 'Gay Muslims' directed by Cara Lavan shown on Channel 4 in 2006,[20] describes how Muslims have faced the problems of reconciling their sexuality with their faith. Some concealed their feelings; others led a covert double life; and a third group who made no secret of their sexual identities experienced rejection by families and wider ethnic communities. In a study of young, white college-age women coming out as bisexual or lesbian in the Unites States, Ramona Faith Oswald (2000) found that building a community, by bringing queer-positive information and relationships into the person's network, was a crucial aspect of coming out. Coming out is not simply something that individuals do first, and *then* reveal to their families and friends later. Announcing and sustaining a non-heterosexual identity is an ongoing process embedded in the events and interactions of everyday life, as Oswald confirms.

Pre-existing relationships often need to be redefined so as to be supportive of the newly identified bisexual or lesbian network member: 'Building community was also an opportunity to decrease tolerance for bigoted ideas and behaviour, as well as to create relationship structures to resist homophobia and heterosexism' (Oswald, 2000: 81). Oswald found that self-disclosure and questioning of the self and others is often accompanied by increased distance from family of origin and increased closeness with friends and peers. These findings indicate that non-heterosexual identities are more than internal orientation claimed by individuals. A queer identity is negotiated in the context of both supportive and rejecting relationships. Activity groups, category sports and artistic production can therefore be important for non-heterosexual individuals and groups marginalised in mainstream cultures, as a way of expressing themselves and subverting cultural norms through physical and/or creative accomplishment and expression.

The significance of gaining access to queer women's communities has been confirmed in a study of queer, lesbian, bisexual and transsexual (QLBT[21]) women's networks by Mary Bryson (2004). Queer communities offer a safe space where people can experiment with non-normative identities. And as Bryson (2004: 251) states, these spaces offer the opportunity 'to take up an improvisational role on a stage populated with other variant characters who also serve the function of an audience'. Bryson (2004) undertook an exploratory study of the ways in which Internet technologies and communities re/mediate the narrativisation of queer lives and communities, and the articulation of queer desire. She found that Internet tools and communities provide a vital space for interaction with other queer women in a relatively safe space; opportunities to experiment with sexual identity and practices; and entry into a cultural context in which to learn how to be queer through immersion and participation in a sexually specific subculture.[22]

Sport can be a hostile, homophobic environment for most masculine defined sports yet it has, surprisingly, been identified as a context that can provide social integrative meanings and functions in terms of 'sexual preference' (Elling, De Knop and Knoppers, 2003). The increasing social acceptance of sexual 'difference' in Western nations, coupled with the simultaneous persistence of homophobia in sport, has contributed to the rise of gay and lesbian sports clubs. This contradictory situation has created the circumstances, over the last two decades, for a rise in lesbian and gay men's participation in lesbian/gay sports clubs and for informal gay sports groups. Communal gay and lesbian sports groups and events present opportunities to create and enjoy gay, lesbian and queer spaces that contest hegemonic heterosexual sports culture (Elling, De Knop and Knoppers, 2003).

The queering of public spaces and events now constitutes a significant challenging and queering of community. The *Mardi Gras* in Sydney and *Europride* in Manchester are examples of major public performances that place queer politics on the international map through the celebration of a global gay discourse. Manchester's gay village, which emerged in the 1990s as a response to a homophobic policing campaign, is an example of a queering of community through the queering of urban space by challenging and subverting the kinds of nostalgic community clung on to in the thesis by Putnam. The success of the gay village as an established public space is illustrated by its co-option as a gentrified, cosmopolitan gay space (Binnie and Skeggs, 2004). A range of activities and architectural styles mark out the space as an identifiably gay men's urban cultural setting. For example, the Manto bar which stands on the site of the Worker's Reading Library, in easy reach of train and bus stations, offers a bold architectural statement of visibility. Only one lesbian space exists, a bar called Vanilla, revealing the privileging of white male inhabitants of public space. 'Cosmopolitan' is a label frequently used to mark out Manchester's gay village as a mechanism for promoting the neighbourliness of the space as non-threatening. In this way, it broadens its appeal to consumers in general, whether straight or gay. The gayness of the village is promoted as a 'non-threatening authentic commodity'. However, Binnie and Skeggs (2004) suggest that marketability rather than sexuality may be the driving force behind the carving out of queer spaces as 'Other authentic', leading to the tendency for gay spaces to become commodified. They point out that, through a process of incorporation, via imaginary cosmopolitanism, 'gay men, lesbians and transgendered people become objects for the fetishisation of difference' (2004: 57). Nevertheless, the queering of community through the creation of supportive networks within queer identified spaces indicates the importance of new communities of belonging.

Families of choice

Weeks, Heaphy and Donovan (2001:12) emphasise that reflexivity is crucial as a process of both giving meaning to and legitimating non-heterosexual ways of living, confirming Giddens's 'reflexive project of the self' (see Chapter 2). New values and meanings are forged out of sexual nonconformity. Ken Plummer (1995) draws on Giddens's idea of the reflexive project of the self as an evolving biography by using the term 'narratives' to indicate the ways that individuals affirm their sexual identities and authenticate their relationships. He views the construction of a personal narrative as an important device for expressing aspirations and understanding sexual and intimate relationships in same-sex commitments. In the 1970s and 1980s, when sexual communities and post-identity queer politics became distinguishable, the discourse of familialism was strongly critiqued for being an oppressive institution and for inciting antagonism towards homosexuality. The rise in alternative ways of living coincided, in terms of timing, with the emerging popularity in the idea of 'friends as family' from the 1980s onwards.

At the same time as contesting the institution of the family, Lesbian and Gay Pride events used the term 'family' to embrace notions of both *broad community* and *smaller unions*. During the 1980s and 1990s, emphasis was placed by some on the process of queering the notion of 'family' (Goss, 1997), at the very same time as others were rejecting the term (Rofes, 1997). These debates, in which the experiences of being shunned by family and community were being articulated and analysed, were crucial in contributing towards an understanding and transcendence of traditional social ties and creating new forms of belonging. 'Families of choice' is a term now adopted by friends and by gay and lesbian couples to valorise non-heterosexual relationships (Weeks, Heaphy and Donovan, 2001). As mentioned in Chapter 2, the term 'friends as family' signifies, among heterosexual groups, a democratisation of intimate relationships by deploying 'friendship' to denote the non-hierarchical nature of chosen relationships and the potential to reinvent narratives of self. 'Families of choice' signifies, then, the transition to more diverse styles of bonding, fluid sexual identities and discretionary sexual unions.

While friendship provides a vital source of support for those who have been rejected by relatives after having taken on a non-heterosexual identity, many object to linking friendship to the term 'family' to describe non-heterosexual relationships. For many, it evokes hierarchy, bigotry and constraint. Since several self-identified non-heterosexual people have become reliant on chosen relationships with friends after being shunned by their families of origin, it isn't surprising that, as Weeks, Heaphy and Donovan (2001: 11) state: 'people slide easily between viewing the family as a site of hostility, and as something they can invent.' They point out that '[F]riends are *like* family; or they *are* family. The family is something external to you, or something you do' (Weeks, Heaphy and Donovan, 2001: 11). The ambivalence in language reveals the profound challenges faced in contesting the norms governing social and personal relationships. And the uncertainty surrounding the use of the term 'family' to describe non-heterosexual unions reveals a lack of available terms to describe intimate relationships, and underlines the dominance of familialism (Weeks, 1991; Weeks, Heaphy and Donovan, 2001). Those who use the term 'families of choice' to describe non-heterosexual relationships generally stress two points: first, the importance of *belonging* and *commitment* to a circle of friends who are seen as corresponding to the familial ideal; and second, the sense of *choice* and *agency* (Weeks, Heaphy and Donovan, 2001: 10).

From the 1980s, the HIV/AIDS epidemic required the building of a community of care-giving, to support those who were suffering and dying from the illness and to offer counselling to loved ones. This community of care consisted of a tight network of friends, experts and relatives and forced hospitals to relax family-centric visitation policies to include same-sex partners and wider circles of friends (Weston, 1991). Weeks, Heaphy and Donovan (2001) describe the risks faced by sexual minorities as a consequence of being deprived of rights that are taken for granted by heterosexual families:

> The HIV/AIDS epidemic dramatized the absence of relational rights for non-heterosexuals in a climate of growing prejudice and enhanced need. Same sex partners were often ignored or bypassed by medical authorities as their lovers lay sick or dying. Insurance companies refused cover for same sex couples. Mortgage companies insisted on HIV tests before agreeing (or more likely, not agreeing) housing loans. Individuals were cast out of joint homes when their lovers died, and were often denied inheritance rights.
>
> (Heaphy, Weeks and Donovan, 1999)

The denial of full citizenship to non-heterosexuals also led to child custody disputes, first experienced in the 1970s by lesbian mothers and then extended to fostering and adoption problems experienced by gay and lesbian couples. Controversies involving the care of children confirmed that the term 'family' was much more than just a cosy metaphor applied to non-heterosexual living arrangements. It was an essential political tool for the advancement of non-heterosexual politics (Nardi, 1999; Weeks, Heaphy and Donovan, 2001).

Non-standard intimacies

Berlant and Warner (2000) argue, in contrast to Weeks, Heaphy and Donovan, that the term 'families of choice' is profoundly conservative and contains an integrationist intent. To describe gay and lesbian relationships and friendship networks by using the label 'family' diverts attention from the counter-normative nature and radical potential of many such relationships. 'Non-standard intimacies', according to Berlant and Warner (2000), involve non-normative sexualities. They argue that a queer approach should therefore be used to emphasise the radical nature of alternative, non-heteronormative ways of living. Queer and other kinds of sexual dissenters strive to foster what were once regarded, and still are in many quarters, as 'criminal intimacies'. 'We have developed relations and narratives that are only recognised as intimate in queer culture: girlfriends, gal pals, fuckbuddies, tricks ...' (Berlant and Warner, 2000: 322). 'Non-standard intimacies' are highlighted in order to rupture and subvert the heteronormativity of relationships. They argue for queer counter-publics: the creation of a queer world which calls for the cultivation of forms of intimacy that have no affiliation with 'domestic space, kinship, the couple, property or the nation' (Berlant and Warner, 2000: 322).

This approach challenges the dominance and the privileging of sexual relationships within academic and public discourses on personal relationships (see Budgeon and Roseneil, 2002). It also exposes the hetero-normativity of the discipline of sociology, exemplified by the use of the heterosexual family as the standard against which other relationships are rendered abnormal (Stacey, 1999; Van Every, 1999). The homosexual/ heterosexual dichotomy is therefore gradually being undermined by a move towards the pure relationship and a series of 'queer tendencies' (Budgeon and Roseneil, 2002), including the decentring of heterorela-tions and cultural validation of queer identity in popular culture.

Significantly, then, friendship plays a vital role in both viewpoints, of 'families of choice' and 'non-standard intimacies', symbolising a liberation from and transcendence of hierarchical relationships. The fluidity of the term 'friendship' allows the diversity of relationships involved in queer cultures to be embraced. It is a label that has the potential to blur the boundaries between the sexual and the non-sexual. Weeks, Heaphy and Donovan (2001) regard the friendship ethic as a discourse by which diverse relationships can be authenticated. They concur with Marilyn Friedman (1993: 5), who reminds us that the voluntary nature of friend-ship 'contributes to the potential of friendship to provide support for persons with unconventional values. With the support of friends, such persons are more able than they would otherwise be to challenge and alter existing traditions and practices.'

In asserting the freedom to choose lifestyles and identities outside the traditional family form, non-heterosexual politics has asserted the radi-cal democratisation of social and personal relationships that Giddens (1992) identifies as a 'pure relationship' (see Chapter 2). However, Giddens did not account for the fact that children are often placed at the centre of new living arrangements that transcend heteronormativity, demonstrating that commitment and care remain crucial issues (Budgeon and Roseneil, 2002). Thus, the voluntary nature of friendship and the contingency of intimate relationships, whether heterosexual or queer in nature, raise concerns about the kind of commitment needed for the upbringing of children and care of the sick and elderly in diverse relationships. This matter is addressed in the final chapter.

Conclusion

Putnam's thesis of declining social cohesion privileges certain forms of sociality over others: namely those more likely to be engaged in by the middle classes, and more likely to have been practiced in the early to mid-twentieth century. Furthermore, because he favours the nuclear family over other associations as the central unit of society and defines social interaction in terms of direct, face-to-face interaction and locality, he overlooks the significance of emergent identities beyond the nuclear family. The tendency to disregard other sites of new 'capital' is a feature of Putnam's thesis: the rise of more fluid and diverse communities and identities; and new postsocial forms of human collectivity contingent on new sexual identities and new media technology. Queer politics has given rise to emergent communities founded on a new discourse of identity that acknowledges the fluid and provisional nature of all social identities. Moreover, as the following chapters show, the fluidity and power of informal friendship networks is being revealed by the use of new communication technologies: by mobile phone use among young people and Internet use by all age groups. Young people may not be 'joiners' of traditional associations such as scout groups, churches and trade unions in the same way as older generations have been, especially since current trends show that civic engagement increases with age, peaking among individuals in their forties to fifties. But the young are, crucially, engaging in novel forms of community-building through networking, as addressed in Chapter 8.

More recently, the Internet has transformed the nature of interaction, including that of ethnic groups at home and abroad. Since the 1970s, certain ethnic communities have used modern information communication technologies, such as faxes and television's global coverage of news to assist in exchanging information between dispersed ethnic groups. The interactivity of the Internet has facilitated a number of changes: it fosters the local dissemination of news and cultural objects, augmenting communal education; it allows the creation of economic, cultural and political resources and support, leading to the development of trans-state political communities; it facilitates communication with local and global NGOs; and not only contributes to the rise of a global civil society, but also to the creation of virtual 'nations' as Gabriel Sheffer and Michael Dahan (2001: 87) point out. This leads us, in the next chapter, to those debates that emphasise a regeneration of the *social* through network society and globalisation. Community is being reshaped and reformed. It is no longer just based on geographical belonging but also on, for example, diasporic communities stretching across time and space.

6
Network Society

In contrast to theories of social disintegration, certain scholars argue that new modes of sociality are emerging from new relations between individuals and being regenerated by new information communication technologies. Here, and in the following chapter, I explore the idea that the 'regeneration of the social' involves a technology-based recovery of community life through networks (Knorr-Cetina, 2000). Before looking at how new information technology is implicated in changing *personal* relationships in the next chapter, it is helpful to consider first the wider *social* context in which these new kinds of relationships are embedded. This chapter focuses, then, on global and macro social, economic and cultural changes. The rise of a network society is identified by Manuel Castells (1996–98) who argues that information communication technologies are facilitating emergent social identities and communities. The chapter begins by exploring changing patterns and meanings of work in network society. This is followed by an account of some of the ways the Internet is being integrated in the lives of individuals before going into the detail of the following chapter. Emergent diasporic networks are then addressed by charting the rise and significance of diasporic networks: intra-state, trans-state and 'virtual nations'.

New communication technologies such as the Internet, e-mail and mobile phones are characterised by interconnectivity, speed, immediacy, and decentralised use. In contrast to old technologies, they are highly personalised and part of everyday life. Mark Poster (1995) argues that these new technologies collapse past distinctions between 'real' and 'unreal' community. Bryan Turner (2001) talks of the Internet as a global market of strangers. This allows us to think in terms of virtual communities composed of 'thin' rather than 'thick' associations, based on anonymous ties with information exchanged anonymously. While thinned out relations is a feature of postsocial ties, the Internet also sustains 'thick' associations given that it is also used to cement other forms of more traditional, face-to-face communication. The immediacy of Internet communication to its users is complemented by wide access to information which, in contrast to the printed form, is unfixed, mobile and changeable. Thus, local, community and national distinctions are being reconfigured by a global sign economy in which computer-mediated communication (CMC) becomes a key symbol of change. Mutual help is provided through Internet support groups and new forms of belonging are expressed through virtual or cyber-communication.

One of the first people to popularise the term 'virtual community' is Howard Rheingold (1993), who saw the Internet as an alternative reality that provides an opportunity to rejuvenate the public sphere by constructing new, technological forms of community. Perceiving a decline in 'real' community life, he argued that the Internet creates new communities that would not have existed without it. While it is accurate that the Internet has the potential to promote open, democratic discourse and foster collective action,[1] the idea of a *'virtual* community' is misleading since it evokes two worlds: one real and one virtual. Rheingold invoked the idea of a split between a mediated and unmediated reality rather than a convergence between virtual and face-to-face relations. The rise of a *virtual* community that takes over from *real* community life suggests that people are withdrawing from everyday life into a virtual world. However, the next chapter shows that chat room experiences are just as real as those associated with communicating by telephone. Online interactions can complement other forms of communication since they often facilitate face-to-face interactions (Wellman, Quan Haase, Witte and Hampton, 2001). Early users were right in predicting that borderless global societies would flourish (Baym, 1997; Sproull and Kiesler, 1991). The discussion of diasporic networks, below, proves the accuracy of the forecast.

The networked individual

For Castells, network logic has become the dominant form of social organisation in a new age of 'informationalism'. Contributing to ideas about emergent postsocial relations, he argues that computer-mediated communication is not only reconfiguring work and employment but is also organising social relationships and cultural identities. Castell's network society emphasises the importance of knowledge-based systems of production in which two spatial logics operate. Network society characterises the social structure of the Information Age, a period between 1945 and 1995 but which began accelerating around 1970. In his trilogy, *The Information Age* (1996–98), Castells identifies a new set of social relations, new perceptions of the self and new institutions emerging from the technology of electronic communication which impact on existing social formations within urban life. Cities are being changed by the interfaces between electronic communication and physical interaction. The tensions between individual-directed and community-directed activities coexist within forms of social interaction mediated by information and communication technology. This tension is overlaid by a further tension between communal spaces of living, working and belonging, and the flow of communication in virtual, non-space. The network is, then, an organising principle in the transformation of contemporary society. For Castells, virtual communities become a form of social reality that, in turn, transforms social relations.

The network enterprise becomes the new form of economic activity with decentralised but coordinated networks and management systems. Multimedia production sites emerge from the old industrial buildings of cities like San Francisco as a kind of informational production for the 'production of dreams, the most powerful manufacturing in our world' (Castells, 2002: 550). Urban centres with advanced software-based industries, such as London, Tokyo, Beijing, Taipei, Barcelona and Helsinki, are characterised by similar work–living arrangements with flourishing multiethnic and multicultural communities with people working, living and socialising in the same space.

The decline of traditional patterns of communication between individuals and cultures is a trend that provokes the rise of defensive spaces, leading to deep divisions between 'gated communities for the rich, territorial turfs for the poor' (Castells, 2002: 551). However, Castell's concern about gated communities differs from Putnam's. While Putnam's anxieties centre on the problem of *social isolation* in these kinds of communities, Castell's concern is about *social division* of rich and poor. He emphasises that the financially rich are also information-rich and have no problems in communicating with one another across their gated communities. This is borne out by confirmation of the 'social capital-rich' middle classes.

For Castells, social networks are either no longer being drawn from the location in which people live, or become less important to them than those beyond it. The example of class differences in friendship networks comes to mind, with the middle classes less likely to have 'local' friends and less likely to have relatives who live nearby compared to the working classes, as mentioned earlier. The middle classes typically have social networks drawn from work, and past contacts such as through university study. Dispersed social networks are a feature of middle-class social networking, sustained by the use of the Internet, telephone and transport as important ways of keeping contact that were not possible until recently. Thus, an individual's community may be unrelated to where they live, which suggests the rise of the 'networked individual' (Wellman, 2001). Following Wellman, Castells refers to 'personal communities' centred on the individual and embedded in networks. Postsocial communities can no longer be assumed to be composed of 'locality': they can no longer be assumed to be synonymous. The key changes involve high social and geographical mobility, fast economic change, breakdown in family ties and fragmentation of family networks. Under these circumstances, individuals cannot ensure that a local community will be drawn on as a social resource. In later work, Castells (2001) emphasises that it is the rise of a networked individualism that is driving change by reshaping social relations. This replaces his earlier technological deterministic argument that new technology is driving the changes.

Networked work

Castells (2000) argues that work and employment are transformed by the new information economy of network society, with the boundaries between work and leisure being obscured. But in the context of work, network culture is mainly benefiting the lives of urban elites, and in particular, elite men. The world's migrant works and unskilled labourers continue to experience poor and sometimes dangerous working conditions. The notion of the 'network society' encourages an overemphasis on the advantages of change enjoyed by urban professionals. On the one hand, the social disadvantages caused by work schedules and hazardous working conditions remain for guest workers, migrant workers and seasonal agricultural workers directed by gang masters, prostitutes and other workers caught in the hidden economy. On the other hand, new urban work cultures are arising out of new corporate cultures such as in branding, marketing and PR which seem to be characterising new metropolitan centres. Castells (2000) focuses on new work values leading to a new network society in metropolitan centres such as New York, London, Paris and Berlin where the divisions between private and public time are collapsing.

For middle-class professionals, the physical and social setting of the workplace and organisational hierarchy are important factors that influence work friendships. Cool office design, café-style eating areas, and sociable group-work zones are generating new forms of work-based sociality for these urban elites. Flexible work in new media and culture industries constitutes an important change in employment patterns, becoming a prevalent type of working arrangement for the urban professional through the rise of part-time and temporary work, contract work, self-employment, and a range of informal or semi-formal labour arrangements within continual occupational mobility. Yet the lifestyles of these privileged groups are precisely dependent on the exploitation of unskilled labourers.

Given that networks between women have already been identified as weaker than men's as a consequence of exclusionary male networking activities, this emphasis on networking has serious gender ramifications that need to be taken into account. In the world of e-business, for example, women networking groups such as Hightech-Women, Webgrrls and *E-Women* have been created in order to combat a male-dominated form of business communication (Wittel, 2001). Online sociality may benefit women in some ways by possibilities for immediacy and flexibility in disembedded forms of networking, but the shift to short-term contracts, long hours, high-risk projects, weak work identities and high physical mobility are all examples of work conditions that favour people who are not expected to take on caring roles in society.

A growing gap is emerging, then, between those who identify with their paid employment and those who do not. The movement to a 'work commitment' culture is exemplified by the tendency for professionals to work above contracted hours in the United States and Britain, where it is seen to be essential to job retention/career success. Career-risks are individualised as part of the system of discipline and governance of the self, and the burden of this shift continues to be placed on the shoulders of women who juggle work and family commitments as shown in Chapter 4. Moreover, as Pahl (2000: 90) points out, personal relationships are being undermined by the 'superficial glad-handedness' which is becoming a feature of much corporate culture. The implication is that an authentic kind of friendship can be contrasted with this superficial network culture. Instrumental work relationships, deemed as 'false friendships', are contrasted with affectionate associations, raising issues about the balance between exploitation and indebtedness, and echoing the ongoing problems of men's instrumental relationships in the public sphere where friendship is commonly offered out of duty or sought for personal gain.

The individualisation of labour is affecting people in different ways, then. Among vulnerable groups of the population such as migrant labour, women and unskilled labourers, this individualisation leads to a weakening of the power of labour. By contrast, authors such as Castells and David Brooks (2000) are celebrating the rise of an emergent middle-class professional. Brooks identifies a 'new' American bourgeoisie: a privileged social group that attempts to take control of their careers or workloads in order to develop new lifestyles based on a better balance between work and leisure. For this elite group, work is a vocation, a calling. Thinking like artists or activists by viewing work as a form of self-expression, these highly motivated employees actually work harder for the company. They treat their work as leisure. For some, high-pressure careers and the accompanying high incomes are relinquished for a less frantic and more creative life, for example through self-employment (Brooks, 2000). Thus, the blurring of work and leisure is the experience of a privileged few in this bold new networked age. The repositioning of 'work as leisure' as an exciting context in which meaningful personal relationships are forged, is exclusive to Western and Third World upper-middle-class professional elites in cosmopolitan centres. This division between the rich and poor is mirrored in terms of access to computer technology (see Mossberger, Tolbert and Stansbury, 2003).

Online and offline sociality

Castells (1998) does not undertake a detailed study of the relationship between the macro-social frameworks and micro-social contexts that influence and condition social action. So how is the Internet being used and integrated in people's lives at an individual level? Bearing in mind that the objects and experiences of new technology at the micro-level are constantly changing, it is only possible to outline the patterns that have begun to emerge in today's early research on the subject. Indeed, constant change is a crucial feature of this mode of social interaction. There are discrepancies in research findings about whether Internet competes for time with other activities. A longitudinal study of 'newbies' (newcomers) to the Internet discovered that as Internet use increases, offline social interaction decreases, leading to isolation and loneliness. Computerisation and the Internet can blur the boundary between home and work, with people attending to work e-mails instead of interacting with family and friends (Nie and Erbring, 2000). The Internet enhances global interactions, but the concern is that it 'keeps people indoors' and that people neglect local interactions at home and in neighbourhood (Nie, 2001). Online interaction may be homogenous in the sense that the interaction evolves around a single interest such as sports, hobbies, politics, family trees, thereby restricting access to new information and new social interactions (Wellman and Guila, 1999). Despite these findings, the arguments about an increase and decrease in social capital tend to overstate the role of the Internet by treating it as something that radically changes how people communicate *offline* (Wellman, Quan Haase, Witte and Hampton, 2001).

Another argument, however, is that the Internet *supplements* social capital. Wellman and colleagues (2001) claim the technology plays less of a central role in shaping social trends when placed in the context of a person's overall life. The Internet is viewed as something integrated in daily rhythms with online activity seen as an extension of offline activity (Flannagan and Metzger 2001: 153). With the growing amount of information on the Web, and with more user-friendly search engines and hyperlinks, it is now easier to locate groups with similar interests, promoting a massive increase in network communities. The Internet does have the potential, then, to increase social capital if defined as interaction with friends, family, neighbours and workmates for companionship, emotional support, services and a sense of belonging, according to Wellman and team (2001). Important gender differences are discussed in the following chapter which focuses on research findings of interactions on the Internet.

Class differences are confirmed by research on Internet use. The Wellman team (2001) found that those with a university degree were more likely to be involved in synchronous online activities and those with lower qualifications were more likely to play multi-user games online, concurring with other research (Howards, Rainie and Jones, 2001; Katz, Rice and Aspden, 2001). Latecomers to the Internet are more likely to play multi-user games and to chat online. The longer individuals have been online, the more types of Internet activities they are likely to engage in (Wellman, Quan Haase, Witte and Hampton, 2001: 443). They found that telephone remains the most used technology at 40 per cent, with e-mail at 32 per cent, face-to-face visits at 23 per cent, and postal letter writing at 4 per cent. Significantly, the communication with kin and friends is distributed in the same way as pre-Internet days, at 46 per cent with kin and 54 per cent with friends. Moreover, distance continues to constrain communication in the Internet era. Most contact is still with relatives and friends who live nearby. And the telephone remains the most used medium for contacts with network members living nearby (Wellman 1992; Wellman and Wortley, 1990). The Internet can enhance existing relationships yet can also foster long-distance communication.

Wellman and colleagues (2001) bear out the thesis that the Internet offers a new mechanism for social engagement. They found that Internet use supplements and increases both organisational involvement and political participation. The fear that Internet communication leads to a weakening of face-to-face ties is not borne out. The more people use the Internet and the more they are involved in online organisational and political activity, the more they will be involved in such activity offline. People participating offline will use the computer to augment and extend their offline activity and vice versa. Age is significant in this context: for people aged 40 to 65 there is a significant association between political participation and Internet use. As with organisational activities, the more people are involved in political activities offline, the more they are likely to be involved online (Wellman, Quan Haase, Witte and Hampton, 2001: 447). Yet unlike organisational participation, older adults are less likely to be involved in online political discussions and Asian-Americans are significantly less involved. The following section looks at ways that participation on the net enhances network communities. Wellman's (1992) suggestion that each individual is at the centre of a unique personal network, consisting of kin, friends, neighbours and workmates, which extends over long distances is convincing. 'Personal community' is not, then, a grouping of people bound by physical space, but an *individualized network* that crosses space, emphasising the coexistence of local and disembedded social relationships.

Virtual communities of care and 'real virtuality'

The formation of self-help groups on the Internet indicates that the medium is now an important vehicle for providing social support on a local and global scale (Pleace, Burrows, Loader et al., 2000). These kinds of postsocial ties may no longer be based on locality, but the nurturing values of ideal and imagined traditional community ties based on neighbourly social support seen to be kept alive in virtual space. Beyond these 'virtual communities' of care, quite different forms of computer-mediated 'communities' have emerged, based on a myriad of Internet multi-user games, prompting scholars to suggest that a new kind of virtual reality has been created: one that transcends conventional notions of 'community'.

Looking first at virtual communities of care, research on self-help groups suggests that the Internet has the power to shape 'communities' into new configurations. Like the examples above, these new social ties transcend geographical boundaries of local neighbourhood and traditional community, leading to virtual associations based on particular interests (Baym, 1997; Sproull and Kiesler 1991; Wellman 2001). Most information comes from research on self-help groups, with a focus on Usenet and use of newsgroups for social support. Pleace and colleagues (2000) examined an Internet Relay Chat 'room' (IRC) by a self-help group made up of problem drinkers transnationally. Instead of relying on professional services, the group insisted on social support to help members deal with their alcohol problems. Does this kind of networking lead to virtual 'communities' of care? The answer seems to be 'yes'.

The shrinking of the welfare state and a questioning of professionals is prompting individuals to search for alternative information, treatments or services on the Internet even where traditional health services are still available, such as in the United Kingdom. But new uses of alternative services require the resources to pursue them. For example, increased use of the Internet by the middle classes as a source of alternative information on health is marked (Hardy, 1999; Burrows and Nettleton, 2000). With high social and geographical mobility and the fragmentation of family networks, individuals are unable to ensure that a local community can act as a social resource. This questions the whole basis of the notion of 'community care', a term that implies there is still a 'community' out there. In the past, those with health or social care needs would have turned to female relatives living locally as carers within the extended family. Without such local connections, individual's social networks can collapse if they lose their jobs (Pleace, Burrows, Loader et al., 2000).

Virtual communities of care are, then, Internet-based self-help groups operating by computer-mediated communication, used as a source of information and support. The logistics of organising meetings at a site at a fixed time are superseded. The number of participants can be large or small. Participants often have no face-to-face contact with one another. With the use of Internet etiquette, 'netiquette', to monitor those who abuse the chat room conventions of communication, support groups can be 'safe' environments in which individuals can discuss personal problems without being insulted. Multiple identities are often adopted to experiment or advocate a particular position in self-help groups, like problem drinking where the group only supports AA (see Reid 1996b).

Research by Pleace and colleagues in 2000 found that despite the site being designed to give support to problem drinkers, much of the activity was social. However, while the group did not have a particularly pronounced role in the delivery of informational support, it could be suggested that it played a role in providing both esteem support and social companionship, both of which could have had potentially beneficial effects on the regular participants. These benefits may have been reinforced by the one-to-one contact via e-mail and the telephone that regular participants made reference to, as well as the face-to-face meetings that were apparently occurring (Pleace, Burrows, Loader et al., 2000: 8). People may have built up confidence by introducing themselves through friendly and playful exchanges.

A further finding of this research was that references to family, partners and social activities and life outside the room were frequent, and no-one claimed the room to be their main source of social support. As Wellman and Guila (1999: 167) point out, assumptions by early research that CMCs would create new forms of community or destroy traditional ones were far too simplistic. These more moderate results by Pleace and colleagues' (2000: 8) support Welman and colleagues' (2001) argument that the Internet enhances rather than replaces other modes of social interaction. The early work ignored the fact that CMC does not work in isolation as 'virtual communities'. Early researchers confined themselves to CMC thereby ignoring how the information and symbolic content are embedded in a broader social context.

Studies of Internet use among socially disadvantaged and minority groups indicate that the Internet has great potential for enhancing social equality and empowerment (Mehra, Merkel and Peterson Bishop, 2004; Nelson, Tu and Hines, 2001). For example, a research project by Bharat Mehra of computer mediated communication among sexual minorities in the United States conducted in 2000 shows how the internet is used by a lesbian, gay, bisexual and transgender (LGBT) community to express their marginalised 'queer' identities and improve the quality of their living environment (Mehra, Merkel and Peterson Bishop, 2004). The LGBT members perceived online communication to be a positive development in their sexual identities. Posting information on the electronic mailing list enhanced individuals' offline lives by promoting LGBT participation in local activities such as political events and rallies, by contributing to policy and planning on issues affecting their lives, and by fostering support groups and cultural events. As well as promoting cultural empowerment by exchanging information, face-to-face communication and friendships were augmented among members through the use of the online mailing list.

In the field of community health, African-American women in the United States have empowered themselves and gained confidence as a group by participating in Internet training in order to share information about healthcare (Bishop, Mhera, Bazzell and Smith, 2000). Led by SisterNet, a grassroots organisation of African-American women, the conditions and relationships that affect the health of black women are being addressed at a community level by developing participative techniques for Internet content development, access and training. These skills and new forms of networking are allowing Black women to break down race- and gender-based stereotypes in community health information. For example, their involvement in the SisterNet website has allowed participants to decide how Internet content and services can serve their needs and objectives. They have acquired the expertise needed to develop their own suite of digital tools and information resources. Informational health profiles on common diseases prevalent among black women are created online by SisterNet community action researchers, based on scenarios that record local health issues and practices.

By allowing social groups to participate in the processes of knowledge creation, existing imbalances in local social and power dynamics are being shifted by this kind of online community, thereby providing the resources to challenge discriminatory practices (Bishops, Mhera, Bazzell and Smith, 2000). SisterNet women do not perceive their roles in Internet use as only a technology-related matter. They see the use of the technology as something that generates community action, as an initiative embedded in a wider community setting. Importantly, the Internet is applied as a 'problem-solving' device to empower a marginalised group through shared community experience.

In contrast to the generation of community action exemplified by SisterNet, computer mediated communication has the potential to stimulate the formation of a culture of 'real virtuality', according to Castells (2002), demonstrating the extraordinary versatility and fluidity of new media in constituting new social ties. The emphasis here is on the technological potential of gaming to constitute a multimedia system founded on interactive networks (network, satellite and cable broadcasting, and also VCR and DVD as well as the Internet). For example, Sherry Turkle (1995) was among the first group of researchers to look closely at the formation of identities on the Net by exploring Multi-User Domains, commonly known as MUDs. These are computer programmes made available through the Internet that allow users to adopt new identities. Derived from, and inspired by, *Dungeons and Dragons*, these multi-user computer games create imaginary worlds in which people use words or programming languages to improvise melodramas, and build their own worlds and the objects within them. MUDs put people in virtual spaces that they are able to navigate, like a new kind of virtual parlour game (Turkle, 1995: 12). Turkle claimed that these kinds of interaction generated a new form of community by bringing individuals together to engage in creative activities ranging from script writing to performance art and improvisational theatre. The process of creating new virtual communities enables people to generate and experiment with new identities. In the past, most players were middle class and male (Turkle 1995: 12), but the explosion in Internet access and popularity in use expands this kind of interaction to much wider and diverse social groups.

Online 'virtual world' role-playing games such as *EverQuest, Asheron's Call, Ultima Online* and *Lineage* have proved to be remarkably popular. These kinds of games allow hundreds of thousands of people to gather online to create digital civilizations:

> players erect cities, businesses, form governments, muster armies, commit crimes, take jobs, earn decent wages, make friends, marry and die. The virtual money they earn has real value: they can trade it for U.S. dollars at online auction sites. Thousands of players consider themselves citizens of their virtual world, and some spend more time there than in ours.
>
> (Plotz, 2003)

Ominous examples of the blurring of reality and virtuality in computer games include *Kuma War*, launched by an American company in 2004 and featuring graphic video footage captured by US troops during the Iraq war. The game includes licensed frontline footage from ITN, Reuters and Associated Press from Iraq and Afghanistan. Raising ethical issues, it has been pointed out that the company, Kumar Reality Games, is cashing in on a conflict in which thousands of people have died (Timms, 2003). The aim of the game is to allow players to go on recreated missions including the bomb raid that killed Saddam Hussein's two sons, Uday and Qusay, and with the same munitions involved in the raid. Each mission is introduced by a TV-style broadcast presenting the licensed war footage. Each mission is presented by an anchor in the style of a CNN or Fox News bulletin. Former ABC news producer, William Davis, who produced news magazine show *20/20*, was drafted in to contribute to designing the game. The chief executive of Kuma Reality Games, Keith Halper remarked that 'We're watching all the real-world events very carefully here, and we're able to jump in a story and make a game mission very quickly.'[2] Such virtual war worlds are habitually structured to reinforce the power struggles that shape real world events, making them potentially dangerous tools of official dogma.

The US Defence Department have advanced online games by asking computer game companies to develop virtual worlds to be used for anti-terrorist training. The Defence Advanced Research Projects Agency signed up an online gaming expert as a consultant in 2003. The US government argues that these kinds of games may offer useful training in rebuilding broken nations in the real world (Plotz, 2003). Worrying though such examples are, they involve the production of a virtuality involving interaction between individuals who reinvent their identities. For instance, *Kuma War* is a game targeted at enhancing a particular kind of masculine identity. The symbolic environment of the hypertext may be 'virtual' in nature yet is nevertheless an essential aspect of reality, in the sense that it offers us the codes and images that we use reflexively to order our lives. Real virtuality, then, is a new kind of culture. Castells (2000) argues that while there are few common codes, a common language is used in this context. The language of the hypertext is the agency of communication and provider of shared cultural codes. However, participation in this new technology does not guarantee the emergence of new social ties. Cultural fragmentation and a recurrent circularity of the hypertext can lead to the individualisation of cultural meaning in communication networks, with the only shared meaning being the sharing of the network. Nevertheless, as the next chapter shows, new technology can foster and reshape sociability by offering new structures and values of interaction.

Ethnic identity politics and diasporic networks

The transformation of social ties by processes of globalisation and the spread of information technology are advanced by identity politics, provoking the disintegration of former shared identities and the rise of various single-focus resistance identities. The growing mode of engagement in political debate known as 'blogging' (web logging) has emerged as a form of public communication. Using the Internet, citizens can bypass government and go straight to the electorate to plan and generate direct action such as demonstrations and rallies on issues ranging from local concerns such as traffic safety in a small market town to global issues such as Third World debt. Blogging has the potential to fundamentally change the nature of politics since individuals can post ideas on websites that can be set up by anyone.

In the context of asylum politics, we find that political organisations, non-government organisations and the citizenry are using the Internet to advance minority activism (Siapera, 2004a and b). The term 'virtual community' has been used to describe some of these groupings. New kinds of social and personal relationships, based on particularistic interests, are emerging from new forms of communication technology. At the same time, the development of a European identity encountered in public discourses is identifiable in areas including the media and being traced by ventures such as the European Identity project.[3] The paradox is that individuals are invited to participate in trans-territorial networks and yet are often spatially segregated at the local level (Castells, 2002). These kinds of identities fix power in the network society where the central energy is generated by a tension between globalisation and communal identities rather than class struggle or state operation. The relevance of the metanarrative of social change forged around information is restricted, however, by the problem of accessibility of the Internet for social groups in developing countries such as the People's Republic of China, where access is highly controlled by the state but nevertheless gradually expanding, at last, with the introduction of an albeit restricted version of the search engine, *Google* to China in 2006. Indeed, issues of differential access to information and communication technologies (ICT) are crucial for ethnic identities.

The digital divide between white and black and minority ethnic groups

Despite an increasing reliance on information technology in Western societies, certain social groups are being left out and left behind through lack of access. In Britain, the government has been 'concerned with the consequences of the "information age" for a society that is already divided socially and economically' (Owen, Green, McLeod et. al., 2003: 1). Recent research evidence from the United Kingdom indicates that many differences in levels of access and use of ICT can be accounted for by age, household structure and income (Department of Trade and Industry, 2000). The report states that:

> An additional 'digital divide' may be said to be emerging, with the 'information rich' benefiting from enhanced access to the economy and government, while the 'information poor' face a new form of exclusion: the inability to fully participate in the emerging economy and society based on new forms of ICT.
>
> (Owen, Green, McLeod et al., 2003: 1).

The overall proportion of families in the United Kingdom owning a computer reached 50 per cent by 2001 (Owen, 2003a). However, research shows that income has a very strong influence on the ability to make use of ICT. Among households with below average income, the adoption of home computers is much slower than among households with above average income. In households with above average income, the proportion of adults with access to a home PC was more than twice as high as in households with below average income (Owen, Green, McLeod et al., 2003: 3).

Ethnic group is also a key social factor that shapes computer and Internet access. Black and minority ethnic groups living in deprived areas are likely to have a relatively low awareness of newer ICT and less access to home computers than white neighbours, particularly among South Asian and Black respondents. And among those that do have access, they tend to use older and cheaper models due to their lower income. In a study commissioned by the Department of Education and Skills, 1585 households in deprived urban neighbourhoods were surveyed. It was discovered that 37 per cent of white families owned computers compared to 31 per cent of black and minority ethnic families (Owen, Green, McLeod et al., 2003).[4] While the figure was higher among Asian households, with 42 per cent owning a computer, this group was less likely to use the Internet. Use of the Internet in the home was lowest among black respondents (22 per cent), followed by South Asians at 26 per cent. The highest use of the Internet was among the relatively younger group of respondents with mixed parentage (38 per cent), followed by Chinese and other groups (35 per cent), with a figure of 31 per cent among white groups. Over a third of white respondents (34 per cent), used their computers to access government services on line, but only 20 per cent of Asian people and 26 per cent of black people used computers for this purpose. When controlling for other factors such as household type and income, it was concluded that being black was significant in forecasting the likelihood of lack of Internet use.

These findings indicate that black and minority ethnic groups in deprived areas tend to have less access to vital facilities such as government online services. White respondents were more likely than those from other ethnic groups to use their home PC for most other purposes such as leisure activities, e-mailing, web surfing, work purposes, buying goods and services. However, while white families who owned a PC were more likely to use it for surfing the net, black and minority ethnic families were more likely to use it for work and educational purposes. And, significantly, a higher proportion of black and minority ethnic respondents than white groups used the Internet to access information of importance to ethnic/religious background (21 per cent of black and minority ethnic group users compared to 9 per cent of white). This signals the importance of the Internet as a potential tool for fostering ethnic, religious and cultural networks, as outlined below in the context of diasporic networks.

Regarding barriers against the use and ownership of ICT, a number of reasons were cited by respondents. Lack of skills in English was stated as a barrier by 25 per cent of black and minority ethnic groups. Lack of computer literacy, cost, problems in reading and writing, and lack of interest or need were also cited. Interviews uncovered gender as a likely barrier for some South Asian women (Owen, Green, McLeod et al., 2003: xvii). The paucity of usage of ICT by people from black and minority ethnic groups is referred to in the report as 'the digital divide' (Owen, Green, M. McLeod et al., 2003). The findings were published at a crucial time, in 2003, when the British government was embarking on a drive to encourage more people to learn to use computers so as to enhance employment prospects. Social groups in deprived areas have therefore been targeted in order to offer them a better chance of learning these vital skills of information retrieval.

Diasporic networks

Lower access to ICT among black and minority ethnic groups in deprived areas of Western nations such as the United Kingdom is a serious problem in an age when people are clearly using the technology to foster a sense of community and personal identity since both are closely associated with ethnicity (Adams and Ghose, 2003: 414). ICT has demonstrated its potential to enhance the emergence of diasporic networks (Dahan and Sheffer, 2001). As Paul Adams and Rhina Ghose (2003: 414) argue, ethnic identity is often associated with a past spatial anchoring: 'the concept of ethnicity gestures to a real or imagined time when a "people" lived together in a particular space.' As such, technological advances in communication can facilitate new ties and strengthen old ones in overcoming the tyranny of distance.

On the one hand, globalisation has accelerated regional unification and the rise of cross-national and cross-state similarities, leading to the possibility of reconfiguring national and ethnic identities. On the other hand, tribal groups, ethnic minorities and ethno-national diasporas have also been cemented by new information communication technology use. The kinds of new media being used by ethnic groups include e-mail, Usenet, Internet Relay Chat and the web. Most studies have tended to approach 'ethnic groups' in general as if they were all of the same form, but the distinctions between various types of ethnic groups and their differing uses of new media need to be emphasised in order to develop effective policies to aid them as Sheffer and Dahan (2001) assert.

For example, Aborigines in regions such as Australia and North and South America are able to use new media for intrastate, trans-state and global exchanges. Dahan and Sheffer identify three categories of ethnic groups who use new media. First, indigenous ethnic minorities permanently in their own homelands, such as nomadic tribes, native nations and rural and urban ethnic minorities are citizens of the same states who do not have extensively organised diasporas, speak the same language and establish and use intrastate networks. A second group is ethno-national diasporas who are dispersed in various states usually not adjacent to the borders of the homeland. They continue to be minorities in their host countries, maintain an ethno-national identity connected to their homelands, and continuous contacts with social and political groups in these homelands. Some become hybrid communities[5] after a while, but the cores of diasporas maintain a considerable amount of cohesion and are able to perform as organised groups.

The third category is made up of completely virtual states or 'national communities', referring to groups who generate new national identities as well as virtual states not based on primordial ethnic elements, who have fragile ties with specific territories and who lack any actual organisation. Such groups may be based on a singular political ideology such as monarchism, libertarianism or economic projects. Virtual 'nations' are not traditional ethnic groupings, since their members may not be of the same ethnic origins. As Dahan and Sheffer (2001) point out, Cyber Yugoslavia, Freedonia, Nova Arcadia, the Republic of Lomar, the Kingdom of Melchizedek and Virtual Afghanistan are all examples of virtual nations.[6]

New media are deployed by intrastate ethnic groups to preserve cultural heritage, history and language, to combat dominant cultures' demands for assimilation. Indigenous ethnic groups participate in networks that promote equal rights for all minorities, affirmative action and social justice for all disadvantaged groups, and the return of land to native nations such as the current demands of the Australian Aborigines (Mele, 2000). Native American tribes in the United States and Canada are preserving their native languages by using the Internet.[7] Diasporas' trans-state networks use new technologies to communicate with member of local communities, other ethnic groups, and with NGOs and IGOs[8] such as Amnesty International, the UN and Human Rights groups at the global level. New media technologies are often the only way they can communicate in nations where their views are censored by hostile governments.[9]

In some cases, though, homeland governments are financially supporting diasporic networks loyal to them, such as the Turkish government
which supports networks operated by activists in Turkish diasporas in
the United States. Palestinians used diasporic networks during the
Intifada, and Iraqi Kurds did the same during Iraqi offensives against
them. These networks have contributed to increasing self-assertiveness
with demands being made about the actions of homeland governments,
as demonstrated by American Jewish organisations communicating their
criticisms of Israeli government policies, Palestinian Americans demanding stronger PLO positions in relation to Israel, and overseas Chinese networks communicating anti-homeland government propaganda in the
struggle for human rights demands (Sheffer and Daha, 2001). Diasporic
networks also extend financial support to their homelands and facilitate
international trade.

Research by Adams and Ghose (2003) on Indian citizens living in the
United States, and immigrants from India and their descendants, referred
to as the 'Indian diaspora', shows how this diverse set of ethnicities maintain websites for a variety of purposes. They use the Internet to preserve
culture, maintain ethnic identity, support cosmopolitanism, intercont-
nental lifestyles and consumption customs. Demand for online versions
of Indian newspapers, business sites, cultural sites and sites for the
search of marriage partners is high among overseas Indians, for whom
the Internet is the only contact with news and culture from India.
Related to the words 'mediascape', 'ideospace', 'financescape', and
'technoscape' used by Appadurai (1996) to explain processes of globalis-
ing culture, and supporting the needs of a particular kind of ethnoscape,
Adams and Ghose (2003) use the term 'bridgespace' (Froehling, (1999:
170) to describe the incorporation of the Internet and other media.
Ranging from music CDs to films, a number of interrelated communicative links are forged between differing media so that 'bridgescape'
becomes a facilitator, a space enabling certain kinds of movements, of
people, goods, capital and ideas to occur.

Challenging Putnam's thesis of decline of voluntary associations in
the United States, Adams and Ghose assert that ethnic groups with high
levels of foreign-born members form strong social ties in the United
States, along the lines of Putnam's 'bowling league' pattern. Temporary
and permanent immigrants to the United States from India form a wide
variety of voluntary groups, which also have a presence in bridgespace
to promote the perpetuation of cultures, economic advancement,
charities, adjustment to American society, arrange trips and so on.
The web becomes a space in which these voluntary associations are

interconnected and become part of an international system linked to India, to Indian diasporas across the world and to the host culture. As described in the following chapter, arranging marriages is one of the most important uses of the Internet by this set of communities.

The use of new media by minority ethnic groups demonstrates that during the era of global information, 'network' has the potential to become a source of power. This counteracts the notion that globalisation inevitably brings about a homogenisation of cultures. Fear of alienation and fragmentation where people no longer understand others outside their cultural set are expressed in many quarters, but evidence suggests that dominant cultures are being challenged by a shift towards 'a co-existence and multiplicity of sources of meaning and expression' as Castells (2002: 555) asserts.

Conclusion

For Castells, one of the key features of network society is not the erosion of social connectedness but, rather, its reconfiguration by flows of information. The 'social' is no longer welded to a physical centre or organic structure. The shift in modes of social interaction from closed systems to open 'networks' implies the rise of a network sociality which is set in opposition to Tonnies's idea of organic community associations. Instead, the social is becoming anchored within the reality of the cultural. With the dissolving of the spatial and temporal categories of modernity, network society is characterised by a shift from territoriality and a functionally integrated society to a world of ephemeral and virtual flows of knowledge and experience. The information society is characterised by transitory symbolic communication. It is a network society whose cultural realm is ordered principally by an integrated system of electronic media. It is also becoming more individuated as Castells (2002: 555) says: 'Communalism is collective individualisation *vis-à-vis* the rest of society.'

For Castells, virtual communities have the potential to give people control over their lives by strengthening social networks and identities through new communities of belonging. His employment of the Internet as a metaphor for society is useful, but only so long as it is not treated as an absolute theoretical construct (Megoran, 1999). However, the intersection between global change and local experiences of network society are not pursued by Castells (1998). Further research needs to be conducted on how 'thick' or 'thin' this new set of social relations is going to be and how far existing socially disadvantaged or marginalised groups are likely to be empowered: ethnic minorities, migrant workers, women and the working class. Nevertheless, Castells states that: 'Cultural expressions of all kinds are increasingly enclosed in or shaped by this electronic hypertext' (2000:12). And this leads us to the issues addressed in the next chapter: new ways of communicating in the form of online chat, gaming, intimacy, dating and social support; as well as the integration of the mobile phone in the lives of young people.

7

Virtual Intimacy and Online Sociality

We have seen, in previous chapters, that identity is increasingly being marked by fluidity and variability with traditional indicators of identity such as family and community being transformed. What are the implications for Giddens's concept of self-identity and the project of the reflexive self if, as Castells (2000) claims, we have now entered a culture of 'real virtuality'? Is networking in urban virtual space more comforting now that we can reinvent or conceal our 'real' selves? And is this really the way new technology is being used?

This chapter examines the impact of new communication technologies on personal relationships, with an emphasis on the Internet, e-mail and mobile phone. Via these new communication technologies, individuals are experiencing new forms of interaction beyond those of face-to-face communication by overcoming barriers of time and distance. *Internet-initiated* interaction has been increasing in relation to forms of communication including chat rooms, Internet dating and self-help groups. Revealing the adaptability of personal relationships, past theories about maintaining friendship either stressed that it needs to be sustained by embedding friendship in the routines of everyday life (Duck, 1988) or claimed that interaction is not essential to friendship since individuals often continue to identify as close friends people they have not seen for years (O'Connor and Brown, 1984). With the rise of Internet-initiated interaction, the point is that relationships appear to be sustainable for long periods without individuals ever having 'met' one another at all. Many factors of identity may shape or interrupt new communication technology-based interaction, including differences of social class, age, ethnic identity, gender, sexuality and disability. To exemplify some of these key changes, in this chapter I will focus mainly on factors of gender and ethnicity in relation to online romance. I shall also explore mobile phone use by concentrating on interaction among young people.

Internet-initiated intimacy

The widespread use of the Internet since the 1990s has not only led to modes of computer-mediated communication that enhance existing personal networks but also sparked an explosion in a distinctive kind of relationship: one formed *without* or *before* initial face-to-face contact. Internet-initiated intimate contact is now taking place on a grand scale through chat rooms, Internet dating agencies and computer-mediated friendships. Internet-initiated relationships are often interpreted by researchers as inherently short-term, transient interactions exemplified by the fleeting and fragmented contacts of the chat room. Although each short-term computer-mediated friendship or romance implies the potential to develop into a long-term one, Internet-initiated interaction can be viewed as a key example of the trend towards ephemeral modes of personal association. However, the whole notion of 'behaviour' needs to be reconceptualised in order to be freed from spatial constraints when we come to explore the Internet as a context for the development of friendships (Adams, 1998: 176).

One of the difficulties in studying computer-mediated communication is that standardised methodologies for the analysis of these kinds of exchanges are yet to be established (Pleace, Burrows, Loader et al., 2000).[1] Most research has involved conventional face-to-face interviews with individuals and groups who use the Internet rather than both individuals and their textual interactions. We still know little about the individual characteristics of those who use the Internet for developing online friendships, although new research is emerging regularly as the examples below testify. The findings outlined in this chapter offer clues about the kinds of patterns now evolving.

Internet etiquette

A popular form of Internet-initiated friendship takes place in Internet chat rooms where individuals meet by sharing electronic space. Involving communication through 'typed conversation' or Internet Relay Chat (IRC) enables people across the world to be joined together in cross-cultural chat. Like mobile phone use discussed below, IRC has given rise to a new postsocial communication etiquette. This form of communication allows people from any location to experiment with communication and self-representation. Internet communication is unlike direct experience as the medium itself enables a masking and distancing of users' identity. As Rheingold states: 'The grammar of computer-mediated conversation involves syntax of identity play: new identities, false identities, multiple identities, exploratory identities' (2000: 151). He approaches this development in a positive way: it enriches and transforms the process of self-formation and also produces a new kind of intimacy that differs fundamentally from the intimacy characteristic of face-to-face interaction.

Some chat rooms are regulated, by the use of a 'host' or 'wizard' who can eject individuals who break the rules of the room with abusive or harassing messages. Computer-mediated communication is often used playfully by employing new or modified signs such as punctuations like hieroglyphics used to represent physical contact (Reid, 1996b). Relationships in groups can thereby be expressed in a number of complex ways, such as flirting through wordplay. Exchanges typically provide social companionship, romantic or sexual intimations, and between members of self-help groups that provide mutual support (Pleace, Burrows, Loader et al., 2000). Chat room conversations may often lead on to the more private form of e-mail or phone contact. The Internet can therefore be an important stepping-stone to more conventional relationships. Chat rooms are popular with teenagers but, unfortunately, also with certain adults who make forays into these sites to connect with children and often use insulting language. However, chat room hosts can use the 'kick' command to remove individuals who are misbehaving.

The fact that children can be fooled online and drawn into unpleasant encounters continues to haunt us in this period of Internet-initiated sociality. Five million British children are now regular online visitors either at school or at home.[2] In fact, many Internet service providers rely on customers to tell them if chat rooms are breaking the rules, or the law. But several newsrooms and chat rooms are unregulated, with no hosts present so that users can say anything without being monitored. Accordingly, there is a danger that vulnerable people can be exposed to ideas that may be harmful to them (Pleace, Burrows, Loader et al., 2000: 8). MSN's teen chat area includes dozens of chat rooms such as 'GIRLS + GUYS THAT JUST WANNA DO IT' and 'INNOCENT GIRLS LOOKING FOR BAD BOYS'. Research by the UK Home Office (Internet Crime Forum, 2001) shows that one in five teenage Internet users receive a sexual solicitation or approach online. The study also demonstrates, like observations made about patterns of mobile phone use in Japan and the United Kingdom discussed below, that many children are exposed to 'inappropriate conversations', forced to listen to depraved fantasies or sent pornographic pictures. 'Grooming' – where a paedophile encounters children on the web or over the phone and plans a meeting – is not yet illegal.

Early research by Parks and Floyd (1996) found that women were more likely to develop personal relationships on the Internet than men, with age making no difference. This departs from research findings on conventional modes of personal interaction, which have repeatedly shown that women are more likely than men to develop relationships based on verbal exchanges (Adams, 1998; Wright, 1982). With different rules operating online compared to the face-to-face communication, it should come as no surprise that traditionally gender-patterned meanings and practices of intimacy are being disrupted or reinvented. For example, Hala Haidar-Yassine's (2002) study of computer-mediated friendships differ from those of Parks and Floyd by showing that face-to-face friendships were perceived by users to be more intimate than computer-mediated friendships for cross-sex friendship dyads. For female–female friendships, however, both face-to-face and Internet communication were rated as *equally* intimate while for male–male friendship dyads computer-mediated friendships were rated as *more* intimate. This indicates that, in the use of chat rooms and e-mail, men were persuaded to self-disclose more online, which may be linked to stronger experiences of 'control' offered by the medium's ability to slow down the pace of interaction from immediate and hurried face-to-face rejoinders to prepared and considered responses.

In Parks and Floyd's (1996) study, online friendships were far less homogenous than those which were formed face-to-face, in the sense that they were less likely to share the same social structural characteristics of gender, race, age and so on. Access to parts of the Internet is restricted by age and income but once on-line, individuals are less constrained by their social characteristics than in offline contexts. In particular, Parks and Floyd found that 51 per cent of the online friendships reported were with members of the opposite sex, indicating that it is being practised in a far more heterogeneous way than among face-to-face friendships. It seems that cross-sex relationships can flourish in a context where the social barriers posed by gender status and power can be rendered opaque when participants do not reveal their gender identity. Early research on computer-mediated interaction revealed that women and ethnic minorities indicate they have more scope to communicate their opinions online than they do in face-to-face contexts even if their gender and ethnic identities are revealed (Walther, 1992). Where sites are interest-based, social status is defined according to the value of the information the participant can offer others in the context of the online world.

Online romance

At the start of the Internet revolution, one of the first niche markets on the web was online personal ads. Online dating is so popular that the stigma attached to matchmaking is gradually diminishing. The image of the type of person who becomes a client of a dating service as a desperate, lonely individual on the hunt for a partner is rapidly receding. In New York, Internet dating is sufficiently fashionable for it to be referred to as 'man shopping' or 'hyperdating' (France, 2002). In fact, Internet dating not only evokes the idea of consumption, with surfing the 'personals' being compared to catalogue shopping, but it also evokes the notion of marketing the self. Internet dating ads involve profiles and photos in which individuals do an advertising pitch on the self (France, 2002). Participants use phrases to place themselves in the best light in an effort to 'market' themselves.

Not only have professional match-making services changed the way people meet one another, but those that provide an Internet service have enjoyed a new boost in customers. Over a million people in the United Kingdom currently use online matchmaking services to find dating partners (Gavin, 2002). There are several reasons why Internet dating agencies have exploded in popularity. First, searching for partners on the Internet offers anonymity and personal control. While participants are expected, at some point, to come out of cyber space and meet virtual partners 'for real', the Internet offers important filtering devices. Writing skills and the attachment of photographs of participants' faces act as a filter before people meet, and so does the fee. Most sites charge a regular fee. The higher the fee, the more exclusive and excluding the market becomes. A sense of control over the development of the relationship is commonly felt by users when relationships are being established on the Internet. 'If it doesn't work out and you don't like the sound of someone, you can always press delete. It's the easiest thing in the world not to reply to an email',[3] as journalist Louise France comments. Second, time-deprived professionals and shiftworkers on antisocial work schedules are finding it increasingly difficult to meet like-minded people outside the context of work. Third, a boom in the population of singletons (both unmarried and divorced) has happened across all Western nations. This growing single population comes at a time when there are more online opportunities for people to meet.

Although many people are going online to find friends rather than, or as well as, in search of romance, one-third of all Internet users turn to the web to establish some sort of personal relationship.[4] It is predicted that within three years, more than half of singletons will meet a partner online. France identifies another group of Internet daters: 'Nowadays there are teenagers who will have cybersex before they have real sex. Where their parents kissed at a Rolling Stones gig, they're just as likely to hook up on a chat room or an internet site. Or maybe they'll meet at a club and then go home to continue contact on the net.'[5]

The rising popularity of Internet romances is transforming the dating patterns of young people as well as the 'maturing' members of society.[6] The anonymity offered by online communication is often experienced as liberating. Men tend to state that they find they are able to be more revealing and intimate online, and women often say they have the freedom to be more flirtatious in a safe environment when compared to the constraining contexts of bars, clubs and restaurants (Gavin, 2002; Whitty and Gavin, 2001). The sense of freedom offered by Internet romance highlights the extent to which people feel the pressures and discomforts of face-to-face interaction, with its concomitant visual and verbal conventions and bodily scrutiny. More than half of the 42 regular users of Internet chat rooms interviewed by Jeff Gavin (2002) had developed a romantic relationship with a person they had met online, with the interaction developing from chat, to e-mails, to 'phone calls and then finally to face-to-face encounters.

In a further study of 300 students in Australia, Whitty and Gavin discovered that half had experienced their first 'meaningful' romantic relationship with a person they had first met online (Gavin, 2002; Whitty and Gavin, 2001). Indeed, some research indicates that romances starting on the Internet are more likely to succeed than those that develop from encounters in the more conventional settings of pubs and nightclubs (Gavin, 2002). Gavin states: 'It [online communication] is the reverse of traditional meetings because it starts off with the intimate stuff, then people find out more mundane things and finally they meet in person.'[7] Curiously, online anonymity seems to encourage individuals to be more emotionally open at the very beginning of a romance, thereby providing a seemingly sound basis on which to build the relationship.

However, in case Internet dating is sounding like the perfect platform on which to stage a new relationship, a website dedicated to Internet dating disasters – www.wildxangel.com – contains enough horror stories to convince us of the extent to which the Internet lends itself to misunderstandings and deceit. Individuals who fall in love on the Internet may discover vast discrepancies in age between the Internet identity and the person behind it when a face-to-face encounter ensues. Individuals may find that their true love is married with no intention of divorcing their spouse, or that the new partner is more interested in their bank account than the relationship. Notwithstanding such problems, disembodied friendships and romances are clearly defining postsocial relations, whether as a new form of communication, the groundwork for a long-term relationship, or as a means by which individuals can create and experiment with new identities online.

Arranged marriages online

Detectable ethnic differences in Internet use for the purposes of arranged marriages signals the importance of the Internet among ethnic minority communities and diasporic populations. The arrangement of marriages is one of the most popular uses of the Internet among immigrants to the United States from India. A single matrimonial site studied by Adams and Ghose (2003) had over 88,000 members, with a likely total of hundreds of thousands of participants across all sites. In the United Kingdom, hundreds of Muslim women are turning to the Internet to find a husband, according to journalist, Aisha Khan in 2003,[8] to overcome the disadvantages of traditional modes of networking.

Matrimonial websites that are popular in the United States integrate domestic and international marriage markets since they are also regularly used by families in India searching for eligible men and women in the United States, Canada, the United Kingdom and other countries as well as India. As Adams and Ghose (2003: 430) state, 'the betrothals arising from this part of the bridgescape form a dense web of transoceanic family ties.' Intercultural contact and dissemination to India is accelerated by this important cultural process, but Adams and Ghose speculate that it may inhibit marriages across ethnic or sub-ethnic lines. Matrimonial websites vary in type from conservative, family-directed markets to unorthodox self-directed markets that have more in common with Western matchmaking sites. While family-directed matrimonial sites often contain a small, low-resolution photograph, they consistently include high-definition information about caste, religion, ethnicity, education and employment, signifying the greater emphasis placed on these factors for a marriage than on physical appearance. Indeed, one site (www.matrimonialonline.net) lists 520 'caste' options, underlining the importance of this characteristic in deciding suitability. These services are distinctive because their focus is on religion and culture. Questions can be asked about which branch of Islam users follow, how often they pray and so on. As Adams and Ghose point out, Western dating sites typically identify individuals with similar interests and mutual physical attraction, a form of use rare in Indian society and Indian diasporas due to traditional Indian attitudes to the body (see, for example, Angelo, 1997: 103). The traditional Indian notion of sex as something to be encountered only in marriage is compromised by the Western concept of dating.

However, complexion is one physical feature that is regularly listed on these matrimonial ads. In the space provided for describing complexion, most skin tones are labelled 'wheatish'. Dark complexion usually prompts an explanation, with an example from www.bharatmatrimony.com cited by Adams and Ghose (2003: 432): 'NEGATIVE POINTS: My daughter is not of fair complexion. Of course she is not very dark, but with no amount of extrapolation she can be called as fair.' This statement signifies the social pressure to conform to social hierarchies that also include educational and professional qualifications of the prospective marital partner and their parents.

British-born Pakistani women are arranging marriage online in the United Kingdom in response to the difficulties of conventional methods of networking which are often unable to fulfil the demands of their culture. Sites designed especially for Muslim populations have grown rapidly, helping those young Muslims who do not date or cohabit before marriage to scrutinise potential partners online. One website (Muslimmatch.com) was launched in January 2002 specifically for this purpose and now has 15,000 members across the world. The membership fee is £14.99 for a three-month period, at the time of writing. Within this period, messages can be sent and received from interested participants. One of the founders of the website, Waleed Saeed, explains that this kind of service gives Muslims greater command over the process of selection and introduction than the postal-based marriage service that it replaced. It allows rapid updating of the site and individuals can log on any time of the day or night.

This matrimonial service overcomes some of the dilemmas of recruiting the help of friends and relatives, or placing an advertisement in an Asian-language newspaper such as the *Daily Jang* or *Eastern Eye*, based in the United Kingdom. A successful search on the net usually leads to the arrangement of a visit between the young man and his parents with the young woman's family. The two are introduced to one another and briefly left alone. A British-born Pakistani user of the internet interviewed by Aisha Khan refers to this short meeting as a 'limited window of opportunity' which allows the pair to chat and find out more about each other in terms of likes and dislikes, jobs, education, martial status of siblings and current living arrangements. The parents then rejoin them and further discussion then takes place. One woman interviewed about the process admitted that the first meeting is 'excruciating' because there is so much pressure placed on the pair to make things work out successfully.

Ali Hassan, who runs a site (muslim-marriages.co.uk) with his wife, began by offering a postal service. But he found that the Internet allowed participants to view potential partners without committing to a match:

> If a boy is found in the traditional way – through friends or family – and a meeting is arranged, then there is more pressure for the match to work because the meeting indicates a level of commitment from both sides. You can learn about a potential match by going online. You can look at more than one match at a time, something you can't do in real life.[9]

Khan points out that although this kind of service is popular among young Muslim men and women in the United Kingdom, their parents are yet to be convinced, as Hassan admits: 'There's a stigma attached to finding a partner through a website because it's seen as a sign of failure – that you couldn't find someone among your friends or family. People don't want others to know that their daughter's husband was found online. And I've yet to be invited to a wedding, although I can understand why.'[10]

Most sites protect users' identities by not giving out contact details, so anonymity and control are crucial. But this can cause the same kinds of difficulties experienced on other, Western-style dating sites with users being older than they claimed, or holding incompatible views. It may be some time before this kind of approach becomes the norm among Muslim communities, however. One users' brother stated:

> OK. So the Internet wasn't around during the Prophet Mohammed's time but the principle is the same. A man and a woman shouldn't have any kind of relationship before marriage. It doesn't matter that they haven't met, it's what's going on in their heads and hearts while they're emailing each other that is the problem. Just because marriage sites are becoming popular and socially acceptable, it doesn't make it right.[11]

The emergent practice of online arranged marriages illustrates not only the flexibility of the Internet for matchmaking purposes but also the notable compatibility between new technology and the demands of particular diasporic cultures. In a situation where meeting or getting to know prospective marriage partners is prohibited in advance of parental or community consent, and where the social customs and networks for arranging marriage have been disrupted by migration, the Internet can serve an important role. Moreover, as Adams and Ghose (2003: 432) argue, in matrimonial websites, the Internet functions as a device for breaking the 'seeing/being seen dyad' that Foucault (1977) talks about in his description of the prisoner in the panoptican. He cites Foucault (1977: 200) who states: 'He is seen, but he does not see; he is the object of information, never a subject in communication.' In a sense, the prospective bride, and to some extent the groom, are the objects rather than subjects of information. However, the British example cited by Khan implies the potential for more control on the part of the prospective marriage partners. Nevertheless, Adams and Ghose (2003: 432) contend that the Internet presents a technological solution in circumstances where geographical dispersion and relocation in an alien culture jeopardises the 'traditional place-based martial panoptican'.

Interestingly, the inscription of the self by complexion, caste, professional and academic qualifications is being contested on websites (such as indya.com) where the Indian body is evaluated by a Western hierarchy of values: physical appearance, desire for the other's body, courtship as play and so on. Yet, not surprisingly, as Adams and Ghose point out, such sites are ineffective since very few women register on such websites given the constraints placed on women.

Friends reunited

Simmel's (1950a and b) claim that life in modern society is becoming more fragmented and impersonal, with social ties increasingly being characterised as unwelcoming and fleeting, is a condition apparently borne out by the increasing tendency for people to loose touch with former friends. However, the Internet has the powerful appeal of stepping in to reunite individuals who lost contact with one another during childhood and teenage years. Launched by Steve and Julie Pankhurst from their spare bedroom in the suburbs of London in 2000, Friends Reunited (www.friendsreunited.co.uk) is an enormously popular website that reconnects old school friends. It has now turned into a thriving industry with nearly nine million registered users – 15 per cent of the UK adult population – with 50,000 visitors a day and rising. Friends Reunited has also been launched in Australia, New Zealand and South Africa with plans to be extended to Spain, Italy and the Netherlands. In his study of the reasons why Friends Reunited (FR) is so popular, journalist Peter Martin captures today's public anxieties about social disintegration:

> The FR phenomenon has tapped into a huge desire to reconnect with the diaspora of our lives, with those formative friendships lost in the search for education and work or to family demands – the very stuff of social displacement captured in Margaret Thatcher's apocalyptic declaration that 'There is no such thing as society'. By the time she said it, the nuclear family had gone pear-shaped, with a soaring divorce rate and alarming levels of teenage drug-taking and suicide. We'd already become a curiously indoor culture – characterised by sofa-bound kids – when, according to fashionably dire expectation, the advent of e-mail and the internet was going to mark the end of real-life interaction.[12]

The anxiety associated with the idea of rampant social disintegration is, then, resolved by a service like Friends Reunited. As Martin points out, the first group of Friends Reunited users were individuals in their forties, 'those most beleaguered by midlife duties and attendant crises'.[13] Today, the average age of users is mid-thirties. Contact through the website is typically followed by e-mail exchanges, then phone call, then face-to-face contact. School memory boards have been set up; with personal notes posted by individuals allowing users to assess how school friends, from bullies to old flames, have since fared in life. As a unique form of social connection with no antecedents, Friends Reunited fuels nostalgia by reconnecting individuals with their past lives. It allows people to construct identities through their roots, with friends from the age of 5 onwards unlocking memories unique to those relationships.

In addition to renewing friendships, the site performs the service of inspiring school reunions and group holidays and bringing together lost relatives and relocating birth parents. As Martin remarks, 'Plainly, FR answers a profound longing for community.' He goes on to say: 'When you factor in Friends Reunited's unique access to past and present, it's safe to say that never in human history has there been such heavy traffic in collective memory and personal disclosure as that now whizzing back and forth online.'[14] Friends Reunited allows former bullies to apologise to their victims for their past misdemeanours after years of pent up guilt. Whether this makes victims feel any better is another matter. However, since Friends Reunited's name-search facility allows users to search for individuals without knowing the school they went to, the site can be used for tracking down the backgrounds of celebrities and politicians. Like many other facilities on the Internet, this website can be exploited as a form of surveillance and harassment, and is even used by the police in crime-solving cases.

The Friends Reunited website is famous for the role it plays in rekindling thousands of old romances that first blossomed at school according to its co-founder, Steve Pankhurst.[15] Of course, there is a downside as Denise Knowles from marriage counselling service, Relate, claims. One in ten of Relate's clients whose marriages have failed blame Internet chat rooms, dating services or Friends Reunited. Technology offers a wider range of ways of reconnecting people with past friends but, as Knowles says, '[B]laming a website is like citing the telephone for divorce in previous decades.'[16] Moreover, romances rekindled on Friends Reunited are no less real or more deluding than couples who meet in other ways.

Online queer communities

Research on use of the internet by queer, lesbian, bisexual and transsexual (QLBT[17]) women shows how important the Internet is in the formation of queer identities and online communities (Correll, 1995; Munt, Bassett and O'Riordan, 2002; Wakeford, 1996; Wincapaw, 2000). Shelley Correll conducted an ethnographic study of an Internet bulletin board system (BBS) called the Internet Café, which shows how individual and community identities are negotiated in the formation and membership of an online lesbian bar. The study demonstrates the positive effects of online interactive spaces for women at risk of being stigmatised and marginalised. Such research also reveals the tendency in work by Turkle (1995) and others, to conflate sex with gender and to obscure differences between women – whether in terms of sexual orientation, race, age or social class.

In her exploratory study of the use of the internet by queer, lesbian, bisexual and transsexual (QLBT[18]) women, mentioned in Chapter 5, Bryson (2004) investigated the ways in which Internet technologies and communities re/mediate the narrativisation of queer lives and communities. She found that internet tools and communities present a crucial space for interaction with other queer women in a relatively safe space. The Internet also provides opportunities to experiment with sexual identity and practices. It offers an important entry into a cultural context in which to learn about queer identity through immersion and participation in a sexually specific subculture. Bryson explains that the net performs a similar role to that of books in the formation of QLBT identities. Past studies show how important texts such as books, movies and community newspapers are to individuals within the formation of queer identities, providing a sense of belonging to a queer culture. They are carriers of the kinds of social and cultural scripts that offer readers the pleasure of finding themselves represented in the text (Lynch, 1990). In the same way, websites with email bulletin boards and chat rooms provide an important source of knowledge and cultural engagement and a valued toolkit for what Bryson (2004: 245) calls 'community apprenticeship' in the shaping of sexual identity. Online lesbian identities (butch, femme, grrrl, etc.) were viewed by participants in somewhat inflexible, literal terms but as Bryson points out, these were performances that opened up the possibility of transgressing the rigid limitations imposed in everyday face-to-face interactions.

Interaction and intimacy on the mobile phone

Conspicuous social interaction

In Chapter 6, I discussed new forms of sociality being configured through technology-based sets of personal networks in which individuals reach beyond, and redefine, cultural spaces in their interactions. In this section I explore ways that young people are reshaping sociability on the mobile phone as part of a new combination of electronic and face-to-face communication which is characterising urban interaction (Castells, 2002: 556). Mobile phone use forms part of the rising pattern of what Castells calls 'individual networks of socialisation'. It is important to emphasise, first, the diverse communicative potential of the mobile phone. The mobile phone offers the remarkable flexibility of both binding and avoiding face-to-face interaction. On the one hand, this communication device can *cement* face-to-face relationships, not only through regular contact with friends and loved ones, but also through mobile phone sharing – a custom practised by young people, as discussed below. On the other hand, the mobile phone can be used to *fragment* face-to-face contact by allowing individuals to withdraw from engagement with physically present others by concentrating on the virtual moment.

A Vodaphone advertisement shown on UK commercial television in March 2002 emphasises this quality, with individual family members in the same room compelled to text one another in order to gain their attention. So the disembedding quality of the mobile phone lends itself not only to *social intimacy* but also to *social distancing*. Not only can individuals swiftly withdraw from interacting with their immediate surroundings by sending or answering a mobile phone spoken or text message, but they can disguise their location to receivers of spoken calls through the use of *audio alibis*. Fake background noises can now be activated while you conduct your phone call. Garcia-Montes, Caballero-Munoz and Perez-Alvarez (2006: 73) suggest that the 'dilemmas of identity (and of trust in others) can be exacerbated by the use of the mobile phone'. Drawing on clinical psychology, they suggest that this adoption and management of *distancing* from the current situation when interrupted by the phone call, leads to a 'transcendent' and more unified sense of self. At the same time, it creates a 'present extensive', an extension of the present by the flexibility in being able to arrange and re-arrange appointments. Being immediately available for whoever might call leads Garcia- Montes and colleagues (2006) to argue that the distinction between public and private spaces are becoming blurred by the need to manage the intersection of private and work life through the receipt of work-related calls at leisure and personal calls at work. They suggest that, in turn, the frontiers between the 'public self' and the 'private self' are blurring.

It was in 2001 that it became clear how far mobile phone use had spread to children and adolescents. An EU survey showed that 80 per cent of young people aged 15 to 24 used mobile phones regularly (Wilska, 2003). And in a British survey of 2001[19] around 60 per cent of secondary school pupils in the United Kingdom owned a mobile phone, with the largest ownership being among 14- to 16-year-olds. Despite its ability to both cement and fragment interaction, this form of personal communication is now so extensive among young people that public anxiety about its use, particularly by children, is widespread. Child sexual exploitation by adults, a breakdown in traditional forms of face-to-face interaction among children, and spiralling costs of children's mobile phone bills have fuelled parental concerns. These kinds of anxieties form part of wider concerns about the collapse of traditional modes of communication in the face of individualised forms of new technology, exemplified by personal CD players and mobile phones, that operate beyond the radar of traditional community and family guardians of children.

By 2005, 25 per cent of the 75 million mobile phone users in Japan were using third-generation (3 G) cell phones with Internet access. Japanese parents are alarmed about the problems of children being exploited by online dating via the mobile phone. Dating sites have been used as a cover for paedophile activity and child prostitution, with a reported 22 per cent of girls and 18 per cent of boys between 15 and 18 years of age in Japan having access to such sites on mobile phones.[20]

In the United Kingdom, child protection charities, such as NCH Action for Children[21] have persuaded mobile phone operators to shield children under the age of 18 from access to adult services on the Internet via the mobile in order to curb the spread of Internet paedophile activity. New regulations agreed by six of the largest mobile phone operators in the United Kingdom (Orange, O2, T-Mobile, Virgin, Vodaphone and 3) to prevent children entering chat rooms, porn sites and gambling services have been introduced in 2004.[22]

Mobile phones have an added disadvantage of being used for offensive calls or bullying, with 14 per cent of 7- to 16-year-olds having received such a call or text message. Yet research suggests that not owning a mobile phone could lead to social exclusion by limiting young people's interaction with peers, by impeding their sense of belonging, and by restricting their opportunities to keep pace with changing technologies. A division between the 'haves' and the 'have-nots' has emerged, with the latter being left behind in the information revolution (Charlton, Panting and Hannan, 2002; Leung and Wei, 1999). As Garcia-Montes and colleagues (2006) point out, there are indications from a US survey that those who do not use mobile phones come from socially disadvantaged groups as they are largely from lower income, and less well educated social groups.

Despite the fears of parents and child protection agencies about Internet paedophilia, the short messaging service (SMS), commonly known as 'texting', is now commonplace, especially among young people. Mobile phone texting is not just functional in the sense of being fast, simple and inexpensive. The intensity with which mobile phones are handled, prodded and fondled indicates their importance to a teenager's identity. While for parents mobile phones may symbolise secrecy and lack of parental surveillance, for young people they can continue to symbolise *conspicuous social interaction*. These devices are marketed and used as fashion accessories with a range of different, brightly coloured designs of mobile phone covers targeted at young people. Mobile phones are, in effect, displayed as a central part of the performance of identity. They are often pulled out of bags and pockets and placed on desks and tables by owners so that the phone can be displayed, and even shared, by others. However, this device cannot be dismissed as a fleeting status symbol, given its explosion in use (Charlton, 2002: 153).

While many teenagers are bought mobile phones by parents as a form of parental surveillance, the technology is being used by teenagers precisely to evade this surveillance and emphasise independence and sociability with other young people. A survey conducted by British youth culture research group, Roar,[23] found that one in ten prefer to flirt over the mobile rather than face-to-face,[24] indicating that the mobile phone shares the same qualities as the Internet: giving individuals the confidence to communicate more intimately from a distance through communication technology than they would do face-to-face. Notwithstanding the flexibility of the mobile phone for both binding and avoiding face-to-face interaction, public fears remain rife that young people are replacing human contact with virtual contact.

Reciprocity among teenagers

Among 16- to 19-year-olds, the mobile phone forms a central part of social intimacy through exchange ceremonies, according to research by Alexander Taylor and Richard Harper (2003). Text messages, call-credits and, indeed, the actual mobile phones themselves are used as forms of *gift-giving* among young people for the purposes of cementing social relationships. As Taylor and Harper point out, the mobile phone is a form of new technology that also forms part of a *ritual of exchange* (Berking, 1999). Forms of reciprocity have been studied in anthropology and sociology, exemplified by the work of Ervin Goffman (1972) on *interaction rituals* and Alvin Gouldner (1973) on *norms of reciprocity* as well as more recent studies of gift-giving rituals. The meaning of a gift is not simply conveyed in the artefact itself but also in the manner of giving as a ritual, in the sense of being ceremoniously delivered (Cheal, 1987; Schwartz, 1967: 7). The mobile phone plays a central role in the ceremonial display of friendship and intimacy. Importantly, this new technology mediates gift exchange as a ritual performance of offering, receiving and reciprocating gifts for building and establishing personal relationships. It is a culture of gift-giving which encourages creativity, with young people producing carefully composed messages by playing with language and symbols. Concerns that the short messaging service (SMS) harms a child's level of literary have therefore been disputed.[25] In fact, mobile phones are being used as a way of developing the literacy levels of young people with poor educational skills at the Learning and Skills development Agency in London.[26]

Value is allocated to the way text messages are written. The absence of punctuation is often regarded as irritating to the receiver since it is difficult to read and indicates saving of money. Sentimental, thoughtful and amusing text messages from lovers or friends are treasured as embodied memories – so much so that teenagers often declare they are reluctant to delete them. Interestingly, then, the electronic message is being treated as something sufficiently unique and personal that it can display the characteristics of a special offering. 'More particularly', Taylor and Harper (2003: 9) state, 'the text message comes to mean more than merely an exchange of words, but becomes an offering of commitment to the relationship.' Boyfriends text their girlfriends with 'goodnight' messages after spending a considerable amount of time on the phone to them during the day.

This kind of texting is considered by many teenagers to be part of 'the rules' of a romantic relationship in order to signify desire, intimacy and commitment. However, important differences between men's and women's uses of the mobile phone are being recorded by researchers. For example, in a study of 18- to 30-year-olds by Simeon Yates conducted in 2005,[27] volunteers kept diaries of patterns of phone use and recording of text messages. The research, which also drew on focus group discussions, revealed that women tend to write longer text messages than men, especially when communicating with other women. While men tend to use an average of 68 characters and to use fewer characters when texting each other, women tend to use an average of 82 characters. Yet swearing, typically used as a form of communication by men, is often a sign of emotional support. Without warning or provocation, they might text 'Fuck Off', and the reply might be something like 'You arse', meaning 'I'm here, how are you?'

The research also found that men were more prone to speaking on the mobile phone while in company, indicating some kind of kudos associated with using the phone in public. But speaking to girlfriends or mothers was more likely to take place in private away from the group, implying that intimate conversation is still publicly unacceptable among men. By contrast, if women were in a group they were less likely to answer the phone. Men divulged that they tended to use texting as a method of communication when they didn't want people in their company to know what they were saying, indicating that secrecy is valued by men who fear disapproval by the group. Both men and women disclosed that they use text messages to avoid difficult social exchanges. In focus groups, young people pondered over the rights and wrongs of texting kisses at the end of a message and whether women should text men on the Monday that fail to phone them after a night out the previous Saturday. 'Text etiquette' is clearly still evolving. Young women revealed disapprovingly that boyfriends have dumped them by text message. Ending a relationship via a text message or the Internet is considered to be the most shameful use of mobile phones as it is considered impersonal (Taylor and Harper, 2003).

Mobile phones may symbolise privacy and independence yet, as Taylor and Harper point out, these devices are also shared between friends, with a phone being passed around a group of three or four boys or girls in localised, phone-mediated interactions, in the college canteen, café or a pub. A phone will be placed on the table with the expectation that others will pick it up and use it in a responsible way, indicating that trust is being extended by the owner to the user. Trust is therefore conveyed in the ritual of sharing.

Examples of Gouldner's (1973) *norms of reciprocity* include actions such as the use of friends' phones to text boyfriends or girlfriends and the exchange of credit to pay for the charges, as a crucial symbol of friendship. Sharing a mobile phone can be expensive, with the charges mounting up, so swapping and trade-offs come to be part of reciprocation and an unspoken part of the establishment of friendship. In fact, friends who reply to text messages via the Internet on one of its free text messaging services rather than using credit on the mobile phone are sometimes condemned for saving money because the exchange is not seen as mutual and fair. The message is not deemed reciprocal if the services are of different values, as Taylor and Harper point out.

Gouldner (1973) provides an analysis of the 'cycle of reciprocity', where exchange between individuals as a mechanism to cement relationships relies on a sequence of mutual reinforcement as a moral obligation. Taylor and Harper draw on this to explain phone-mediated gift-giving where teenagers are bound to one another through unspoken contracts such as the obligation to reply to a text message, and to reply to the reply and so on. They also refer to Goffman's (1972: 90) notion of 'supportive interchange', wherein mobile phone conversation and texting affirm personal ties and wider social allegiances. The centrality of reciprocity means that mobile phones can be used effectively to reject or exclude a person from a social network, by not replying to messages. 'Alice: Oh, there are some days when my phone does not beep at all. I'm like "ok nobody likes me. NOBODY knows me!" ...' (Taylor and Harper, 2003: 279). So text messaging is perceived as inherently intimate in some contexts, as a crucial way of cementing social relationships and expressing intimacy in general, with the use of word abbreviations and smiley faces to imply affection. Yet, conversely, it is perceived as a highly impersonal mode of communication when ending a romantic relationship. Moreover, the inability of a mobile phone to lock or hide messages means that personal messages cannot be hidden from friends within the sharing culture. Privacy can only be expressed through shared secrets and understandings between individuals.

The arrival of multi-media mobile phones will no doubt offer new modes of interaction as yet unforeseen. The attachment of still pictures or video provides a new dimension to messaging at a number of levels: surveillance and voyeurism, evidence and documentation, as well as sentimental interaction and shared memories. Although the mobile phone is often portrayed as a form of global imagination technology that renders face-to-face interaction secondary to virtual communication, ethnographic studies demonstrate, then, that the mobile phone has been appropriated in localised ways, allowing a rearticulation of traditional forms of sociality (Taylor and Harper, 2003; Yoon, 2003). There is, as yet, no evidence that young people have been disembedded from local sociality (Yoon, 2003). On the contrary, evidence suggests that trust and reciprocity are central to mobile phone use among teenagers. Phone-mediated gift-giving and ritual reciprocation cement moral commitment within young people's relationships by denoting friendship and solidarity. Importantly, if mobile phone use enhances young people's communication with peers and nurtures confidence in operating other communication technologies, then the 'have-nots' will be at an increasing disadvantage, demonstrating the need for an understanding of the distinctions made between the information-rich and the information-poor.

The mobile phone is, then, a form of *conspicuous social interaction* precisely because it is a relatively novel communication device, a fashion item nevertheless likely to be rapidly rendered mundane and yet a vital mode of interaction among the young. And, like the Internet chat room, it is the ideal technology for the exploration and communication of intimacy, in the form of loyalty and privacy as well as solidarity. So Castells (2002) is right in claiming that the mobile phone is among the new forms of technology that form the rising pattern of 'individual networks of socialisation'. While the examples of mobile phone use among the young show how this new technology can strengthen social ties through trust and reciprocity, wider debates about computer mediated communication are characterised by the accent on transience.

Conclusion

Ideas about collective disembodied systems of social interaction that originate in a symbolic space, such as the Internet and mobile phone, are important examples of 'postsocial' forms of communication. We can define the 'postsocial', then, as 'forms of human interaction mediated by and constituted through communication technologies' (Knorr-Cetina, 2001: 532–3). Postsocial forms of interaction are conceived in circumstances where interaction, space and even communication mean something quite distinctive from the conventional uses of terms about social connection once founded on face-to-face interaction. While 'global hyperspace' contains features of shallowness, triviality and exploitation, it also harbours the potential to foster new collectivities.

Moreover, although computer-mediated communication holds the promise of creating a separate social space and a separate reality; examples such as virtual communities of care indicate that these new forms of community are not necessarily constituted at the expense of existing traditional support networks of family, neighbourhood and partners. They often run parallel to, or become embedded within, other modes of interaction as demonstrated by mobile phone use among the young. In other words, new technologies become part of already established social contexts which, in turn, shape the use of those technologies (Taylor and Harper, 2003).

However, Internet-initiated interaction raises a number of profound questions about shifting ground rules for forming and conducting personal relationships. Within non-proximate interaction initiated over the Internet, structural and dispositional characteristics such as age, class, gender, ethnic identity and race operate in quite different ways from that of face-to-face interaction. Internet-initiated relationships are often, but no longer necessarily, based on a shared history, shared biography, shared physical community space or some other common experience. The kinds of rituals and conventions associated with face-to-face meeting contexts – whether leisure, work or neighbourhood community contexts – are reconfigured through different modes of sharing such as mutual interest Internet websites.

Within computer mediated communication, the idea of permanence in personal relationship is disrupted by an emphasis on ambivalence, unpredictability, flexibility and individualism. It throws into relief the socially constructed nature of the self, emphasised by postmodernism. It undermines the modernist idea that personal relationships constitute a privileged realm of self-fulfilment. Personal relationships are transient, mobile and experimental. Friendship sometimes merges with, and sometimes separates from, family, sexual relationships and work relationships. This causes, however, a number of problems in an era when the rules are no longer telling us what the boundaries are. It has important implications for the way that sex and gender are being reconfigured. The instability and fluidity of sexual identity is emphasised through experimentation within Internet chat.

One of the consequences is that this new form of communication can provoke a weakening of trust and responsibility. The contemporary disembedding of time and space entails a greater need for trust than in modern society given that transactions are no longer predominantly face-to-face. While time-space distanciation allows the development of new links between the global and local, traditional social relations are gradually 'lifted out' from their ties to specific spatial contexts. As systems of organisation such as monetary exchange and expertise become more abstract, faceless and depersonalised, the problem of trust increases, given that interactions are fused by relations of trust. This need for trust is all the more urgent in a society whose social ties are increasingly being characterised by uncertainties and contingencies. This is therefore an issue dealt with in the following chapter in relation to questions of responsibility, care and morality raised by postmodern social ties.

8
The Politics of Social and Personal Relationships

This book has explored the ways in which the exclusive nature of associations of family, community and place are being challenged and reconfigured by alternative social relationships involving local and global political movements, urban voluntary associations, and new face-to-face and computer-mediated forms of belonging. New social ties are characterised as thinned out, fluid and transient. Yet they are also often expressed as intense associations and offer possibilities for confronting old inequalities. My central argument is that a friendship discourse is being used as a way of managing these rapid changes in social ties. Friendship's flexibility and adaptability ensures that it appeals to different and sometimes contradictory discourses and social trends: neoliberal discourses and processes of individualisation as well as discourses of equality, justice and democracy. I argue that friendship is being monitored as a form of governance in Western societies, within a social capital discourse. And, conversely, by offering a discursive framework for claiming intimate relationships as non-hierarchical, friendship becomes a powerful metaphor for the postmodern condition. Alongside new, disembedded 'postsocial relations' mediated by Internet and cell phone technology, traditional ties are being reshaped not only by informality, speed and interactions over distance but by new ideas of the 'self'.

The quality of kin relationships is being gauged by the moral value of friendship. In turn, friendships are increasingly being authenticated by association with the alluring and nostalgic aspects of family and community bonds. The deployment of the metaphor of friendship to describe family relationships serves, then, a chain of aspirations within the search for the pure relationship. However, while friendship signifies a challenge to old hierarchies, this bond contains no obligations or guarantees of responsibility and guardianship in the way that older, traditional ties such as 'family' and community have done. The problem with friendship is that mutual trust, interdependence and care for others are apparently undermined by the fluid and indecisive nature of this personal tie. Friendship is unable to call upon the same kinds of legal and bureaucratic regulations that privilege and preserve kin relations over non-kin relationships.

The fear among scholars of postmodernity is that the culture of individualism, in which the celebrated concept of friendship is anchored, is undermining the moral regulation of individuals and may be leading to moral indifference. The literature on subjectivity thinking about the modern and postmodern individual is conceptualised in terms of relational inadequacies. As Knorr-Cetina (2001: 525) states, the individual is characterised as 'uprooted', 'disembedded', 'thrown back upon its own resources', 'inward turning', 'individualised', 'atomised', 'ontologically insecure'. This subject is now signified as self-reliant yet potentially confused and apathetic. The precarious nature of this set of social conditions highlights the urgency of a common moral framework for connecting people together.

These issues are focused on in this final chapter by addressing the problems of trust, justice and care associated with new, fluid and elective social ties. Higher divorce rates and a crisis of care of both children and the elderly are trends coinciding with new-found freedoms, increasing elective relationships and women's growing autonomy. These concerns lead to a questioning of the ideological and physical onus placed on them to take responsibility for caring for dependents. Not only is the level of trustworthiness of non-face-to-face interaction, such as Internet-initiated communication, brought into sharp relief but so is the level of trust in governments, political leaders during a period when leadership and hierarchy are being questioned. Trust in the integrity of the self and of others cannot be taken for granted in an individual-centred society of opportunism. Giddens (1991) argues that a new type of politics is needed to deal with the rise of new uncertainties, knowledges and social movements brought about by globalisation, expanded self-reflexivity and a post-traditional society. He argues that life politics must restore solidarity and recover or devise *new* traditions to create a meaningful context for people's lives. For Giddens, only through the creation of a new politics can trust be generated. This new, radical politics involves a revaluation of the ways in which we care for citizens and share out the material resources to support the collective well-being of members of society in the form of the modern welfare state.

In the following section, I look at the ways that 'trust' is being defined, measured and interpreted by governments today. Trust is being conceived of, in Western societies, within a social capital discourse. This discourse, assessed in Chapter 5, is influencing the definitions, arguments and findings about the relationship between trust and morality in an age of rapidly changing social relationships. The implications for social justice and ethics of care are addressed thereafter. Post-structuralist writers such as Derrida examine the role of friendship in recovering the social and a search for morality. Within the Aristotelian ideal, friendship signifies a moral quest for the pure expression of voluntary individual agency and elective interpersonal affinities. The need for a more equitable sharing of responsibilities of care between men and women is something that governments have not yet tackled centrally. This problem is addressed by a feminist ethics of care in response to Derrida's politics of friendship and identifies the challenges associated with the postmodern moral subject.

Decline in trust and rise in moral standards?

Both pessimistic and positive accounts of postmodern values and conditions share a concern with the status of morality and a desire for the recovery of ethical life within new modes of sociality. Their differences reflect the contradictory elements of postmodernity itself, as a set of social and cultural processes. On the one hand, it apparently leads to a more *tolerant* society in which people are more open-minded and more charitable. On the other, it is characterised by an intensified *mistrust* of all forms of authority as a feature of the desire for a shift from rigid, controlling social relations to democratic social relations. A distinctive feature of changing individual and collective existence is a rapid decline in social and political trust, causing a dilemma for governments who need to validate their authority. Crucially, particular versions of 'trust' have been coopted by governments and political analysts as part of the apparatus of the administration of political democracy and social policy: levels of trust among social groups are being regularly monitored.

Governments are ruling in new ways to adapt to the demands of the postmodern condition, characterised by a questioning of authority and loosening of ties of loyalty. They are attempting to demonstrate 'good government' by appealing to ethical issues. Rather than targeting birth rates, income distribution or employment patterns as such, governments are now targeting the civility, the level of trust in society, the intensity of community feeling, the extent of voluntary endeavour (Rose, 1999: 390). Sentiments, values and beliefs now provide a new 'medium' through which self-government of the autonomous individual is being connected up with the imperatives of ethical government. This trend is part of a shift from biopolitics with its emphasis on populations and territories (Foucault, 1997), to an ethical politics that emphasises ethical issues like social capital, health and well-being. Yet despite the fact that these values are less tangible and therefore more difficult to measure, they are becoming powerful signifiers of good government. This is why friendship is under the spotlight now. It is being surveyed as a form of governance, treated as a factor that has the potential to contribute to the productivity of social capital. Rose's term, 'ethopolitics', highlights the way social capital is being used by policy makers and in public debates to promote discourses that have ethical appeal (Walters, 2002).

'Trust' is, then, among the factors used in measurements of 'social capital' in the sense used by Putnam (1993a, 2000) to measure the productivity of community activity and sharing, described in Chapter 5. An examination of the empirical data generated by surveys of social and political trust, outlined below, demonstrates the growing suspicion of authority within changing patterns of social and political trust. The concept of 'trust' used by governments and academics is categorised as a feature of social capital. Government findings have shown that two kinds of trust have declined in the postwar period of Western nations such as the United Kingdom and the United States: 'social trust', defined as trust in fellow citizens and 'political trust', defined in terms of voting in political elections. For instance, findings of the World Values[1] and British Social Attitudes surveys of the late 1980s[2] show a decline of social trust in five Western nations since the 1950s. Here, 'trust' is defined as people's general inclination to trust their fellow citizens. This decline is matched by a similar drop in *political trust* between 1950s and 1980s,[3] and the proportion of people who trusted British governments fell in 2000.[4] A similar decline in electoral turnout for local, national and European elections has also been witnessed, especially in the last decade, as mentioned earlier.

The general downturn in social and political trust from the late 1950s to the late 1980s has been attributed to urbanisation, and the erosion of the collectivist traditions (Hall, 1999; Putnam, 1993a, 2000). From the 1980s, conservative governments promoted a more 'individualistic' entrepreneurialism encouraging people to become more competitive, and less trusting in others according to Hall (1999). He suggests that experiences of divorce, migration to a larger city and unemployment are likely to lower people's trust. Echoing Putnam, Hall (1999: 448) asserts that those whose value systems are self-interested tend to have significantly lower levels of social trust. Those who grew up in a more individualistic society in the 1980s are more likely to hold self-interested values, but many show more support for moral relativism. However, the rise in computer-mediated communication may also be another factor encouraging distrust. The speed with which individuals and action groups can obtain accurate information about local and world events, and communicate with one another in organising political action, is sharpening awareness of the wrongdoings of governments and multinational corporations, from human rights violations to world pollution.

The lack of trust in world leaders could be interpreted in a more positive light: as an example of the high standards of morality that people hold these days. This seems to be verified by a global public opinion poll study conducted in 15 countries for the World Economic Forum in 2003.[5] The study reveals that trust in *institutions* across the world is not declining but that *leaders* have suffered declining trust, and that they enjoy less trust than the institutions they lead. The survey asked respondents how far they trusted leaders to 'manage the challenges of the coming year in the best interests of you and your family'. Leaders of non-government organisations (NGOs) are the only leaders out of eight leadership categories that enjoy the trust of citizens across the nations surveyed.[6] The second most trusted of leaders tested are the United Nations and spiritual and religious leaders, with over 40 per cent stating they have a lot of trust in them. The least trusted leaders are leaders of the United States (27 per cent). The only nation where US leaders are trusted is the United States itself, with 75 per cent of Americans trusting the US leaders to manage the challenges of the next year.

Four in ten citizens across the 15 countries said that the terrorist attacks of 11 September 2001 caused their trust in government leaders to decrease, while just over one in ten said it increased their trust in national leaders. The attributes of leadership that most affect trust levels are honesty, followed by vision, followed by experience and intellect. Compassion is the least important of the attributes tested. Most citizens distrust leaders because they do not *do* what they say (4 out of 10), are self-interested (3 out of 10), and are secretive or arrogant (1 in 10). Interestingly, character flaws are the least important of the five factors tested. In response to the survey's identification of a crisis of trust in leaders, Doug Miller states that 'leaders of NGOs, the UN, and religious groups (as well as others enjoying high public trust) will need to be included as part of any solution.'[7]

The lack of trust in society could, then, be a feature of the *enhancement of morality* as a characteristic of postmodernity, rather than proof of a rise in self-interested values. Making this point, Bauman (1993) argues that postmodernity coincides with a *strengthening* of morality and that past obsessions with rationality and utility are now being challenged. This allows morality to become a stronger issue and to work towards benefiting mutual security and individual well-being. Such a shift is inferred by the fact that, globally, people are engaging in more political protests and becoming increasingly *intolerant* of leaders who cannot be trusted to act morally and follow through what they promise to do. For instance, from the mid-1980s to the present, political action has risen in the United Kingdom at the very same time that voting in elections has declined. The signing of petitions, contacting Members of Parliament, and protest movements have steadily increased over the decades.

The new style of political protest in the form of anti-globalisation demonstrations that began in the 1990s brings together a variety of groups of campaigners from across the world under one banner, with anti-capitalist marches and environmentalist protests against corporations such as McDonalds, Shell and Esso; against representatives of global capital such as the World Trade Organisation, the International Monetary Fund and the Organisation for Economic Cooperation; as well as against governments and big business for the damage being inflicted on the planet by global warming. Among issues being protested against on a local and global scale are, for example, child labour in the Third World, the destruction of the world's rainforests, GM crops, animal cruelty, global warming, and the elimination of local cultures by multinational corporations, global brands, Third World debt and defence spending.

Anti-capitalist demonstrations have accelerated, taking place at major world conferences and summits. Tens of thousands of protestors from almost 1200 non-governmental organisations in 87 countries called for the wholesale reform of the World Trade Organisation on 30 November 1999 in Seattle. On May Day in 2000, several thousand protestors descended on Whitehall and on April 24, 2001, activists disrupted the Summit of the Americans in Quebec City, Canada. Police used tear gas, water cannons and rubber bullets against the demonstrators. Although May Day now represents a day of world protest, these demonstrations have often taken the establishment by surprise in many countries since they are mainly organised on the Internet by activists working under the radar of the mainstream news media. Some of the largest peace marches ever known have been generated in response to the bombing of cities and invasion of Iraq in February 2003. The global peace movement, known as the Stop the War Coalition displayed mass direct action in a series of coordinated demonstrations involving 400 cities in 60 countries across five continents with peace rallies, vigils and marches. Importantly, then, the decline in associations devoted to public interest issues such as political party membership and affiliation to religious groups has been accompanied by a rise in communities of dissent: membership of environmental and protest movements. A shift from traditional to new modes of political participation, including identity politics, is identifiable from voting to political agitation and direct action.

These forms of political protest confirm that people are coming together in new and important collectivities. The communitarian view that individualism threatens community by eroding civic pride, voluntarism and social capital is questioned by social movement research. For example, Paul Lichterman (1996) argues that a sense of public responsibility and collective commitment is linked to expressivist individualism, a cultural trend whose foundations lie in the counter-cultural movements of the 1960s and 1970s. Radical democratic politics empowers individuals and offers them a stronger sense of identity by providing them with the opportunity to unite through communal activism. Alberto Melucci (1996) highlights the declining importance of older social movements such as trade unionism and the rise of new movements characterised by collective identities such as identity politics. He argues that individuals affirm their identities and relate to one another through collective expression. New social connections are being created, then, through social action thereby questioning the communitarian claim that lack of trust coincides with breakdown of social ties and social morality.

Trust as a form of social regulation

There is strong evidence to suggest that a key feature of late modernity is the explosion of discourses and programmes that have an overtly ethical appeal and build ethical political variables (Walters, 2002: 391). Communitarianism, social cohesion, stakeholding and the Third Way are among these ethical political concepts and movements given a special priority. Social capital comes under this umbrella. It combines the language of community and trust, with the quantitative force of modern economic analysis. Social capital has the appeal of words like 'community', 'civility' and 'civil society' and the cachet of academic precision. What is being measured in the case of ethopolitics 'appears to be *natural* property' according to Walters. He exemplifies this by quoting from Putnam, Leonardi and Nanetti (1993b: 177): 'Trust itself is an emergent property of the social system, as much as a personal attribute.'

Social capital represents a new way of conceiving social processes that can be exploited by governmental projects. The metaphor of capital deployed in Putnam's analysis defines processes of cooperation and network building as capital accumulation. This discourse is, then, an attempt to convince us that society is self-governing and that it possesses its own dynamics (Walters, 2002: 391). We are persuaded to *invest* in community through a discourse of social capital that attempts to reconfigure the relationship between the social and the economic in the administration of national economies. Civility, association, cooperation and other social values and practices are reaffirmed not for their intrinsic merit but because social capital boosts the benefits of 'investment in physical and human capital' (Putnam, 1993a). Social capital places *economic performance* at the forefront of today's social mission, rather than wealth distribution, social need and social justice. As Walters maintains, it encourages us to regard cooperation, trust and community as mechanisms for improving the performance and competitiveness of societies. Public or social 'investment' replaces public 'spending' in communities instilled with an economic rationality, thereby guaranteeing a community absent of crime and political alienation.

Importantly, then, social capital discourse has regulatory effects. Social capital divides and classifies groups of people according to its own internal norms which appear to be natural expressions of the populace. Social capital can be associated with the binary distinctions between social exclusion and social cohesion, social and anti-social, sane and insane. Related to these distinctions, social capital is about the civic and the uncivil (Walters, 2002: 391). Middle-class norms of trust and civility saturate the social capital debate. Accordingly, a lack of civic attitudes among residents in ghettos and other areas of social deprivation can be cited as the cause of poverty. Social capital has a benevolent image of neighbourly relations. It is the site of power relations which symbolise a consensual political imagination and allow governments to look as if they are attending to social injustice while avoiding the awkward issue of economic exploitation (Walters, 2002: 392–4). This trend is part of the privatisation of social problems and the demotion of the citizen to a consumer in Western societies today. Inequality and injustice, which underlie social fragmentation, are justified by seemingly neutral market forces. Thus, friendship, trust and sociality seem to have been wholly coopted as features of self-absorbed individualisation and 'ethical government'.

Friendship, hospitality and social justice

While friendship has been absorbed as a crucial aspect of the reflexive project of the self, for Derrida the idea is to push friendship in another direction. He uses the ideal not to prop up the unstable self-identity of today's confused individual, but to transcend this idea by searching for a metaphor that promises a wider global peace and understanding. Friendship's attributes of intersecting the private and public domains, the personal and political, gives it the potential to provide insights for an understanding of democracy and citizenship, beyond the superficial treatment of 'trust' under the umbrella of 'social capital', and beyond the personalisation of ethical issues. Following Plato and Aristotle, Derrida privileges friendship as an organising concept in the definition of political experience. In *Politics of Friendship* (1997a), he addresses morality as part of his exploration of democracy by drawing on friendship as a metaphor for the practice of justice. He deals more with lateral relations of fraternity and friendship rather than hierarchical ones of authority and servility.

For Derrida, friendship is a relation that necessitates sacrifice. He treats this association as an ideal which should not be used as an instrument of personal desire to intimidate the other. Instead, it must be non-utilitarian and invoke freedom. Noble friendship demands generosity to enemies as well as friends. When linked with politics, friendship is about integrity, a virtue developed through respect for the other. This approach relates to Bauman's (1993) notion of a postmodern sensibility that, in its positive form, promotes responsibility for the Other in the form of tolerance and solidarity. Derrida undermines the distinction between the public and private, between the personal (the pre-political) and the political. He searches for a politics of friendship as a politics of separation, based on equality and fraternity and ethical and political responsibility.

Derrida proceeds by examining the association between an ethics of hospitality and a politics of hospitality in Levina's (1969) writings. He asks whether the ethics of hospitality, in the classical sense, can enter the spheres of politics and law, but admits that there is no plausible answer as to how this can be achieved. As Elizabeth Grosz (1997) suggests, it is not Derrida's intention to provide political solutions but, rather, to make his readers feel uncomfortable. He argues that the relation between ethics and politics involves a link between a non-traditional conception of friendship (which prioritises the other) and a 'democracy to come'. Derrida asks whether it is possible to think of a 'democracy to come' that does not prescribe fraternity as family, and ethnocentrism. 'Democracy to come' is complex because it has a contradictory structure: it is not simply a future as a modality of a present, but a promise of something in the future yet which happens now.

While democracy means equality, the demand for equality must be reconciled with the demand for singularity, 'with respect for the Other as singular' (Derrida, 1997b: 4). Experiences of togetherness are always at a stage of incompleteness. Derrida defends a new internationalism in relation to a new articulation of the emancipatory promise of modernity: beyond the interests of the nation state and beyond territorial restrictions (Derrida 1997b: 202). Simon Critchley (1998: 275) argues that Derrida's idea of democracy is not a fixed political form of society but a process. It is a process of deterritorialised democratisation.[8] Examples of such processes would be Greenpeace, Amnesty International and *medecins sans frontiers*, since they are organisations of people that work in ways that transcend state territories and make continuous demands on states for emancipation (of humans and of flora and fauna) as a way of continually improving existing democracy (Critchley, 1998: 276).

By drawing on Derrida's deconstructive approach, then, we can use friendship as a metaphor in the quest for a new ethical politics as a response to the moral challenges posed by the postmodern desire for a recovery of the moral dimension of personal life. He uses the theme of unconditional *hospitality* to address the concept of democracy and ethics of friendship. The modern-day problem in Europe, surrounding immigration is 'to what extent we should welcome the Other'. Derrida answers, in a transcribed talk:

> I have to – and that's an unconditional injunction – I have to welcome the Other whoever he or she is unconditionally, without asking for a document, a name, a context, or a passport. That is the very first opening of my relation to the Other: to open my space, my home – my house, my language, my culture, my nation, my state and myself. But of course this unconditionality is a frightening thing, it's scary.
>
> (Derrida, 1997b: 7)

He goes on to say that we therefore organise this unconditionality through laws, rights, conventions, borders, including laws on immigration. Hospitality is about a new relationship to citizenship because it makes us rethink the meaning of this kind of belonging. In Kant the concept of cosmopolitanism contains the conditions for hospitality such as welcoming the stranger. The tradition of cosmopolitanism relates back to the Greek idea of the 'citizen of the world'. However, Derrida argues that the concept of cosmopolitanism is limited because it only refers to the political: the state, authority of the state, citizenship. Addressing the necessity to break down capitalism, Derrida (1997b: 12) states, in response to a question on hospitality:

> the Other is already inside, and has to be sheltered and welcomed in a certain way. We have to negotiate also, that's a complicated unconscious operation, to negotiate the hospitality within ourselves. To this one, in ourselves, to this image that might exclude this other one or be allergic to this other one. We know that someone who doesn't negotiate this hospitality in him or herself in a certain way cannot be hospitable to the Other, that's what the Greeks taught us. That you have to solve the problem within yourself, and it's already a society, a multiplicity of heterogeneous singularities, to be really smiling to the Other. If you are at war with yourself you may be allergic to the Other, that's what complicates the issue.

In summary, Derrida's approach to friendship allows us to approach it as a conceptual device for challenging the separation between the *personal* and the *social*. Friendship offers us clues about processes of recovering the social through the mutual appreciation of differences between self and other. By opposing the centrality of the self and subjectivity, and by refusing to define sociality as exclusively individualism or collectivity, we are offered an idea of friendship that moves beyond the dualism of communitarian political theory to conceive of sociality as the expression of difference and the need to share with and welcome the stranger (Corlett, 1989).

However, while traditional notions of male friendship provide an entrance into the study of justice, Derrida does not expose the mechanisms that repress and eroticise femininity and thereby provide the potential for privileging homosocial bonding. Mariana Valverde (1999) argues that Derrida elevates homosocial masculine practices of friendship and ethics by drawing on an assemblage of texts that marginalise feminine and feminist ideas and practices. Writers such as Elizabeth Grosz (1989) and Eve Sedgewick (1985) explain that the marginalisation of the feminine privileges masculine relationships and shapes the public sphere. This privileging involves, first, the treatment of women as objects of exchange in familial bonds, in political obligations through the sexual contract (Pateman, 1988) and in expert knowledges such as the pathologisation of women's bodies; and second, the treatment of women as objects of desire (Valverde, 1999: 309). We find that it is only when friendship shifts towards a privatised relationship that a context is created in which the feminine is centralised. Women are viewed as the group that performs friendship best as *nurturers*.

A postmodern feminist ethics of care

While Derrida offers the potential of identifying responsibility and care as political issues by linking friendship with hospitality, the philosophical level of discussion provides no concrete examples. And by privileging the public sphere in debates about justice and rights, the gendered power dynamics that shape the meanings and practices of caring go unchallenged. Thus, the kinds of power struggles that go on daily among citizens and government bodies both in bringing up and caring for children and caring for elderly, sick or disabled relatives are not addressed or linked to the wider political and global context. In this section I address ethics of care which have important implications for an understanding of the social and personal problems thrown up by the fluid, elective relationships of postmodernity.

The exposure of inequalities in traditional forms of familial-centred care and the growth of new experimental lifestyles that appeal to more friendship-style, non-hierarchical relationships poses challenges in the need for a new moral framework based on trust, commitment and caring.[9] Governments are concerned that the rise in the number of lone parents, changing patterns of marriage and greater mobility among family members are leading to new kinds of relationships that do not entail informal caring when a person becomes sick or disabled.[10] New social ties have, then, triggered a profound crisis of care. Governments need, however, to address the gendered nature of caring. To take the United Kingdom as an example of broad trends across Western societies, the first national strategy for carers produced in 1999 by the British Department of Health (1999) in recognition that 'caring forms a vital part of the fabric and character of Britain' showed that carers of the elderly and disabled are saving society £57 billion (Department of Health, 1999: 5). The document acknowledges that one in eight people are carers of adults and women are more likely to be carers than men.[11]

With respect to childcare, demand for day care and childminding options for parents with children have risen rapidly in the last decade in Western nations such as the United Kingdom, resulting from changes in the labour market, including more women in the workplace who have dependent children.[12] Despite a substantial increase in the percentage of women in employment and a drop in the percentage of men in employment, women continue to spend longer than men on household tasks.[13] Time use surveys show that women across all types of living arrangements, including those in which women are full-time workers, devote more time to caring for their children than men. Even where two people are sharing the responsibility of childcare, women are more likely to carry the main responsibility for domestic tasks and childcare.[14] Moreover, there has been a doubling in the percentage of households headed by a lone parent since the early 1970s with 90 per cent of lone parents being women.[15]

However, women are not necessarily morally better or more caring than men. Rather, patterns of domination structure caring practices. Caring is a private practice traditionally based on *intimate relationships*, undertaken in the private sphere out of a sense of *duty* arising from a relationship of kinship, but it is also a public market of poorly paid jobs. The fact that the caring and cleaning professions are among the lowest paid jobs in society is justified by the essentialising logic of a subordinated feminised set of caring, nurturing values. The modern women's movement of the twentieth century aimed to liberate women from the inevitable burden of responsibility associated with women's caring work. However, today feminists recognise care as a crucial aspect of life that should not necessarily be incompatible with independence and self-realisation.

In her work on feminist ethics of care, Carol Gilligan's (1982, 1987) explored differences between two key moral orientations: justice and rights, and care and personal relationships. She identified a 'care–justice' dichotomy on the basis of interviews with women about moral development. Gilligan (1982) found that women conceptualised ethics differently from men. Men tended to express moral problems in terms of a conflict of abstract rights and rules, while women tended to view moral dilemmas as conflicts of responsibilities in particular contexts. The ethics of care is therefore a set of practices and considerations rather than a way of producing and applying rules and principles to unambiguous moral dilemmas. However, Gillian has been fiercely criticised for essentialising women, and reinforcing their traditional social role. Her work was based on interviews with white, middle-class, heterosexual women and failed to address differences between women involving factors of sexual orientation, race, class, religion, ethnicity, age and ableness. Later empirical research indicates that types of moral reasoning are not so clearly divided between men and women, that there are considerable overlaps and similarities between their moral approaches (Sevenhuijsen, 1998).

Moreover, research on the relationship between First and Third World women shows how important it is not to essentialise women. It uncovers the processes by which women in wealthy countries follow careers by asking elderly parents or paying women from the developing world to care for their children. Millions of poor women are forced to leave their own children and families in regions such as Thailand and the Dominican Republic and migrate to wealthy regions such the United States and Western Europe to serve as nannies, maids or sex workers. This global transfer of the services associated with the traditional role of 'wife' from poor countries to rich ones demonstrates a 'care deficit' resulting from the pressures placed on women and their families by the intersections of patriarchy and global capitalism (see, for example, Ehrenreich and Hochschild, 2003). Importantly, the recent stress on a caring fatherhood, which has prompted governments to offer paternity leave to employed men in nations such as the United Kingdom, forms a central part of public debates about child custody and post-divorce parenting (Lupton and Barclay, 1997; Smart and Neale, 1999).

Thus, Selma Sevenhuijsen (1998: 52) calls for a postmodern feminist ethics of care. Ethnocentrism and the Western ideal of autonomous individuals is a standard of moral agency and moral identity that needs to be confronted. This standard devalues the moral considerations that people (whether male or female, black or white) derive from their responsibility for others. The atomistic individual, as a moral subject, is expected to practise self-sufficiency and independence: 'In this way vulnerability and dependency easily become separated from the ideal self and localised in, or projected onto others: weak or 'needy' people' (Sevenhuijsen, 1998: 52). A feminist ethics of care places vulnerability, ambiguity and dependency within rather than outside the moral subject. Sevenhuijsen argues for the recognition of multiculturalism in a feminist ethics of care, of 'self' and 'other', placing the feminist ethics of care in the framework of a postmodern moral and political philosophy and connecting it with psychodynamic ideas of moral subjectivity. The relational idea of human nature does not involve a radical separation of self and other in a feminist ethics of care. Instead, moral subjectivity, care and responsibility are viewed as interactive, applied not just to 'others' but also to moral subjects themselves.

The erosion of the ideal complete and fixed self of the rationalist tradition and the rise of the postmodern self allows a recognition of a multiple, ambiguous moral subject who is vulnerable and prepared to accept responsibility according to Sevenhuijsen. Altruism and egoism are no longer set in opposing registers. Thus, 'other' isn't separated from the self and projected on to 'Women' or 'Foreign Cultures' but is experienced within the self. The ethics of care rests on the recognition of responsibilities by gaining knowledge of the situation through communication, interpretation and dialogue. Instead of pursuing autonomy and independence, the feminist ethics of care emphasises connection and dependence as intrinsic to human life and moral subjectivity. Sharing with Derrida a search for the moral subject, Sevenhuijsen (1998: 67) calls for a 'caring solidarity', arguing that the ethics of care needs to occupy a more important place in public morality. In doing so, it can be conceived as a form of political ethics though communal interaction and collective deliberation rather than private charity. Moving away from conceptualising citizenship in terms of a liberal rights model, she calls for situated rights, and a politics of needs-interpretation and caring solidarity.

Responsibility for the Other

One of the most important questions posed by the postmodern condition, then, is whether new social ties legitimate self-centredness and indifference or are capable of recognising and extending hospitality to the Other. Under postmodernity, as Bauman (1995: 2) reminds us, responsibility for the Other is saturated with uncertainty because it offers no guidelines on how to manage this relationship. Defined by the collapse of the kind of consensus and established reason that characterised the modern project, postmodernity offers no comfortable solutions. Postmodernist social theory has apparently recuperated the autonomy of the Self, emphasised through choice and freedom in new social ties, but at the same time has uncovered profound anxieties about morality, commitment, trust, responsibility and caring. How we should connect personal independency and intimacy with the public domain of politics and citizenship in the search for a social equality across social and personal relationships is the question facing us. The appeal of friendship and the aspiration for new relationships based on equality and mutual respect signifies the desire for a better future with a new kind of belonging. It also signifies the critical need for a new ethical understanding in order to recover the self as a social subject on which to build a new solidarity of care and responsibility.

Notes

Introduction

1   Henley Centre and Salvation Army, *The Responsibility Gap: Individualism, Community and Responsibility in Britain Today* (Henley Centre/Salvation Army, 2004) available at: http://www.salvationarmy.org.uk/en/responsibilitygap/home.htm.

2   See, for example, S. Heath and E. Cleaver, *Young, Free and Single? Twenty-Somethings and Household Change* (London, Palgrave, 2003); J. Chandler, M. Williams, M., Maconachie, T. Collett, and B. Dodgeon, 'Living alone: Its place in household formation and change', *Sociological Research Online*, 9:3 (2004), available at: http://www.socresonline,.org.uk/9/3/chandler.html. Longitudinal data from UK Censuses between 1971 and 2001, for example, corroborates other research indicating that increasing numbers of non-retired people are living alone, with single-occupancy households rising by 31 per cent (Office for National Statistics, 2003). This trend of living alone is a characteristic across Europe (J. C. Kaufmann, 'One person households in Europe', *Population*, 49:4/5 (1994), pp. 935–58).

3   Single person households rose from 9 per cent in 1973 to 16 per cent in 2001 (*National Statistics*, 2003: households).

4   This concept was developed and explored by Benedict Anderson (1991).

1   Changing ideas about social ties

1   The Enlightenment was a rationalist, liberal, humanitarian and scientific trend of thought of the eighteenth century, preceded by the scientific revolution of the seventeenth century. It found expression in the writings of men such as Diderot, Voltaire, Montesquieu, J. J. Rousseau, Hume and Kant.

2   See, for example, D. Chambers, *Representing the Family* (London: Sage, 2001); D. Lupton and L. Barclay, *Constructing Fatherhood:* Discourse and Experiences, (London: Sage, 1997).

3   The book was first written in 1835, with a second volume in 1840.

4   See Mills, the 'sociological imagination', 1959.

5   See H. J. Gans, *The Urban Villagers: Group and Class in the Life of Italian-Americans* (New York: Free Press of Glencoe,1962); E. Liebow, *Tally's Corner: A Study of Negro StreetcOorner Men* (Boston, MA, Little Brown, 1967); William F. Whyte, 1943.

6   See Gans, *The Urban Villagers*; William H. Whyte, *The Organization Man* (New York: Simon and Schuster, 1956).

2   Freedom and choice in personal relationships

1   Steven Fletcher and Mhairi McFarlane, 'Speed Dating: Two Post Reporters Went along to the first speed dating event in Nottingham', *Nottingham Evening Post*, 14 February 2002, p. 12–13.
2   Ibid.
3   Featured on *Richard and Judy*, Channel 4 (UK), 11 March 2004.
4   Featured on *Woman's Hour*, BBC Radio 4, 12 March 2004.

3   Hegemonic masculine identities and male bonds

1   D. Hammond and A. Jablow, 'Gilgamesh and the Sundance Kid: The myth of male friendship', in H. Brod (ed.), *The Making of Masculinities: The New Men's Studies* (Boston: Allen & Unwin, 1987), pp. 241–58; P. M. Nardi, ' "Seamless Souls": An introduction to men's friendships', in P. Nardi (ed.), *Men's Friendships* (London: Sage, 1992).
2   Reform Bill, in British history, is a name given to measures liberalising representation in the House of Commons. The Reform Bill of 1832, passed by Earl Grey's Whig ministry, redistributed seats in the interest of larger communities, by extending franchise to middle-class men.
3   Andrew Bonar Law is a British Conservative statesman who became Chancellor of the Exchequer in 1916 under Lloyd George. He led a revolt from the wartime coalition government in 1922 and became Prime Minister, but soon resigned due to ill-health.
4   Examples include television shows such as *Men Behaving Badly* (BBC) and men's magazines such as *Nuts*.
5   We held 16 focus group interviews in four schools with just under 100 pupils in total. The schools included a private all-boys school, two mixed comprehensive schools in inner-city Nottingham and a private all-girls' school in Kent.
6   Will Stott, 'Too Drunk to Feck', *Loaded*, December 2000, p. 61–6.

4   Feminine identities and female bonds

1   The term 'social capital' is critically examined in Chapter 6.
2   See, for example, The General Household Survey (2000/1) in the United Kingdom: National Statistics, *Living in Britain: Results from the 2000/01 General Household Survey* (London: HMSO, 2001).
3   *Working Parents' Health Report*, BUPA 2002. Aavailable at: https://www.bupa.co.uk/intercom/pdfs/news/54715%20-%20Working%20parents.pdf (accessed 17/12/05).
4   The General Household Survey (2000/1).
5   The study was funded by five UK government departments, and a recruitment consultancy: by the Cabinet Office, the Department for Work and Pensions, the Ministry of Defence, the Home Office and the Department of Health, and also by the recruitment agency, Norman Broadbent.

6 EOC Press release: 'Women Heading for Pay Disappointment', available at http://www.eoc.org.uk/cseng/news/timetogeteven.asp. In the United Kingdom, a survey for the Equal Opportunities Commission in 2004 found that although the overwhelming majority of women expect to earn the same as a man with the same qualifications, the difference in average pay between men and women working full time is £559 per month.

7 Ibid.

8 See http://www.eoc.org.uk/cseng/news/5_jan_sexandpower.asp.

9 Ibid.

10 Recent evidence comes from a report from the Science and Technology Committee, UK, in 2002, which focuses on learned societies including the Royal Society and Royal Academy of Engineering (T. Tysome, 'Women set up old-girl network' *Times Higher Supplement*, 14 February 2003). See the East Midlands Local Academic Women's Network (EMLAWN), website is available at: www.lboro.ac.uk/admin/personnel/athena_web/index.htm.

11 EMLAWN ibid.

12 See 'Binge Drinking: Nature, Prevalence and Causes', IAS fact Sheet, Institute of Alcohol Studies, October 2005. Available at: http://www.ias.org.uk/factsheets/binge-drinking.pdf (accessed 18/12/2005).

13 *Girls Gone Wild* is a collection of DVDs and videos made by Mantra Films, a Southern Californian company famous for filming women flashing their breasts.

14 'Raunch culture' is a term publicised by New York journalist and author, Ariel Levy (2005). Her book, *Female Chauvinist Pigs* documents, in indignant tones, the exploits of American college girls who have breast implants, flash themselves at men, engage in poll dancing, have casual sex and model themselves on celebrity figure, Paris Hilton: A. Levy, *Female Chauvinist Pigs: Women and the Rise of Raunch Culture* (New York: Simon & Schuster, 2005).

15 'Fat slags' and 'Tasha slappa' are characters in the bawdy, satirical comic magazine called *Viz* which is aimed at a male readership and which originated in and satirised England's Northern working-class culture.

16 Alcohol Harm Reduction Strategy for England, Prime Minister's Strategy Unit, Cabinet Office, March 2004. Available at: www.strategy.gov.uk/work_areas/alcohol_misuse/index.asp (accessed 18/12/2005).

17 Ibid., p. 7.

18 Simon Lennon and David Brown, *The People*, 21 March, 2004, pp. 28–9.

19 Christen Pears, 'Why Girls Drink Themselves Stupid', *The Northern Echo*, 12 January 2004. p. 10.

20 Tasha Kosviner, 'My night of booze and pub brawls', *The Evening Standard*, 15 March, 2004, p. 9.

21 See E. Tincknell and D. Chambers (2002) 'Performing the crisis: Fathering, gender and representation in two 1990s films', *Journal of Popular Film and Television*, 29:4 (Winter 2002), 146–55.

22 Longitudinal data from UK Censuses between 1971 and 2001, for example, corroborates other research indicating that increasing numbers of non-retired people are living alone, with single occupancy households rising by 31 per cent (Office for National Statistics, *Social Trends*, 33 (2003). Available at: www.statistics.gov.uk/socialtrends (accessed 20/02/2005). This trend of

living alone is a characteristic across Europe (J. C. Kaufmann, 'One person households in Europe', *Population*, 49:4/5 (1994), pp. 935–58).

23 See, for example, 'Action urged as under-performing boys eclipsed by girls in GCSEs', *The Guardian*, 26 August 2004.

24 Aspects of this section have been published in D. Chambers, D., 'Comedies of sexual morality and female singlehood,' in M. Pickering and S. Lockyer (eds), *Beyond a Joke: The Ethics of Humour*, (Basingstoke: Palgrave/Macmillan, 2005).

25 See A. Oram, 'Repressed and thwarted, or bearer of the New World? The spinster in inter-war feminist discourses, *Women's History Review*, 1:3 (1992), 413–33.

26 *Sex and the City* (HBO) was aired from June 1998 to February 2004 on US and British television networks.

27 Episode 16.

28 Quoted in K. Akass and J. McCabe (2004) 'Introduction: Welcome to the age of un-innocence', in *Reading Sex and the City* (London: I. B. Tauris, 2004), pp. 8–9.

5 The decline and rise of 'community'

1 See for example, the UK government document, *Bringing Britain Together: An National Strategy for Neighbourhood Renewal* (Social Exclusion Unit, 1998); and the Henley Centre/Salvation Army charity report, *The Responsibility Gap: Individualism, Community and Responsibility in Britain Today* (Henley Centre/ Salvation Army, 2004) available at: http://www.salvationarmy.org.uk/ en/responsibilitygap/home.htm (accessed 13/05/04).

2 This is demonstrated in the United Kingdom by a string of examples, such as the discussion paper, 'Social Capital', produced for the British government's Cabinet Office by the Performance and Innovation Unit in 2002 (see S. Aldridge and D. Halpern with S. Fitzpatrick, *Social Capital: A Discussion Paper*, (London: Performance and Innovation Unit, Cabinet Office, 2002); and the Health Education Authority report, *Social Capital and Health* (C. Campbell, with R. Wood and M. Kelly, *Social Capital and Health* (London: Health Education Authority, 1999). Examples of cross-national studies of social capital include an OECD (2001) report, *The Well-Being of Nations: The Role of Human and Social Capital, Education and Skills* (Paris, OECD, 2001). In the United Kingdom, the periodical, *Social Trends, 33* (2003), which analyses government data including census statistics, has confirmed that increased academic and official interest in social capital and its policy implications have resulted in more surveys being commissioned and a greater range of data becoming available.

3 http://pages.ebay.com/sell/givingworks/giving_statistics.html.

4 *Social Trends*, 33 (2003), 19.

5 National Council for Voluntary Organisations, *The Voluntary Agencies Directory* (London: National Council for Voluntary Organisations, 1996), quoted in P. Hall, 'Social capital in Britain, *British Journal of Political Science*, 29 (1999), 417–61.

6 *Social Trends*, 33 (2003), Fig A3, p. 21.

7 National Statistics, *Living in Britain: Results from the 2000/01 General Household Survey* (London: HMSO, 2001), Table 13.5, p. 226.

8 Ibid., Table 13.5, p. 226.
9 *Social Trends*, 33 (2003), Fig A3, p. 22.
10 Ibid.
11 Ibid.
12 *Living in Britain: 2000/1General Household Survey.*
13 Longitudinal data from UK Censuses between 1971 and 2001, for example, corroborates research indicating that increasing numbers of non-retired people are living alone, with single-occupancy households rising by 31 per cent (Office for National Statistics, *National Statistics Omnibus Survey* (London: Office for National Statistics, 2001)). This trend of living alone is a characteristic across Europe (J. C. Kaufmann, 'One person households in Europe', *Population*, 49:4/5 (1994), pp. 935–58).
14 Ibid.
15 C. Attwood, G. Singh, D. Prime, R. Creasey et al. (2001) *Home Office Citizenship Survey: People, Families and Communities*, Home Office Research Study 270. Home Office Research, Development and Statistics Directorate. (London: HMSO, 2003); *Social Trends*, 33 (2003); Hall, 'Social capital in Britain', pp. 417–61.
16 Attwood et al. 2001; *Social Trends*, 33 (2003).
17 For information, see http://www.nationmaster.com/graph-T/dem_par_ele_re_vot_turn/EUR
18 *Social Trends*, 33 (2003): 19–20.
19 With same-sex relationships continuing to be defined in relation to heterosexual norms, the term 'non-heterosexual' is neutral at least in the sense of being inclusive of lesbian, gay, bisexual, transgender, queer and other dissenting sexual identities (J. Weeks, B. Heaphy and C. Donovan, *Same Sex Intimacies: Families of Choice and Other Life Experiments* (London: Routledge, 2001)).
20 'Gay Muslims', directed by Cara Lavan, executive producer Richard McKerrow, Channel 4, 23/01/06.
21 As Mary Bryson (2004: 251 fn) states, 'the QLBT acronym does not imply a naive assumption about any kind of a straightforward relationship between arbitrary markers of identification and universal aspects of being, ontology, or essence' (M. Bryson, 'When Jill jacks in: Queer women and the Net', *Feminist Media Studies*, 4:3 (2004), 251 fn). She emphasises that these signifiers are contested because they are deeply problematic in discursively mediating the visibility of groups. Depending on the social context, they have either negative effects of subordination or positive effects of liberation.
22 See Chapter 8 which addresses this topic further, in the context of Internet communities.

6 Network society

1 See E. Schwartz, *Netactivism: How Citizens Use the Internet* (Sebastopol, CA: Songline Studies, 1996); L. S. Sproull and S. B. Kiesler, *Connections: New Ways of Working in the Networked Organization* (Cambridge, MA: MIT Press, 1991); S. Tarrow, 'Fishnest, Internets and catnets: Globization and transnaional collective action', in M. Hanagan, L. Moch and W. TeBrake (eds), *The Past and Future of Collective Action* (Minneapolis: University of Minnesota Press, 1998), pp. 228–44.

2 D. Timms (2003) 'Iraq war game comes under fire', *The Guardian*, 15 August
   2003. Available at: http://www.mediaguardian.co.uk (accessed 08/05/04).
3 Available at: http://webdb.iue.it/FMPro?-db=RSidnet&-lay=web&-format=
   RSidnet/search.htm&-view
4 The survey was carried out in deprived areas of London, Birmingham, Leeds,
   Bradford, Cardiff and Glasgow.
5 Dahan and Sheffer refer to P. Werbner, 'The dialectics of cultural hybridity',
   in P. Werbner and T. Modood (eds), *Debating Cultural Hybridity* (London: Zed,
   1997), pp. 1–26, who addresses the dialectics of hybridity.
6 See, for example: http//:www.virtualnation.org.
7 See, for example: http://www.nativeweb.org/.
8 NGOs refers to non government organisations and IGOs to international
   government organisations.
9 Various Tibet sites include: http:www.tibet.org/ and http://freetibet.org.

7 Virtual intimacy and online sociality

1 Within early research a view was held that because exchanges in public were
   publicly accessible they could be reported on without declaring it to participants (F. Sudweeks and S. Rafaeli, 'How do you get a hundred strangers
   to agree: computer mediated communication and collaboration', in
   T. M. Harrison and T. D. Stephen (eds), *Computer Networking and Scholarship in
   the 21ˢᵗ Century* (New York: SUNY Press, 1996)). Ensuring the anonymity of
   the groups was seen to be sufficient to conform to ethical research standards.
   This view has been questioned by authors such as E. M. Reid, 'Virtual worlds,
   culture and imagination', in S. J. Jones (ed.), *Cybersociety : Computer-Mediated
   Communication and Community* (California: Sage, 1996a). Most work done so
   far does not even report whether permission was sought or not (N. Pleace,
   R. Burrows, B. Loader, S. Muncer & S. Nettelton, 'On-line with the friends
   of Bill W: Social support and the Net', *Sociological Research Online*, 5:2 (2000).
   Available at: http://www.socresonline.org.uk/5/2/pleace.html.
2 Oliver Owen 'Chat rooms and the exploitation of children by paedophiles:
   Our Worst Nightmare', *The Observer*, 18 March 2001, p. 17.
3 L. France, 'Love at first site: discos and singles bars are a distant memory for
   today's lonely hearts', *Observer Magazine*, 30 June 2002. Available at:
   http://observer.guardian.co.uk/magazine/story/0,11913,746525,00html.
4 Ibid. Also see J. Gavin, J., 'Chat-room relationships', paper presented at
   British Psychological Society conference, Bath University 2002; M. Whitty
   and J. Gavin, 'Age/sex/location: Uncovering the social cues in the development of online relationships', *Cyberpsychology and Behavior*, 4 (2001), 441–8.
5 Ibid.
6 Jeff Gavin, cited in 'Love online "can be stronger" ' *Telegraph on-line*, filed
   16/03/2002.
7 Ibid.
8 Aisha Kahn, 'How to Net a Husband', *The Guardian*, 19 May 2003, G2, pp. 8–9.
9 Ibid., p. 8.
10 Ibid., p. 9.
11 Ibid., p. 9.
12 Peter Martin, 'We'll mate again', *Sunday Times Magazine*, 27 April 2003, pp. 23–4.

13 Ibid., p. 24.
14 Ibid., p. 24.
15 Cited in Martin: 'We'll mate again', p. 25.
16 Cited in ibid.
17 As Mary Bryson states, 'the QLBT acronym does not imply a naive assumption about any kind of a straightforward relationship between arbitrary markers of identification and universal aspects of being, ontology, or essence.' She emphasises that these signifiers are contested because they are deeply problematic in discursively mediating the visibility of groups. Depending on the social context, they have either negative effects of subordination or positive effects of liberation. M. Bryson, 'When Jill jacks in: Queer women and the Net', *Feminist Media Studies*, 4:3 (2004), 251 fn.
18 Ibid.
19 National Opinion Poll Research group Internet Surveys (2001) 'Half of 7–16s Have a Mobile Phone'. Available at: http://www.nop.co.uk/news/news_survey_half_of_7–16s.shtml (accessed 29/01/2001).
20 Ibid.
21 NCH Action for Children published a report on 12 January 2004) warning of the dangers posed by mobile phones with Internet access. See John Carr, Child Abuse, Child Pornography and the Internet: Executive Summary (NCH, 2004). The summary is available at: http://www.nchafc.org.uk/downloads/children_internet_report_summ.pdf.
22 'Children to be shielded from abuse via mobile', by David Batty and Justin McCurry, *The Guardian*, 12 January 2004, p. 3.
23 'Have young people developed a new communication etiquette?', Roar (2003), available at: http://www.roar.org.uk/press40.htm.
24 Ibid.
25 For example, Michael North, 'My Summr Hols Wr Cwot. B4, We Usd 2 Go 2ny 2c My Bro, His Gf & Thr 3 :- @kds Ftf', *The Times Higher Education Supplement*, 19 September 2003, p. 22.
26 Ibid.
27 See 'Sexes in battle of the texts', *Sheffield Hallam University News*, 9/11/2005. Available at: http://www.shu.ac.uk/cgi-bin/news_full.pl?id_num=PR862&db=05.

8 The politics of social and personal relationships

1 For details of the World Values Survey see: http://www.worldvaluessurvey.com/.
2 The British Social Attitudes survey of 1989 compared questions asked in the 1959 Civic Culture Study (Almond, G. A., and S. Verba (eds), *The Civic Culture: Political Attitudes and Democracy in Five Nations* (Princeton, NJ: Princeton University Press, 1963); G. A. Almond and S. Verba (eds), *The Civic Culture: Political Attitudes And Democracy In Five Nations* (Newbury Park, CA: Sage, 1989).
3 In Britain, 56 per cent of adults agreed that 'most people can be trusted' in 1959, falling to 44 per cent in 1989 according to the British Social Attitudes Survey (R. Jowell, J. Curtice, A.Park, K. Thomson, L. Jarvis, C. Bromley and N. Stratford (eds)), *British Social Attitudes: Focusing on Diversity*, 17th Report, (London: Sage, 2001).

4 The proportion of people who agreed that they trusted British governments 'just about always' or 'most of the time' fell from 39 per cent in 1974 to 16 per cent in 2000; the down turn in trust has been accompanied by a small rise in the 1990s (Jowell et al., 2001).

5 The poll was conducted by Environics International for the World Economic Forum, an independent organization committed to improving the state of the world, which was awarded NGO consultative status with the Economic and Social Council of the United Nations in 1995. See World Economic Forum, 'Declining public trust foremost a leadership problem', 14 January 2003, available at: http://www.weforum.org/pdf/AM_2003/Trust-in-Leaders.pdf (accessed 1/7/03).

6 Participating research institutes included those from Argentina, Canada, China, Germany, Great Britain, India, Italy, Mexico, Netherlands, Nigeria, Russia, Qatar, South Korea, Turkey, United States (ibid.).

7 Ibid.

8 Here, Critchley (S. Critchley, S., 'The other's decision in me (What are the politics of friendship?)', *European Journal of Social Theory*, 1:2 (1998), 259–79) draws on William Connolly's (1992) concept of nonterritorial democratisation (W. Connolly, *Identity/Difference* (Ithaca, NY: Cornell University Press, 1992)).

9 See, for example, the important set of research projects currently being conducted by the ESRC Research Group on Care, Values and the Future of Welfare, University of Leeds, available at: http://www.leeds.ac.uk/CAVA/research.

10 For example, in the British context, see the Department of Health (1999: 20).

11 Fifty-eight per cent of carers are women, and 42 per cent of carers are men. (Department of Heath, 1999:17).

12 'Informal Childcare Arrangements for children Whose Mothers Are in Employment', Labour Force Survey, Autumn 2002, *Social Trends*, 34. Available at: http://www.statistics.gov.uk/STATBASE/ (accessed 26/02/ 2006). The Labour Force Survey (2002) found that over a third of children under 15 whose mothers were in employment had been looked after by a grandparent at some point in the previous week. The sex of the grandparent is not mentioned, but it is likely that grandmothers are more involved in this task than grandfathers.

13 For example, in 2000–1 women living in a couple who worked full time spent on average almost four and a half hours on childcare and other activities with their children every weekday. For men in the same circumstances the comparable figure was an hour less ('Work and Family', Labour Force Survey, Spring 2003, Office for National Statistics published 8 January 2004, source: Census 2001, available at: http://www.statistics.gov.uk/cci (accessed 26/02/2006)).

14 See, for example, UK Time Use Survey 2000, Office for National Statistics. Available at: http://ww.statistics.gov.uk/cci (accessed 26/02/2006). On average, women spend 2 hours 30 minutes a day on domestic chores, that is, 1 hour 30 minutes more than men.

15 'Living arrangements', National Statistics published 8 January 2004, source: Census 2001, available at: http://www.statistics.gov.uk/cci (accessed 26/ 02/2006).

Bibliography

Adams, P. C., and R. Ghose, 'India.com: The construction of a space between', *Progress in Human Geography*, 27:4 (2003), 414–37.

Adams, R. G., 'The demise of territorial determinism', in R. G. Adams and G. Allan (eds), *Placing Friendship in Context* (Cambridge: Cambridge University Press, 1998), pp. 153–82.

Adams, R., and G. Allan (eds), *Placing Friendships in Context* (Cambridge: Cambridge University Press, 1998).

Adams, R., and R. Blieszner, 'An integrative conceptual framework for friendship research', *Journal of Social and Personal Relationships*, 11 (1994), 163–84.

Adkins, L., *Gendered Work: Sexuality, Family and the Labour Market* (Buckingham: Open University Press. 1995).

Afshar, H., 'Marriage and family in a British Pakistani community', in S. Jackson and S. Scott (eds), *Gender: A Sociological Reader* (London: Routledge, 2002), pp. 238–47.

Aitchison, C., *Gender and Leisure: A Social-Cultural Nexus* (London: Routledge, 2003).

Akass, K. and McCabe, J. (2004) 'Ms Parker and the Vicious Circle: Female narrative and humour in *Sex and the City*', in K. Akass and J. McCabe, *Reading Sex and the City* (London: I. B. Tauris, 2004), pp. 177–98.

Aldridge, S., and D. Halpern with S. Fitzpatrick, *Social Capital: A Discussion Paper* (London: Performance and Innovation Unit, Cabinet Office, 2002).

Allan, G., *A Sociology of Friendship and Kinship* (London: George, Allen & Unwin, 1979).

Allan, G., *Friendship: Developing a Sociological Perspective* (Hemel Hempstead: Harvester Wheatsheaf, 1989).

Allan, G., 'Class variation in friendship patterns', *British Journal of Sociology*, 41 (1990), 389–92.

Allan, G., *Kinship and Friendship in Modern Britain* (Oxford: Oxford University Press, 1996).

Almond, G. A., and S. Verba (eds), *The Civic Culture: Political Attitudes and Democracy in Five Nations* (Princeton, NJ: Princeton University Press, 1963).

Almond, G. A., and S. Verba (eds), *The Civic Culture: Political Attitudes And Democracy In Five Nations* (Newbury Park, CA: Sage, 1989).

Anderson, B., *Imagined Communities: Reflections on the Origin and Spread of Nationalism*, rev. edn (London and New York: Verso, 1991).

Anderson, M., *Family Structure in Nineteenth-Century Lancashire* (Cambridge: Cambridge University Press, 1971).

Andrew, A., and J. Montagie, 'Women's friendships at work', *Women's Studies International Forum*, 21:4 (1998), 355–61.

Angelo, M., *The Sikh Diaspora: Tradition And Change In An Immigrant Community* (New York and London: Garland, 1997).

Appadurai, A., *Modernity at Large: Cultural Dimensions of Globalisation* (Minneapolis: University of Minnesota Press, 1996).

Aristotle, *The Ethics of Aristotle: The Nichomachean Ethics*, trans. J. A. K. Thomson, Book 9 (Harmondsworth: Penguin, 1955), pp. 1169 a23–b11.

Aristotle, *Eudeminan Ethics*, with translation and commentary by Michael Woods (rev. Oxford translation, 1982), p. 1234b, 18ff.

Aronwitz, S., J. Cutler and S. Aronowitz (eds), *Post-Work: Wages of Cybernation* (London: Routledge, 1998).

Arthurs, J., '*Sex and the City* and consumer culture: Remediating postfeminist drama', *Feminist Media Studies*, 3:1 (2003), 83–98.

Asher, S. R., and J. M. Gottman (eds), *Development of Children's Friendships* (Cambridge:Cambridge University Press, 1981).

Attwood, C., G. Singh, D. Prime, R. Creasey et al. (2001) *Home Office Citizenship Survey: People, Families and Communities*, Home Office Research Study 270. Home Office Research, Development and Statistics Directorate (London: HMSO, 2003). Available at: http://www.renewal.net/Documents/Research/Homeofficecitizenship.pdf (accessed 10/04/2004).

Ballard, R. (ed.), *Desh Pardesh: The South Asian Presence in Britain* (London: Hurst, 1994).

Barker-Benfield, G. J., *The Culture of Sensibility* (Chicago: The University of Chicago Press, 1992).

Barrett, D. V., *Secret Societies: From the Ancient and Arcane to the Modern and Clandestine* (London: Cassell, 1997).

Barrett, M., and M. Macintosh, *The Anti-Social Family* (London: Verso, 1982).

Bauman, Z., *Legislators and Interpreters: On Modernity, Postmodernity and Intellectuals* (Oxford: Blackwell, 1987).

Bauman, Z., *Modernity and the Holocaust* (Cambridge: Polity Press, 1989).

Bauman, Z., 'Modernity and ambivalence', in M. Featherstone (ed.), *Global Culture: Nationalism, Globalisation and Modernity* (London: Sage, 1990), pp.143–70.

Bauman, Z., *Intimations of Postmodernity* (London: Routledge, 1992).

Bauman, Z., *Postmodern Ethics* (Oxford: Blackwell, 1993).

Bauman, Z., *Life in Fragments: Essays in Postmodern Morality* (Oxford: Blackwell, 1995).

Bauman, Z., 'Morality in the age of contingency', in P. Heelas, S. Lash and P. Morris (eds), *Detraditionalisation: Critical Reflections on Authority and Identity* (Oxford: Blackwell, 1996), pp. 49–58.

Bauman, Z., *Community: Seeking Safety in an Insecure World* (London: Polity, 2001).

Bauman, Z., *Liquid Love* (London: Polity 2004).

Baxter, S., and G. Raw, 'Fast food, fettered work: Chinese women in the ethnic catering industry', in S. Jackson and S. Scott (eds), *Gender: A Sociological Reader* (London: Routledge, 2002), pp. 165–9.

Baym, N. K., 'Interpreting soap operas and creating community: Inside an electronic fan culture', in S. Kiesler (ed.), *Cultures of the Internet* (Mahweh, NJ: Lawrence Erlbaum, 1997), pp.103–20.

Beck, U., *Risk Society: Towards a New Modernity* (London: Sage, 1992).

Beck, U., *The Invention of Politics* (Cambridge: Polity Press, 1997).

Beck, U., *Democracy Without Enemies* (Cambridge: Polity Press 1998).

Beck, U., and E. Beck-Gernsheim, *The Normal Chaos of Love* (Cambridge: Polity Press, 1995).

Beck, U., and E. Beck-Gernsheim, 'Individualisation and "precarious freedoms": Perspectives and controversies of a subject-oriented sociology', in P. Heelas,

S. Lash and P. Morris (eds), *Detraditionalisation: Critical Reflections on Authority and Identity* (Oxford: Blackwell, 1996), pp. 23–48.

Beck, U., and E. Beck-Gernsheim, *Individualisation* (London: Sage, 2002).

Beck-Gernsheim, E., *Reinventing the Family: In Search of New Lifestyles* (London: Polity, 2002).

Bell, C., 'Mobility and the middle-class extended family', *Sociology*, 2 (1968), 173–84.

Bell, R., *Worlds of Friendship* (Beverley Hills, CA: Sage, 1981).

Bellah, R., R. Madsen, W. M. Sullivan, A. Swidler and S. M. Tipton, *Habits of the Heart: Individualism and Commitment in American Life* (London: University of California Press, 1996).

Berger, P., and H. Kellner, 'Marriage and the construction of reality', Diogenes, reprinted in M. Anderson (ed.), *The Sociology of the Family* (Hamondsworth, Penguin, 1980), pp. 302–4.

Berger, P., and T. Luckmann, *The Social Construction of Reality* (London:Allen Lane, 1966).

Berger, P., B. Berger and H. Kellner, *The Homeless Mind: Modernisation and Consciousness* (Harmondsworth: Penguin, 1974).

Berking, H., *Sociology of Giving* (London: Sage, 1999).

Berlant, L., and M. Warner, 'Sex in public', in L. Berlant (ed.), *Intimacy* (Chicago: University of Chicago, 2000), pp. 311–30.

Beynon, J., *Masculinities and Culture* (Buckingham: Open University Press, 2002).

Bhabha, H. K., *The Location of Culture* (London: Routledge, 1994).

Bhachu, P., *Twice Migrants: East African Sikh Settlers in Britain* (London: Tavistock, 1985).

Biddulph, S., *Manhood: An Action Plan For Changing Men's Lives* (London: Finch, 1995).

Binnie, J., and B. Skeggs, 'Cosmopolitan knowledge and the production and consumption of sexualised space: Manchester's gay village', *Sociological Review* (2004), 39–61.

Bishop, A. P., B. Mhera, I. Bazzell and C. Smith 'Socially grounded user studies in digital library development', *First Monday*, 5:6 (2000). URL: http://firstmonday.org/issues/issue5_6/bishop/.

Blau, P., *Exchange Power in Social Life* (New York: John Wiley & Sons, 1964).

Blieszner, R., and R. G. Adams, *Adult Friendship* (Newbury Park: Sage, 1992).

Boggs, C., 'Social capital and political fantasy: Robert Putnam's Bowling Alone', *Theory and Society*, 30 (2001), 281–97.

Boswell, J., *Same Sex Unions in Pre-Modern Europe* (New York: Villard Books, 1994).

Bourdieu, P., 'The forms of capital', in J. G. Richardson (ed.), *Handbook of Theory and Research for the Sociology of Education* (New York: Greenwood Press, 1983a), pp. 241–58.

Bourdieu, P., *Sociology in Question* (London: Sage, 1983b).

Bowlby, R., *Shopping with Freud* (London: Routledge, 1993).

Brannen, J., and P. Moss, *Managing Mothers: Dual Earner Households after Maternity Leave* (London: Unwin Hyman, 1991).

Bridenthal, R., 'The family: The view from a room of her own', in B. Thorne and M. Yalom (eds), *Rethinking the Family: Some Feminist Questions* (London: Longman, 1982).

Brooks, D., *Bobos in Paradise: The New Upper Classes and How they Got There* (New York: Simon & Schuster, 2000).

Brown, S. E., 'Love unites them and hunger separates them: Poor women in the Dominican Republic', in R. Reiter (ed.), *Towards an Anthropology of Women* (New York: Monthly Review Press, 1975), pp. 322–32.

Bryson, M., 'When Jill jacks in: Queer women and the Net', *Feminist Media Studies*, 4:3 (2004), 239–54.

Budgeon, S., and S. Roseneil, 'Cultures of intimacy and care beyond "The Family": Friendship and sexual/love relationships in the twenty-first century', paper presented at *International Sociological Association World Congress of Sociology*, Brisbane July 2002. Available at: http://www.leeds.ac.uk/cava/papers/culturesofintimacy.htm.

Burgess, A., and S. Ruxton, *Men and their Children* (London: Institute for Public Policy Research, 1996).

Burgess, E. W., and H. J. Locke, *The Family: From Institution to Companionship* (New York: American Book Company, 1945).

Burghes, L., L. Clarke and N. Cronin, *Fathers and Fatherhood in Britain* (London: Family Policy Studies Centre, 1997).

Burns, A., and C. Scott, *Mother-Headed Families and Why They Have Increased* (Hilldale, NJ: Lawrence Erlbaum, 1994).

Burrows, R., and S. Nettleton, 'Reflexive modernisation and the emergence of wired self-help', in K. Renniger and W. Shumar (eds), *Building Virtual Comunities: Learning and Change in Cyberspace* (New York: Cambridge University Press, 2000).

Busfield, J., *Men, Women and Madness: Understanding Gender and Mental Disorder* (Basingstoke: Macmillan – now Palgrave, 1996).

Butler, J., *Gender Trouble: Feminism and the Subversion of Identity* (London: Routledge, 1990).

Cameron, D., and D. Kulick, *Language and Sexuality* (Cambridge: Cambridge University Press, 2003.)

Campbell, A., P. E. Converse and W. L. Rodgers, *The Quality of American Life* (New York: Russell Sage, 1976).

Campbell, C., with R. Wood and M. Kelly, *Social Capital and Health* (London: Health Education Authority, 1999).

Cancian, F., 'Gender politics: Love and power in the private and public spheres', in A. Rossie (ed.), *Gender and the Life Course* (Hawthorne, NY: Aldine, 1985), pp. 253–62.

Cancian, F. M., 'The feminization of love', *Signs: Journal of Women in Culture and Society*, 4 (1986), 692–709.

Caplan, P., and J. M. Bujra, *Women United Women Divided: Comparative Studies of Ten Contemporary Cultures* (Indiana: Indiana University Press, 1978).

Carnegie, D., *How to Win Friends and Influence People* (New York: Simon & Schuster, 1937).

Carr, J., *Child Abuse, Child Pornography and the Internet: Executive Summary* (London: NCH, 2004). The summary is available at: http://www.nchafc.org.uk/downloads/children_internet_report_summ.pdf.

Carrington, C., *No Place Like Home: Relationships and Family Life among Lesbians and Gay Men* (Chicago and London: University of Chicago Press, 1999).

Castells, M., *The Informational City: Information Technology, Economic Restructuring and the Urban-Regional Process* (Oxford: Basil Blackwell, 1989).

Castells, M., *The Rise of the Network Society* (Cambridge, MA: Blackwell, 1996).

Castells, M., *End of the Millennium*, vol. 3 of *The Information Age: Economy, Society and Culture* (Oxford: Blackwell, 1998).

Castells, M., 'Materials for an exploratory theory of the network society', *British Journal of Sociology*, 51:1 (2000), 5–24.

Castells, M., *The Internet Galaxy: Reflections on the Internet, Business and Society* (Oxford University Press, 2001).

Castells, M.,'Local and global: Cities in the network society', *Tijdschrift voor Economische en Sociale Geografie*, 93:5 (2002), 548–58.

Chamberlain, M., 'Brothers and sisters, uncles and aunts: A lateral perspective on Caribbean families', in E. B. Silva and C. Smart (eds), *The New Family?* (London: Sage, 1999).

Chambers, D., *Representing the Family* (London: Sage, 2001).

Chambers, D., 'Comedies of sexual morality and female singlehood,' in M. Pickering and S. Lockyer (eds), *Beyond a Joke: The Ethics of Humour*, (Basingstoke: Palgrave/Macmillan, 2005).

Chambers, D., L. Steiner and C. Fleming, *Women and Journalism* (London: Routledge, 2004a).

Chambers, D., E. Tincknell and J. Van Loon, 'Peer Regulation of Teenage Sexual Identities', *Gender and Education*, 16:3 (September 2004b), 397–415.

Chambers, D., J. Van Loon and E. Tincknell, 'Teachers' views of teenage sexual morality', *British Journal of Sociology of Education*, November 2004c, pp. 573–86.

Chandler, J., M. Williams, M., Maconachie, T. Collett and B. Dodgeon, 'Living alone: Its place in household formation and change', *Sociological Research Online*, 9:3 (2004). Available at: http://www.socresonline,.org.uk/9/3/chandler.html (accessed 06/01/05).

Charlton, T., C. Panting and A. Hannan, 'Mobile telephone ownership and usage among 10- and 11-year-olds', *Emotional and Behavioural Difficulties*, 7:3) (2002), 152–63.

Cheale, D. J., 'Showing them you love them: Gift giving and the dialectic of intimacy', *The Sociological Review*, 35:1 (1987), 150–70.

Cherlin, A., *Marriage, Divorce, Remarriage* (Cambridge, MA: Harvard University Press, 1992).

Clare, A., *On Men* (London: Chatto and Windus, 2001).

Clarke, D., and D. Haldane, *Wedlocked? Intervention and Research in Marriage* (Cambridge: Polity, 1990).

Clawson, M. A., 'Summer: Early modern fraternalism and the patriarchal family', *Feminist Studies*, 6 (1980), 368–91.

Clawson, M. A., *Constructing Brotherhood: Class, Gender, And Fraternalism* (Princeton, NJ: Princeton University Press, 1989).

Cohen, S., and T. Wills, 'Stress, social support and the buffering hypothesis,' *Psychological Bulletin*, 98 (1985), 310–57.

Coleman, J., *Foundations of Social Theory* (Cambridge, MA: Belknap Press, 1990).

Coleman, J., 'The Rational Reconstruction of Society: 1992 Presidential Address', *American Sociological Review*, 58 (1993), 1–15.

Coleman, J., 'Social capital in the creation of human capital', *American Journal of Sociology*, 94 (supplement) (1998), S95–S120.

Coleman, J., and T. J. Fararo (eds), *Rational Choice Theory: Advocacy and Critique* (London: Sage, 1992).

Colman, M., *Continuous Excursions: Politics and Personal Life* (London: Pluto Press, 1982).

Connell, B., *The Men and the Boys* (Oxford: Polity Press, 2000).

Connell, R. W., *Gender and Power: Society, the Person and Sexual Politics* (Cambridge: Polity Press, 1987).

Connell, R. W., 'Cool guys, swots and wimps: The interplay of masculinity and education', *Oxford Review of Education*, 15:3 (1989), 291–303.

Connell, R. W., *Masculinities* (Cambridge: Polity Press, 1995).

Connolly, W., *Identity/Difference* (Ithaca, NY: Cornell University Press, 1992).

Corlett, W. *Community Without Unity: A Politics of Derridian Extravagance* (Durham, NC: Duke University Press, 1989).

Correll, S., 'The ethnography of an electronic bar', *Journal of Contemporary Ethnography*, 24:3 (1995), 270–98.

Cote, S., and T. Healey, *The Well Being of Nations: The Role of Human and Social Capital* (Paris: Organisation for Economic Cooperation and Development, 2001).

Cott, N. *Bonds of Womanhood* (New Haven, CT: Yale University Press, 1977).

Cotterill, P., 'Interviewing women: Issues of friendship, vulnerability and power', *Women's International Forum*, 15 (1992), 593–606.

Craven, P., and B. Wellman, 'The network city', in M. P. Effrat (ed.), *The Community: Approaches and Applications* (New York: Free Press, 1974).

Critchley, S., 'The other's decision in me (What are the politics of friendship?)', *European Journal of Social Theory*, 1:2 (1998), 259–79.

Dahan, M., and G. Sheffer, 'Ethnic groups and distance shrinking communication technologies', *Nationalism and Ethnic Politics*, 7:2 (2001), 85–107.

Davidoff, L., and C. Hall, *Family Fortunes: Men and Women of the English Middle Class, 1780–1850* (London: Routledge, 1994).

Davidoff, L., M. Doolittle, J. Fink and K. Holden, *The Family Story: Blood, Contract and Intimacy, 1830–1960* (London: Longman, 1999).

Davies, B., *Frogs, Snails and Feminist Tails* (London: Allen & Unwin, 1989).

Davies, B., and R. Harre, 'Positioning: The discursive production of selves', *Journal for the Theory of Social Behaviour*, 20:1 (1991), 43–63.

Debord, G., *Society of the Spectacle* (London: Rebel Press, 1967).

De Kerckhove, D., *Connected Intelligence: The Arrival of the Web Society* (Toronto, Canada: Somerville House, 1997).

Delanty, G., *Community* (London: Routledge, 2003).

Delany, G., *Social Theory in a Changing World: Conceptions of Modernity* (Cambridge: Polity Press, 1999).

Dennis, N., F. Henrique and C. Slaughter, *Coal is our Life: An Analysis of a Yorkshire Mining Community* (London: Tavistock, 1956).

Department of Health and Social Security, *Caring about Carers: A National Strategy for Carers* (London: Department of Health and Social Security, 1999).

Department of Trade and Industry 'Closing the digital divide: Information and communication technologies in deprived areas: A report by the Social Exclusion Unit Policy Action Team 15' (London: Department of Trade and Industry, 2000).

Derlega, V. J., B.A. Winstead, P. T. P. Wang and S. Hunter (1985) 'Gender effects in an initial encounter: A case where men exceed women in disclosure', *Journals of Social and Personal Relationships*, 2 (1985), 25–44.

Derrida, J., *The Politics of Friendship* (London: Verso, 1997a).

Derrida, J., *Politics and Friendship: A Discussion with Jacques Derrida* (Centre for Modern French Thought, University of Sussex, hosted by Geoffrey Bennington, 1 December 1997b). Available at: http:www.sussex.ac.uk/Units/frenchthought/derrida.htm (accessed 12/06/2003).

Derrida, J., *Adieu Emmanuel Levinas* (Paris: Galilee, 1997c).

Dobash, R. E., and R. Dobash, *Women, Violence and Social Change* (London: Routledge 1992).

Donaldson, M., 'What is hegemonic masculinity', *Theory and Society*, 22 (1993), 643–57.

Dovey, J., *Freakshow* (London: Pluto Press, 2000).

Dryzek, J., *Discursive Democracy: Politics, Policy and Political Science* (New York: Cambridge University Press, 1990).

Duck, S., *Friends for Life* (Hemel Hempstead: Harvester Wheatsheaf, 1983).

Duck, S. *Relating to Others* (Milton Keynes: Open University Press, 1988).

Duncombe, J., and D. Marsden 'Whose orgasm is it anyway? "Sex Work" in long-term heterosexual couple relationships', in J. Weeks and J. Holland (eds), *Sexual Cultures: Communities, Values and Intimacy* (New York, St. Martins Press – now Palgrave, 1996).

Durkheim, E., *Sociology and Philosophy* (New York: The Free Press, 1974).

Durkheim, E., [1893] *The Division of Labour in Society* (London: Macmillan, 1984).

Edwards, M., 'Enthusiasts, Tacticians and Sceptics: The World Bank, Civil Society and Social Capital' (n.d.).

Ehrenreich, B., and A. R. Hochschild (eds), *Global Woman: Nannies, Maids and Sex Workers* (London: Granta Books, 2003).

Eldridge, M., 'A study of teenagers and SMS', *Proceedings of Mobile Futures Workshop*. CHI. Seattle, WA, 31 March–5 April 2001.

Elling, A., P. De Knop and A. Knoppers, 'Gay/lesbian sports clubs and events: Places of homosocial bonding and cultural resistance?' *International Review For The Sociology of Sport*, 38:4 (2003), 441–56.

Epstein, D., 'Keeping them in their place: Hetero/sexist harassment, gender and the enforcement of heterosexuality', in A. M. Thomas and C. Kitzinger (eds), *Sexual Harassment: Contemporary Perspectives* (Buckingham: Open University Press, 1997).

Evans, G., 'The decline of class divisions in Britain? Class and Ideological Preferences in the 1960s and 1980s', *British Journal of Sociology*, 44 (1993), 449–71.

Every. J. van, 'From modern nuclear family household to postmodern diversity? The sociological construction of families', in G. Jagger and C. Wright (eds), *Changing Family Values* (London: Routledge, 1999).

Faderman, L., *Surpassing the Love of Men: Romantic Freidnship and Love Between Women from the Renaissance to the Present* (New York: William Morrow, 1981).

Faludi, S., *Backlash: Undeclared War Against American Women* (New York: Vintage 1993).

Fehr, B., *Friendship Process* (Newbury Park: Sage, 1996).

Feinberg, L., '18 women end Cosmos Club's 110-year male era', *Washington Post*, 12 October 1988, p. B3 (quoted in Spain, 1992).

Ferri, E., and K. Smith, *Parenting in the 1990s* (London: Family Policy Studies Centre, 1996).

Festinger, L., S. Schacter and K. Back, *Social Pressures in Informal Groups* (New York: Harper, 1950).

Finch, J., and J. Mason, *Negotiating Family Relationships* (London:Roultedge, 1993).

Finch, J., and P. Summerfield, 'Social reconstruction and the emergence of companionate marriage, 1945–59', in D. Clark (ed.), *Marriage, Domestic Life and Social Change: Writings for Jacqueline Burgoyne (1944–88)* (London: Routledge, 1991), pp. 7–32.

Finch, J., J. Mason, J. Massen, L. Wallis and L. Hayes, *Wills, Inheritance and Families* (Oxford:Clarendon Press, 1996).

Fink, J., and K. Holden, 'Pictures from the margins of marriage: Representations of spinsters and single mothers in the mid-Victorian novel, inter-war Hollywood melodrama and British Film of the 1950s and 1960s', *Gender and History*, 11:2 (July 1999), pp. 233–55.

Fischer, C. S., *To Dwell Among Friends: Personal Networks in Town and City* (Chicago:University of Chicago Press, 1982).

Flannagan, A., and M. Metzger, 'Internet use in the contemporary media environment', *Human Computer Research*, 27 (2001), 153–81.

Flax, J., *Forgotten Forms of Close Combat: Mothers and Daughters Revisited' in Disputed Subjects: Essays on Psychoanalysis, Politics and Philosophy* (London: Routledge, 1993).

Flood, M., 'Men's movements', *Community Quarterly*, 46 (1998), 63–71.

Fortier, A. M., *Gender, Ethnicity and Power: Identity Formation in Two Italian Organisations of London*, unpublished PhD dissertation (Goldsmiths College, University of London, 1996).

Foucault, M., *Discipline and Punish* (New York: Random House, 1977).

Foucault, M., *The History of Sexuality*, vol. 1: *An Introduction* (Harmondsworth: Penguin, 1979).

Foucault, M., 'The birth of biopolitics', in P. Rabinow (ed.), *Michel Foucault. Ethics: Subjectivity and Truth* (New York: New Press, 1997).

France, L., 'Love at first site: Discos and singles bars are a distant memory for today's lonely hearts', *Observer Magazine*, 30 June 2002. Available at: http://observer.guardian.co.uk/magazine/story/0,11913,746525,00html.

Francis, B., and C. Skelton, 'Men teachers and the construction of heterosexual masculinity in the classroom', *Sex Education*, 1:1 (2001), 9–21.

Franklin, C., II, 'Hey, home – yo, bro: Friendship among black men', in P. M. Nardi (ed.), *Men's Friendships* (London: Sage, 1992).

Friedman, M., *What are Friends For? Feminist Perspectives on Personal Relationships and Moral Theory* (Ithaca, NY, and London: Cornell University Press, 1993).

Friedman, M., *Feminism in Ethics: Conceptions of Autonomy* (Cambridge: Cambridge University Press, 2000).

Froehling, O. 'Internauts and guerrilleros: The Zapatista rebellion in Chiapas, Mexico and its extension into cyberspace', in M. Crang, P. Crang and J. May (eds), *Virtual Geographies: Bodies, Space and Relations* (London and New York; Routledge 1999), pp. 164–77.

Frosh, , S., A. Phoenix and R. Pattman, *Young Masculinities* (Basingstoke: Palgrave, 2002).

Fukuyama, F., *Trust: The Social Virtues and the Creation of Prosperity* (London: Penguin, 1996).

Gamman, L., and M. Marshment, *The Female Gaze: Women as Viewers of Popular Culture* (Seattle: Real Comet, 1989).

Gans, H. J., *The Urban Villagers: Group and Class in the Life of Italian-Americans* (New York: Free Press of Glencoe, 1962).

Garcia-Montes, J. M., D. Caballero-Munoz and M. Perez-Alvarez, 'Changes in the self resulting from the use of mobile phones', *Media, Culture and Society,* 28:1 (2006), 67–82

Garrod, J., 'The work-life balance, *Sociological Review,* 13:2 (2003), 30–1.

Gavin, J., 'Arousing suspicion and violating trust: The lived ideology of safe sex talk', *Culture, Health and Sexuality,* 2:2 (2000), 117–34.

Gavin, J., 'Chat-room relationships', paper presented at British Psychological Society conference, Bath University, 2002.

Gearing, F. O., *The Face of the Fox* (Chicago: Aldine 1970).

Giddens, A., *The Consequences of Modernity* (Stanford, CA: Stanford University Press, 1990).

Giddens, A., *Modernity and Self-Identity* (Cambridge: Polity Press, 1991).

Giddens, A., *The Transformation of Intimacy: Sexuality, Love and Eroticism in Modern Societies* (Cambridge: Polity Press, 1992).

Giddens, A., 'Living in a post-traditional society', in U. Beck, A Giddens and S. Lach (eds), *Reflexive Modernisation* (Stanford, CA: Stanford University Press, 1994a).

Giddens, A., *Beyond Left and Right: The Future of Radical Politics* (Stanford, CA: Stanford University, 1994b).

Giddens, A., 'The post-traditional society and radical politics: An interview with Anthony Giddens', in L. B. Kaspersen (ed.), *Anthony Giddens: An Introduction to a Social Theorist,* trans. S. Sampson (Oxford: Blackwell, 2000).

Gilbert, R., and P. Gilbert, *Masculinity Goes to School* (Sydney: Allen & Unwin,1998)

Gilligan, C., *A Different Voice: Psychological Theory and Women's Development* (Cambridge, MA:Harvard University Press, 1982).

Gilligan, C., 'Moral orientation and moral development', in E. Feder Kittay and D. T. Meyers (eds), *Women and Moral Theory* (Savage, MD: Rowman & Littlefield, 1987), pp. 19–33.

Goffman, E., *Interaction Ritual: Essays on Face-to-Face Behaviour* (Harmonsdworth: Penguin Books, 1972).

Goffman, E., *Forms of Talk* (Philadelphia: University of Pennsylvania Press, 1981).

Goldthorpe, J. H., *Social Mobility and Class Structure in Modern Britain,* 2nd edn (Oxford: Clarendon Press, 1987).

Goss, R. E., 'Queering procreative privilege: Coming out as families', in R. E. Goss and A. S. Strongheart (eds), *Our Families, Our Values: Snapshots of Queer Kinship* (Binghampton, NJ: The Harrington Park Press, 1997).

Gouldner, A. W., *For Sociology: Renewal and Critique in Sociology Today* (London: Allen Lane, 1973).

Gouldner, M., and M. Symons Strong, *Speaking of Friendship: Middle-Class Women and their Friends* (New York and London: Greenwood Press, 1987).

Grebler, L., J. W. Moore and R. C. Guzman, *The Mexican-American People* (New York: The Free Press, 1970).

Green, E., S. Hebron and D. Woodward, *Women's Leisure, What Leisure?* (London: Macmillan, 1990).

Greer, G., *The Whole Woman* (New York: Doubleday, 1999).

Griffin, C., *Typical Girls? Young Women from School To The Full-Time Job Market* (London: Routledge, 1985).

Griffiths, M., *Feminisms and the Self: The Web of Identity* (London: Routledge, 1995).

Grosz, E., *Sexual Subversions* (Sydney: Allen & Unwin, 1989).

Grosz, E. 'Ontology and equivocation: Derrida's politics of sexual difference', in N. Holland (ed.), *Feminist Interpretations of Jacques Derrida* (University Park, PA: Pennsylvania University Press, 1997).

Guerrero, E., *Framing Blackness: The African American Image in Film* (Philadelphia: Temple University Press, 1993).

Hacker, H. M., 'Blabbermouths and clams: Sex differences in self disclosure in same-sex and cross-sex friendship dyads, *Pyschology of Women Quarterly*, 5 (1981): 385–401.

Haezewindt, P., 'Investing in each other and the community: The role of social capital', in National Statistics, *Social Trends*, 33 (London: HMSO, 2003).

Haidar-Yassine, H., *Internet Friendships: Can Virtual be Real?*, PhD thesis (Alliant International University, 2002), p. 2651.

Hakim, C., *Key Issues In Women's Work: Female Diversity and the Polarisation of Women's Employment* (London: Glasshouse Press, 2004).

Hall, J., 'The capital(s) of cultures: A nonholistic approach to status situations, class, gender and ethnicity', in M. Lamont and M. Fournier (eds), *Cultivating Differences, Symbolic Boundaries and the Making of Inequality* (Chicago: University of Chicago Press, 1992).

Hall, P., 'Social capital in Britain', *British Journal of Political Science*, 29 (1999), 417–61.

Hall, S., 'Introduction', in S. Hall and B. Gieben (eds), *Formations of Modernity* (Cambridge: Polity, 1992), pp. 1–16.

Halttunen, K., *Confidence Men and Painted Women: A Study of Middle-Class Culture in America, 1830–1870* (New Haven, CT: Yale University Press, 1982).

Hammond, D., and A. Jablow, 'Gilgamesh and the Sundance Kid: The myth of male friendship', in H. Brod (ed.), *The Making of Masculinities: The New Men's Studies* (Boston: Allen & Unwin, 1987), pp. 241–58.

Hansen, K., ' "Our Eyes Behold Each Other": Masculinity and intimate friendship in Antebellum New England', in P. M. Nardi (ed.), *Men's Friendships* (London: Sage, 1992).

Hanson, S., and G. Pratt, *Gender, Work and Space* (London: Routledge, 1995).

Hardy, M., 'Doctor in the house: The Internet as a source of lay health knowledge and the challenge to expertise', *Sociology of Health and Illness*, 21:6 (1999), 820–35.

Harrison, K., 'Rich friendships, affuent friends: Middle-class practices of friendship, in R. G. Adams and G. Allan (eds), *Placing Friendship in Context* (Cambridge: Cambridge University Press, 1998), pp. 92–116.

Harrison, H., *Intimate Relations: A Study of Married Women's Friendships*, PhD thesis, Southampton University, 1999), pp. 50–2972.BL.

Harvey, D., *The Condition of Postmodernity: An Enquiry into the Origins of Cultural Change* (Oxford: Blackwell, 1990).

Harvey, S., 'Hegemonic masculinity, friendship and group formation in an athletic subculture', *The Journal of Men's Studies*, 8:1 (1999), 91–102.

Hayden, D., *Redesigning the American Dream: The Future of Housing, Work and Family* (New York: Norton, 1984).

Bibliography 187

Haywood, C., 'Out of the curriculum: Sex, talking sex, *Curriculum Studies*, 4:2 (1996), 229–51.
Haywood, C., and M. Mac An Ghaill, [1996], 'Schooling masculinities', in M. Mac an Ghaill (ed.), *Understanding Masculinities* (Buckingham: Open University Press, 2000).
Heaphy, B., J. Weeks and C. Donovan, 'Narratives of love, care and commitment: AIDS/HIV and non-heterosexual family formations', in P. Aggleton, G. Hart and P. Davies (eds), *Families and Communities Responding to AIDS* (London: UCL Press, 1999).
Heath, S., and E. Cleaver, *Young, Free and Single? Twenty-Somethings and Household Change* (Basingstoke: Palgrave, 2003).
Heim, M., 'The erotic ontology of cyberspace', in M. Benedikt (ed.), *Cyberspace: First Steps* (Boston, MA: MIT Press, 1992).
Helgeson, V. S., P. Shaver and M. Dyer, 'Prototypes of intimacy and distance in same sex and opposite sex relationships', *Journal of Social and Personal Relationships*, 4 (1987): 195–233.
Heller, Z., 'Girl columns', in S. Glover (ed.), *Secrets of the Press: Journalists on Journalism* (London: Allen Lane, The Penguin Press, 1999), pp.10–17.
Henley Centre and Salvation Army, *The Responsibility Gap: Individualism, Community and Responsibility in Britain Today* (Henley Centre/Salvation Army, 2004) available at: http://www.salvationarmy.org.uk/en/responsibilitygap/home.htm (accessed 13/05/04).
Herdt, G. H., *Guardians of the Flutes* (New York: McGraw-Hill, 1981).
Herdt, G. H., *Ritualised Homosexuality in Melanesia* (Berkeley, CA: University of California Press, 1984).
Herek, G., 'On heterosexual masculinity: Some psychical consequences of the social construction of gender and sexuality', in M. Kimmel (ed.), *Changing Men: New Directions in Research on Men and Masculinity* (Newbury Park, CA: Sage, 1987), pp. 68–82.
Hey, V., *Patriarchy and Pub Culture* (London: Tavistock, 1986).
Hey, V., *The Company She Keeps: The Social and Interpersonal Construction of Girls' Same-Sex Relationships*, PhD thesis, University of Kent, 1988.
Hey, V., *The Company She Keeps: Ethnography of Girls' Friendship* (Milton Keynes: Open University Press, 1997).
Hite, S., *Women and Love* (London: Penguin, 1987).
Holland, J., C. Ramazanoglu and S. Sharpe, 'Power and desire: The embodiment of female sexuality', *Feminist Review*, 46 (1994), 21–38.
Holland, J., C. Ramazanoglu and S. Sharpe, *The Male in the Head: Young People, Heterosexuality and Power* (London: The Tufnell Press, 1998).
Hornsby, A., 'Surfing the net for community', in P. Kivisto (ed.), *Illuminating Social Life* (Thousand Oaks, CA: Pine Forge Press, 1998), pp. 63–106.
Howard, G., 'Love in the office', *New Law Journal*, 23 December 1994, pp. 1762–64.
Howard, P. E. N., L. Rainie and S. Jones, 'Days and nights on the Internet: The impact of a diffusing technology', *American Behavioral Scientist*, 45:3 (2001), 382–403.
Hume, D., *Treatise of Human Nature* (1739–40), Introduction A. D. Lindsay, (London: Dent, 1977).
Hunt, G., and S. Satterlee, 'Darts, drink and the pub: The culture of female drinking', *The Sociological Review*, 35 (1987), 575–601.

Hutcheson, F., [1755], *A System of Moral Philosophy* (Bristol: Thoemmes, 2000).

Institute for Volunteering Research (2003), *Volunteering Facts and Figures*. Available at: http://www.ivr.org.uk/facts.htm (accessed 20/02/03).

Internet Crime Forum (2001). Available at http://www.internetcrimeforum. org.uk (accessed 25/04/2006)

Jackson, C., ' "Laddishness" as a self-worth protection strategy', *Gender and Education*, 14:2 (2002), 37–51.

Jackson, R. M., 'Social structure and process in friendship choice', in C. S. Fischer, R. M. Jackson, C. A. Steuve, K. Gerson, and L. McCallister Jones with M. Baldassare (eds), *Networks and Places* (New York: Free Press, 1977).

Jameson, F., *Postmodernism or the Cultural Logic of Late Capitalism* (London: Verso, 1991).

Jamieson, L., 'Theories of family development and the experience of being brought up', *Sociology*, 21 (1987), 591–607.

Jamieson, L., *Intimacy: Personal Relationships in Modern Societies* (Cambridge: Polity Press, 1998).

Jamieson, L., 'Intimacy transformed? A Critical look at the "pure relationship" ', *Sociology*, 33:3 (1999), 477–94.

Jeffries, S., *The Spinster and Her Enemies: Feminism and Sexuality 1880–1930*, (New York: Routledge & Kegan Paul, 1986).

Johnson, L., *Modern Girl: Girlhood and Growing Up* (Milton Keynes: Open University Press, 1993).

Jones, C., 'Becoming a girl', *Gender and Education*, 5:2 (1993), 157–66.

Jones, C., 'Lara Croft: Fantasy games mistress', *BBC New Online*, 6 July 2001. Available at: http://news.bbc.co.uk/hi/english/uk/newsid_1425000/ 1425762.stm.

Jones, S., 'Information, Internet and community: Notes towards an understanding of community in the information age', in *Cybersociety 2.0*. (London: Sage, 1998), pp. 1–34.

Jowell, R., J. Curtice, A. Park, K. Thomson, L. Jarvis, C. Bromley and N. Stratford (eds), *British Social Attitudes: Focusing on Diversity*, 17th Report, (London: Sage, 2001).

Katz, J. E., R. E. Rice and P. Aspden, 'The Internet, 1995–2000: Access, civic involvement, and social interaction', *American Behavioral Scientist*, 45:3 (2001), 404–18.

Kaufmann, J. C., 'One person households in Europe', *Population*, 49:4/5 (1994), 935–58.

Knopp, L., 'Gay identified spaces', *Space and Society*, 10 (1992), 651–69.

Knorr-Cetina, K., 'Postsocial relations: Theorising sociality in a postsocial environment', in G. Ritzer and B. Smart (eds), *Handbook of Social Theory* (London: Sage, 2001), pp. 520–37.

Kosnick, K., 'Building bridges – media for migrants and the public service mission in Germany', *European Journal of Cultural Studies*, 3:3 (2000), 321–44.

Kraut, R., V. Lundmark, M. Patterson, S. Kiesler, T. Mukopadhyay and W. Scherlis, 'Internet paradox: A social technology that reduces social involvement and psychological well-being?', *American Psychologist*, 53:9 (1998), 1017–31.

Kuhn, A., *Family Secrets* (London:Verso, 1995).

Labour Research, 'The downside of workplace romance', *Labour Research*, 81:12 (1992), 15–17.

Lamont, M., and A. Lareau, 'Cultural capital: Allusions, gaps and glissandos in recent theoretical developments', *Sociological Theory*, 6 (1988), 153–68.

Lasch, C., *The Culture of Narcissism* (London: Abacus, 1979).

Lasch, C., *The Minimal Self* (London: Picador, 1984).

Lasch, C., *The Revolt of the Elites and the Betrayal of Democracy* (New York: Norton, 1995).

Lasch, S., 'Reflexivity and its doubles: Structures, aesthetics, community' in U. Beck, A. Giddens and S. Lasch, *Reflexive Modernisation: Politics, Tradition and Aesthetics in the Modern Social Order* (Cambridge: Polity Press.1994).

Lehne, G., 'Homophobia among men: Supporting and defining the male role', in M. Kimmel and M. Messner (eds), *Men's Lives* (NewYork: Macmillan, 1989), pp. 416–29.

Lejeune, A., and M. Lewis, *The Gentlemen's Clubs of London* (London: Macdonald & Janes, 1979).

Leung, L., and R. Wei, 'Who are the mobile phone have-nots?', *New Media and Society*, 1:2 (1999), 209–26.

Levinas, E., *Totality and Infinity*, trans. A. Lingis (Pittsburgh: Duquesne University Press, 1969).

Levinas, E., *Ethics and Infinity – Conversations with Philippe Nemo*, trans. R. A. Cohen (Pittsburgh: Duquesne University Press, 1985).

Levinas, E., and R. Kearney, 'Dialogue with Emmanuel Levinas', in R. A. Cohen (ed.), *Face to Face with Levinas* (Albany, NY: State University of New York Press, 1986).

Levy, A., *Female Chauvinist Pigs: Women and the Rise of Raunch Culture* (New York: Simon & Schuster, 2005).

Levy, P., *Collective Intelligence: Mankind's Emerging World in Cyberspace* (New York: Plenum Trade, 1997).

Levy Simon, B., 'Impact of shift work on individuals and families', *Families in Sociology*, 71 (June 1990), 342–8.

Lewis, J., 'The power of popular television: The case of Cosby', in T. O'Sullivan and Y. Jewkes (eds), *The Media Studies Reader* (London: Arnold, 1997), pp. 91–100.

Lewis, J., *The End of Marriage? Individualism and Intimate Relations* (Cheltenham: Edward Elgar, 2001).

Lichterman, P., *The Search for Political Community: American Activists Reinventing Commitment* (Cambridge: Cambridge University Press, 1996).

Liebow, E., *Tally's Corner: A Study of Negro Streetcorner Men* (Boston, MA: Little, Brown, 1967).

Ling, R., ' "We will be reached": The use of mobile phone telephony among Norwegian Youth', *Information Technology and People*, 13:2 (2000), 102–20.

Lloyd, G., *The Man of Reason: 'Male' and 'Female' in Western Philosophy* (London: Methuen, 1984).

Lupton, D., *The Emotional Self* (London: Sage, 1998).

Lupton, D., and L. Barclay, *Constructing Fatherhood: Discourse and Experiences* (London: Sage, 1997).

Lyman, P., 'The fraternal bond as a joking relationship: A case study of sexist joles in male group bonding', in M. S. Kimmel (ed.), *Changing Men: New Directions in Research on Men and Masculinity* (Newbury Park, CA: Sage, 1987), pp. 148–63.

Lynch, L., 'Cruising the libraries', in K. Jay and J. Glasgow (eds), *Lesbian Texts and Contexts* (New York: New York University Press, 1990) pp. 37–48.

Lynch, S., 'Aristotle and Derrida on friendship', *Contretemps*, 3 July 2002, pp. 98–108. Available at: http://www.usyd,edu.au/contretempts/3July2002/lynch.pdf (accessed 02/06/2003).

Lynd, R., and H. Lynd, *Middletown: A Study in American Culture* (New York: Harcourt, Brace, 1929).

J.-F. Lyotard, *The Postmodern Condition* (Manchester: Manchester University Press, 1984).

Mac an Ghaill, M., *The Making of Men: Masculinities, Sexualities and Schooling* (Open University Press: Buckingham, 1994).

MacFarlane, A., *The Origins of English Individualism: The Family, Property and Social Transition* (Cambridge: Cambridge University Press, 1978).

McCall, L., *Complex Inequality: Gender, Class and Race in the New Economy* (London: Routledge, 2001).

McCarthy, H., *Girlfriends in High Places* (London: Demos, 2004).

McDowell, L., 'Work, workfare, work/life balance and an ethic of care', *Progress in Human Geography*, 28:2 (2004), 145–63.

McIntosh, M., 'The homosexual role', *Social Problems*, 16 (1968), 182–92.

McLennan, G., 'Maintaining Marx', in G. Ritzer and B. Smart (eds), *A Handbook of Social Theory* (London: Sage, 2001), pp. 43–53.

McRobbie, A., *Postmodernism and Popular Culture* (London: Routledge, 1994).

McRobbie, A. 'Bridging the gap: Feminism, fashion and consumption', *Feminist Review*, 55 (Spring 1997a), 73–89.

McRobbie, A., 'Pecs and penises: The meaning of girlie culture', *Soundings*, 5 (1997b), 157–66.

Maffesoli, M., 'Jeux de Masques: Postmodern tribalism', *Design Issues*, 4 (1988), 141–51.

Maffesoli, M., 'Postmodern sociality', *Telos*, 85 (1990), 89–92.

Maffesoli, M., *The Shadow of Dionysus: A Contribution to the Sociology of the Orgy* (New York: State University of New York, 1993).

Maffesoli, M., *The Time of the Tribes: The Decline of Individualism in Mass Society* (London: Sage, 1996).

Peter Martin: 'We'll mate again' *Sunday Times Magazine*, 27 April 2003, pp. 22–8.

Martino, W., 'Cool boys', 'party animals', 'squids' and 'poofters': Interrogating the dynamics and politics of adolescent masculinities in school', *British Journal of Sociology of Education*, 20:2 (1999), 239–63.

Marx, K., *The Economic and Philosophic Manuscripts of 1844* (New York: International Publishers, 1971).

Marx, K., *Capital*, vol. 1 (Harmondsworth, Middlesex: Penguin in association with London: New Left Review, 1976).

Matheson, J., and C. Summerfield, *Social Trends*, 30 (London: The Stationary Office, 2000).

Mayes, T., 'Submerging in "therapy news" ', *British Journalism Review*, 1:4 (2000), 30–5.

Megoran, N. 'Book review of Castells *The Power of Identity*, Volume 2 of *The Information Age: Economy, Society and Culture* (Oxford: Blackwell, 1999)', *International Journal of Urban and Regional Research*, 23:2 (1999), 398–400.

Mehra, B., C. Merkel and A. Peterson Bishop, 'The internet for empowerment of minority and marginalized users', *New Media and Society*, 6:6 (2004), 781–802.

Mele, C. 'Cyberspace and disadvantaged communities: The Internet as a tool of collective action', in M. A. Smith and P. Kollock (eds), *Communities in Cyberspace* (London: Routledge, 2000), pp. 290–310.

Melucci, A. *Challenging Codes: Collective Action in the Information Age* (Cambridge: Cambridge University Press, 1996).

Messner, M., 'Like family: Power, intimacy and sexuality in male athletes' friendships', in P. M. Nardi (ed.), *Men's Friendships* (London: Sage, 1992).

Messner, M., 'Friendship, intimacy and sexuality,' in *The Masculinities Reader*, ed. S. M. Whitehead and F. J. Barrett (London: Polity, 2004), pp. 253–66.

Mikula, M., 'Gender and video games; The political valency of Lara Croft', *Continuum: Journal of Media and Cultural Studies*, 17:1 (2003), 79–87.

Miller, S., *Men and Friendship* (London: Gateway Books, 1983).

Mills, C. W., *The Sociological Imagination* (Oxford: Oxford University Press 1959).

Mills, M., *Challenging Violence in Schools: An Issue of Masculinities* (Buckingham: Open University Press, 2001).

Mirza, H., 'Redefining black womanhood', in S. Jackson and S. Scott (eds), *Gender: A Sociological Reader* (London: Routledge, 2002), pp. 303–10.

Moody-Adams, M. M., 'Gender and the complexity of moral voices', in C. Card (ed.), *On Feminist Ethics and Politics* (Kansas:University Press of Kansas, 1991).

Morgan, D., 'Men, masculinity and the process of sociological enquiry', in H. Roberts (ed.), *Doing Feminist Research* (London: Routledge & Kegan Paul, 1981), pp. 83–113.

Morgan, D., *Family Connections; An Introduction to Family Studies* (Cambridge: Polity, 1996).

Morris, K., 'Girl Power' – The Lives and Friendships of a Group of Adolescent Girls in a Rural Area, PhD thesis, Bristol University, 1997.

Mosquera, M., 'More than half of U.S. households now have Internet access', *TechWeb News* (2000). Available at: http://www.techweb.com/wire/story/ TWB20001121800011.

Moss, P. (ed.), *Father Figures: Fathers in the Families of the 1990s* (Edinburgh: HMSO, 1995).

Mossberger, K., C. J. Tolbert and M. Stansbury, *Virtual Inequality: Beyond the Digital Divide* (Georgetown University Press, 2003).

Munt, S., E. Bassett and K. O'Riordan, 'Virtually belonging: Risky connectivity and coming out online', *International Journal of Sexuality and Gender Studies*, 7:2 (2002), 125–37.

Murdock, G. P., and D. White, 'Standard cross-cultural sample', *Ethnology*, 8 (1969), 329–69.

Nardi, P. M., ' "Seamless Souls": An introduction to men's friendships', in P. Nardi (ed.), *Men's Friendships* (London: Sage, 1992).

Nardi, P., *Gay Men's Friendships: Invincible Communities* (Chicago, IL: Chicago University Press, 1999).

National Opinion Poll Research Group Archived Surveys (2000), 'Mobile phones: The teens' must-have'. Available at: http://www.nop.co.uk/news/ news_archive_survey2000.shtml (accessed 17/07/2000).

National Opinion Poll Research Group Internet Surveys (2001), 'Half of 7–16s Have a Mobile Phone'. Available at: http://www.nop.co.uk/news/ news_survey_half_of_7–16s.shtml (accessed 29/01/2001).

National Statistics, *Living in Britain: Results from the 2000/01 General Household Survey* (London: HMSO, 2001).

Nayak, A., and M. J. Kehily, 'Playing it straight: Masculinities, homophobias and schooling', *Journal of Gender Studies*, 5:2 (1996), 211–30.

Nelson, A., T. L. N. Tu and A. H. Hines, *Technicolor: Race, Technology and Everyday Life* (New York: New York University Press, 2001).

Nie, N. H., 'Sociability, interpersonal relations, and the Internet: Reconciling conflicting findings', *American Behavioural Scientist*, 45:3 (2001), 419–35.

Nie, N. H., and L. Erbring, *Internet and Society: A Preliminary Report* (Stanford, CA: Stanford Institute for the Quantitative Study of Society, 2000).

Nie, N. H., and H. Sackman, *The Information Utility and Social Change* (Montvale, NJ: AFIPS, 1970).

Nolletti, A., Jnr, 'Male companionship movies and the Great American Cool', *Jump Cut*, December 1976, pp. 12–13,

O'Connor, P., *Very Close Relationships*, unpublished PhD thesis, University of London, 1987.

O'Connor, P., 'The adult mother-daughter relationship: A uniquely and universally close relationship?', *Sociological Review*, 38:2 (1990), 293–323.

O'Connor, P., *Friendships between Women: A Critical Review* (London: The Guilfod Press, 1992).

O'Connor, P., and G. W. Brown, 'Supportive relationships: Fact or fancy?', *Journal of Social and Personal Relationships*, 1 (1984), 159–76.

OECD, *The Well-Being of Nations: The Role of Human and Social Capital, Education and Skills* (Paris, OECD, 2001).

Office for National Statistics, *National Statistics Omnibus Survey* (London: Office for National Statistics, 2001).

Office for National Statistics, *Social Trends*, 33 (2003). Available at: www.statistics.gov.uk/socialtrends (accessed 20/02/2005).

Oldenburg, R., *The Great Good Place* (New York: Marlowe, 1999).

Oliker, S., *Best Friends and Marriage* (California:University of California Press, 1989).

Oram, A., 'Repressed and thwarted, or bearer of the New World? The spinster in inter-war feminist discourses', *Women's History Review*, 1:3 (1992), 413–33.

Orbach, S., and L. Eichenbaum, *Between Women*, 2nd edn (London: Arrow, 1994).

Orlikowski, W. J., 'Learning from notes: Organisatinal issues in groupware implementation', in R. Kling (ed.), *Computerization and Controversy: Value Conflicts and Social Choices*, 2nd edn (Sandiego, CA: Academic Press, 1996), pp. 173–89.

Oswald, R. F., 'Family and friendship relationships after young women come out as bisexual or lesbian', *Journal of Homosexuality*, 38:3 (2000), 65–83.

Owen, D., 'The digital divide', in K. Mossberger, C. J. Tolbert and M. Stansbury, *Virtual Inequality: Beyond the Digital Divide* (Georgetown: Georgetown University Press, 2003).

Owen, D., A. E. Green, M. McLeod, I. Law, T. Challis and D. Wilkinson, 'The use and attitudes towards information and communication technologies (ICT) by people from black and minority ethnic groups living in deprived areas', Centre for Research in Ethnic Relations and Institute for Employment Research, University of Warwick (Nottingham: Department of Education and Skills, 2003).

Paetcher, C., *Educating the Other: Gender, Power and Schooling* (London: Falmer Press, 1998).

Pahl, J., *Money and Marriage* (Basingstoke: Macmillan, 1989).

Pahl, R., *After Success* (Cambridge: Polity, 1995).

Pahl, R. E., *On Friendship* (Cambridge: Polity, 2000).

Pahl, R. E., and E. Spencer, 'The politics of friendship', *Renewal*, 5:34 (1997), 100–7.

Pahl, R. E., and E. Spencer, *Rethinking Friendship: Personal Communities and Social Cohesion*, ESRC report (2001). Available at: http://www.regard.ac.ukcgi-bin/regardng.

Parekh, B., *Rethinking Multiculturalism, Cultural Diversity and Political Theory* (Basingstoke: Macmillan Press – now Palgrave, 2000).

Park, R., *Human Communities* (Glenco: The Free Press, 1952).

Parkman, F., *The Oregon Trail* (Madison: University of Wisconsin Press, 1969).

Parks, M. R., and K. Floyd, 'Making friends in Cyberspace', *Journal of Communication*, 46:1 (1996), 80–97.

Parsons, T., *The Structure of Social Action*, 2nd edn (New York: McGraw-Hill, 1949).

Parsons, T., *The Social System* (New York: The Free Press, 1951).

Parsons, T., 'The social structure of the family', in R. N. Anshen (ed.), *The Family, Its Function and Destiny* (New York: Harper, 1959), pp. 241–74.

Parsons, T., 'Youth in the context of American Society', *Daedalus*, 91 (1962), reprinted in T. Parsons, *Social Structure and Personality* (New York: Collier Macmillan, 1970).

Parsons, T., *Social Structure and Personality* (New York: Free Press, 1964a).

Parsons, T., *Essays in Sociological Theory* (New York: Free Press, 1964b).

Parsons, T., *Societies* (Englewood Cliffs, NJ: Prentice-Hall, 1966).

Parsons, T., and R. F. Bales, *Family Socialisation and The Interaction Process* (London: Routledge & Kegan Paul, 1956).

Pateman, C., *The Sexual Contract* (Cambridge: Polity Press, 1988).

Pease, B., *Recreating Men: Postmodern Masculinity Politics* (London: Sage, 2000).

Pease, B., *Men and Gender Relations* (Melbourne: Tertiary Press, 2002).

Phillips, T., 'Imagined communities and self-identity: An exploratory and quantitative analysis', *Sociology*, 36:3 (2002), 597–617.

Phoca, S., and R. Wright, *Introducing Postfeminism* (Trumpington: Icon, 1999).

Plant, S., *Most Radical Gesture* (London: Routledge, 1992).

Pleace, N., R. Burrows, B. Loader, S. Muncer and S. Nettelton, 'On-line with the friends of Bill W: Social support and the Net', *Sociological Research Online*, 5:2 (2000). Available at: http://www.socresonline.org.uk/5/2/pleace.html.

Pleck, E., and J. Pleck, *The American Man* (Englewood Cliffs, NJ: Prentice-Hall, 1980).

Plotz, D., 'Iraq the computer game: What virtual world games can teach the real world about reconstructing Iraq', *Slate*, 19 June 2003. Available at: http://www.slate.com/id/2084604/device/html40/ (accessed 19/04/06).

Plummer, K., *Telling Sexual Stories: Power, Change and Decline in Modern Societies* (London: Routledge, 1995).

Pool, I., *Forecasting the Telephone: A Retrospective Technology Assessment* (Norwood, NJ: Ablex, 1983).

Poster, M., *The Second Media Age* (Cambridge; Polity Press, 1995).

Pressley, S. A., 'Metropolitan Club ends ban on women members', *Washington Post*, 26 June 1988, p. B1 (quoted in Spain, 1992).

Putnam, R., 'The prosperous community: Social capital and public life', *American Prospect*, 13 (1993a), 35–42.

Putnam, R., with R. Leonardi and R. Nanetti, *Making Democracy Work: Civic Traditions in Modern Italy* (Princeton, NJ: Princeton University Press, 1993b).

Putnam, R., *Bowling Alone* (New York: Simon & Schuster, 2000).

Rainey, N. A., *Successful Ageing: The Role of Friendship in the Psychological Well-Being of Elderly People*, PhD thesis, Queen's University Belfast, 1994, pp. 44–6207, B2b.

Rawlins, W. K., *Friendship Matters: Communication Dialect and the Life Course* (New York: Aldine De Gruyter, 1992).

Raymond, J., *A Passion for Friends* (London: The Women's Press, 1986).

Redman, P., 'Tarred with the same brush: Homophobia and the unconscious in school-based cultures of masculinity', *Sexualities*, 4 (2001), 483–99.

Reeves, R., 'We bowl alone, but work together', *New Statesman*, 2 April 2001, pp. 23–4.

Reid, E. M., 'Virtual worlds, culture and imagination', in S. J. Jones (ed.), *Cybersociety: Computer-Mediated Communication and Community* (California: Sage, 1996a).

Reid, E. M., 'Communication and community on Internet relay chat: Constructing communities', in M. Goodwin (ed.), *High Noon on the Electronic Frontier* (Cambridge, MA: MIT Press, 1996b).

Reid, H., and G.A. Fine, 'Self-disclosure in men's friendships: Variations associated with intimate relations', in P. Nardi (ed.), *Men's Friendships* (London: Sage, 1992).

Reis, H. T., and P. Shaver, 'Intimacy as an interpersonal process', in S. W. Duck et al. (eds), *A Handbook of Personal Relationships* (Chichester: Wiley, 1988).

Renolds, E., 'Other' boys: Negotiating non-hegemonic masculinities in the primary school, *Gender and Education*, 16:2 (2004), 247–66.

Rheingold, H., *The Virtual Community* (Reading, MA: Addison-Wesley, 1993).

Rheingold, H., *The Virtual Community: Homesteading on the Electronic Frontier*, 2nd edn (Cambridge, MA: MIT Press, 2000).

Richards, J., ' "Passing the Love of Women": Manly love and Victorian society', in J. A. Mangan and J. Walvin (eds), *Manliness and Morality: Middle Class Masculinity in Britiana and America, 1800–1940* (Manchester: Manchester University Press, 1987), pp. 92–122.

Ridley, J., *The Freemasons* (London: Constable, 1999).

Riesman, D., R. Denney and N. Glazer, *The Lonely Crowd, A Study of Changing American Character*, 2nd edn (New Haven, CT: Yale University Press, 1951).

Robinson, W. I., *Promoting Polyarchy: Globalisation, US Intervention and Hegemony* (New York: Cambridge University Press, 1996).

Rofes, E., 'Dancing bears, performing husbands, and the tyranny of the family', in R. E. Goss and A. S. Strongheart (eds), *Our Families, Our Values: Snapshots of Queer Kinship* (Binghampton, NJ: The Harrington Park Press, 1997).

Rojek, C., *Decentring Leisure: Rethinking Leisure Theory* (London: Sage, 1995).

Rose, N., *Governing the Soul: The Shaping of the Private Self* (London: Routledge, 1990).

Rose, N., 'Inventiveness in politics', *Economy and Society*, 28 (1999), 467–93.

Ross, C. D., (ed.), *Patronage, Pedigree and Power in Later Medieval England* (Gloucester: Sutton Publishing, 1973).

Rosaldo, M., and L. Lamphere (eds), *Woman, Culture and Society* (Palo Alto, CA: Stanford University Press, 1974).

Rotundo, A., 'Romantic friendships: Male intimacy and middle-class youth in the northern United States, 1800–1900', *Journal of Social History*, 23:1 (1989), 1–25.

Rowe, K., *The Unruly Woman: Gender and the Genres of Laughter* (Austin: University of Texas Press, 1995).

Rubin, L., *Intimate Strangers: Men and Women Together* (New York: Perennial, 1983).

Rubin, L. B., *Just Friends: The Role of Friendship in our Lives* (New York: Harper & Row, 1985).

Rudolph, I., ' "Sex" and the married girl', *TV Guide*, 6 June 1998, pp. 12–14.

Rueschemeyer, D., and T. Skocpol (eds), *States, Social Knowledge, and the Origins of Modern Social Policies* (Princeton, NJ: Princeton University Press, 1996).

Rundell, J., 'Modernity, enlightenment, revolution and romanticism: Creating social theory', in G. Ritzer and B. Smart (eds), *Handbook of Social Theory* (London: Sage, 2001), pp. 13–29.

Salisbury, J., and D. Jackson, *Challenging Macho Values: Practical Ways of Working with Adolescent Boys* (London: The Falmer Press, 1996).

Sapadin, L., 'Friendship and gender: Perspectives of professional men and women', *Journal of Social and Personal Relationships*, 5:4 (1988), 387–403.

Schiller, D., *Digital Capitalism* (Cambridge, MA: MIT Press, 1999).

Schmalenback, H., *On Society and Experience: Selected Papers*, ed. G. Luschen and G. P. Stone (Chicago: Chicago University Press, 1977).

Schwartz, B., 'The social psychology of the gift', *American Journal of Sociology*, 73:1 (1967), 1–11.

Schwartz, E., *Netactivism: How Citizens Use the Internet* (Sebastopol, CA: Songline Studies, 1996).

Sedgewick, E. K., *Between Men: English Literature and Male Homosocial Desire* (New York: Columbia University Press, 1985).

Segal, L., *Slow Motion: Changing Masculinities, Changing Men* (London: Virago, 1990).

Seidler, V., 'Rejection, vulnerability and friendship', in P. M. Nardi (ed.), *Men's Friendships* (London: Sage, 1992).

Seidman, S., *Romantic Longings* (New York: Routledge, 1991).

Seigel, J., V. Dubrovsky, S. Kiesler and T. McGuire, 'Group processes in computer-mediated communication', *Organizational Behaviour and Human Decision Processes*, 37 (1986), 157–87.

Sella, M., 'The electronic fishbowl', *New York Times Magazine*, 21 May 2000, pp. 50–104.

Sevenhuijsen, S., *Citizenship and the Ethics of Care: Feminist Considerations of Justice, Morality and Politics* (London: Routledge, 1998).

Sharpe, S., *Double Identity: The Lives of Working Mothers* (Harmonsworth: Penguin, 1984).

Sheffer, G., and Michael Dahan. 'Ethnic groups and distance shrinking communication technologies', *Nationalism & Ethnic Politics*, 7:1 (2001), 85–107.

Sherrod, D., 'The bonds of men: Problems and possibilities in close male relationships', in H. Brod (ed.), *The Making of Masculinities: The New Men's Studies* (Bostonm MA: Allen & Unwin, 1987), pp. 213–40.

Sherrod, D., 'The influence of gender on same-sex friendships', in C. Hendrick (ed.), *Close Relationships* (Newbury Park, CA: Sage, 1989).

Siapera, E., 'Minority activism on the web: The Internet, minorities and asylum politics', *Journal of Ethnic and Migration Studies*, in print (2004a).

Siapera, E., 'Asylum politics, the Internet and the public sphere', in *Javnost/The Public*, in print (2004b).

Silver, A., 'Friendship and trust as moral ideals: An historical approach', *European Journal of Sociology*, 30 (1989), 274–97.

Silver, A., 'Friendship in commercial society: Eighteenth-century social theory and modern sociology', *American Journal of Sociology*, 95 (1990), 1474–504.

Silver, A., 'Two different sorts of commerce', or, friendship and strangership in civil society', in J. Weintraub and K. Kumar (eds), *Public and Private in Thought and Practice: Persectives on the Grand Dichotomy* (Chicago: University of Chicago Press, 1996).

Simmel, G., 'The metropolis and mental life', in K. H. Wolff (ed. and trans.), *The Sociology of Georg Simmel* (Glencoe, IL: Free Press, 1950a).

Simmel, G., *The Sociology of Georg Simmel*, trans., ed. and introduction Kurt H. Wolff (London: The Free Press, 1950b).

Simmel, G., *Conflict and the Web of Group Affliliations* (Glencoe, IL: The Free Press, 1955).

Simmel, G., *On Individuality and Social Forms*, ed. and introduction D. N. Levine (Chicago: University of Chicago Press, 1971).

Simon, B. L., 'Impact of shift work on individuals and families', *Families in Sociology*, 71 (June 1990), 342–8.

Singleton, A., 'Men getting real? A study of relationship change in two men's groups', *Journal of Sociology, The Australian Sociological Association*, 39:2 (2003), 131–47.

Skeggs, B., *Formations of Class and Gender* (London: Sage, 2002).

Skelton, C., *Schooling the Boys: Masculinities and Primary Education* (Buckingham: Open University Press, 2001)

Skolnick, A., *The Intimate Environment: Exploring Marriage and the Family*, 5th edn (New York: Harper Collins, 1992).

Slouka, M., *War of the Worlds: Cyberspace and the High-tech Assault on Reality* (New York: Basic Books, 1995).

Smart, B., 'Sociology, morality and ethics: On being with others', in G. Ritzer and B. Smart (eds), *Handbook of Social Theory* (London: Sage, 2001).

Smart, C., 'The 'new ' parenthood: Fathers and mothers after divorce', in E. B. Silva and C. Smart (eds), *The New Family?* (London: Sage, 1999), pp. 100–14.

Smart, C., and B. Neale, *Family Fragments?* (London: Polity, 1999).

Smith, A., [1759, 1790], *The Theory of Moral Sentiments* (Oxford, Clarendon Press, 1976).

Smith, C. B., M. L. McLaughlin and K. K. Osborne, 'From terminal ineptitude to virtual sociopathy: How conduct is regulated on Usenet', in F. Sudweeks, M. Mclaughlin and S. Rafaeli (eds), *Networks and Netplay: Virtual Groups on the Internet* (Cambridge, MA: MIT Press, 1998).

Smith-Rosenberg, C., 'The female world of love and ritual: Relations between women in nineteenth-century America', *Signs*, 1:1 (1975), 1–29.

Smith-Rosenberg, C., *Disorderly Conduct* (New York: Oxford University Press, 1986).

Social Exclusion Unit, *Bringing Britain Together: An National Strategy for Neighbour hood Renewal* (London: The Stationary Office, 1998).

Social Exclusion Unit, *Teenage Pregnancy* (London, The Stationary Office, 1999).

Spain, D., 'The spatial foundations of men's friendships and men's power', in P. Nardi (ed.), *Men's Friendships* (London: Sage, 1992).

Sproull, L. S., and S. B. Kiesler, *Connections: New Ways of Working in the Networked Organization* (Cambridge, MA: MIT Press, 1991).

Stacey, J., 'Virtual social science and the politics of family values in the United States', in G. Jagger and C. Wright (eds), *Changing Family Values* (London: Routledge, 1999).

Stack, C. B., *All Our Kin: Strategies for Survival in a Black Community* (New York: Harper & Row, 1974).

Stacey, J., 'Virtual social science and the politics of family values in the United States', in G. Jagger and C. Wright (eds), *Changing Family Values* (London: Routledge, 1999).

Starr, R., 'Fall, Men's Clubs, Women's Rights', *The Public Interest*, 89 (1987), 57–70.

Stehr, N., 'Modern societies as knowledge societies', in G. Ritzer and B. Smart (eds), *Handbook of Social Theory* (London: Sage, 2001).

Stewart, A., 'Hope and despair: Making sense of politics in the twenty-first century', *British Journal of Sociology*, 53:3 (2002), 467–90.

Stock, Y., and P. Brotherton, 'Attitudes towards single women', *Sex Roles*, 7:1 (1981), 73–8.

Stoll, C., *Silicon Snake Oil: Second Thoughts on the Information Highway* (New York: Doubleday, 1995).

Stone, A. R., *The War of Desire and Technology at the Close of the Mechanical Age* (Boston, MA: MIT Press, 1996).

Stone, C., *Networking: The Art of Making Friends* (London: Vermillion, 2000).

Strain, L. A., and N. L.Chappell, 'Confidants: Do they make a difference in quality of life?', *Research on Aging*, 4 (1982), 479–502.

Strathern, M., *After Nature: English Kinship in the Late Twentieth Century* (Cambridge: Cambridge University Press, 1992),

Sudweeks, F., and S. Rafaeli, 'How do you get a hundred strangers to agree: Computer-mediated communication and collaboration', in T. M. Harrison and T. D. Stephen (eds), *Computer Networking and Scholarship in the 21st Century* (New York: SUNY Press, 1996).

Suitor, J. J., 'Friendship networks in transitions: Married mothers return to school', *Journal of Social and Personal Relationships*, 4 (1987), 445–61.

Swain, S., 'Covert intimacy: Closeness in men's friendships', in B. Risman and P. Schwartz (eds), *Gender in Intimate Relationships: A Microstructural Approach* (Belmont, CA: Wadsworth, 1989), pp. 71–86.

Swain, S., 'Men's friendships with women: Intimacy, sexual boundaries and the informant role', in P. M. Nardi (ed.), *Men's Friendships* (London: Sage, 1992).

Tarrow, S., 'Fishnest, Internets and catnets: Globization and transnaional collective action', in M. Hanagan, L. Moch and W. TeBrake (eds), *The Past and Future of Collective Action* (Minneapolis: University of Minnesota Press, 1998), pp. 228–44.

Taylor, A., and R. Harper, 'The gift of the *gab*?: A design oriented sociology of young people's use of "mobilZe!" ', *Computer Supported Cooperative Work (CSCW)*, 12:3 (2003), 267–96.

Taylor, S., *Sociology: Issues and Debates* (Basingstoke: Palgrave, 1999).

Thompson, J. B., *The Media and Modernity* (Cambridge: Polity Press, 1995).

Thompson, K., 'Religion, values and ideology', in R. Bocock and K. Thompson (eds), *Social and Cultural Forms of Modernity* (Cambridge: Polity, 1991), pp. 321–66.

Thomson, R., 'Diversity, values and social change: Renegotiating a consensus on sex education', *Journal of Moral Education*, 26:3 (1997), 257–71.

Tiger, L., *Men in Groups* (London: Nelson, 1969).

Tincknell, E., and D. Chambers (2002) 'Performing the crisis: Fathering, gender and representation in two 1990s films', *Journal of Popular Film and Television*, 29:4 (Winter 2002), 146–55.

Tincknell, E., D. Chambers, J. Van Loon and N. Hudson, ' "Begging for it": "New femininities", social agency and moral discourse in contemporary teenage and men's magazines', *Feminist Media Studies*, 3:1 (2003), 47–63.

Tocqueville, A. de, *Democracy in America*, first published in 2 vols, 1835 and 1840 (New York: Doubleday, 1969).

Tonnies, F., [1887] *Community and Society*, trans. C. Loomis (New York: Harper & Row, 1963).

Tonnies, F., [1887], *Community and Association* (London: Routledge, 1974).

Tremlett, G., *Clubmen: The History of the Working Men's Club and Institute Union* (London: Martin, Secker & Warburgh, 1987).

Turkle, S., *Life on the Screen* (New York: Simon & Schuster, 1995).

Turner, B., 'Outline of a general theory of cultural citizenship', in N. Stephenson (ed.), *Culture and Citizenship* (London: Sage, 2001).

Tysome, T., 'Women set up old-girl network' *Times Higher Supplement*, 14 February 2003, p. 6.

Van Every, J., 'From modern nuclear family households to postmodern diversity?', in G. Jagger and C. Wright (eds), *Changing Family Values* (London: Routledge, 1999).

Valverde, J. M., 'The personal is the political: Justice and gender in deconstruction, *Economy and Society*, 28:2 (1999), 300–11.

Verbrugge, L. M., 'The structure of adult friendship choices', *Social Forces*, 56 (1977), 576–97.

Virilio, P., *Polar Inertia* (London: Sage, 2000).

Wakeford, N., 'Sexualised bodies in cyberspace', in W. Chernaik, M. Deegan and A. Gibson (eds), *Beyond the Book: Theory, Culture and the Politics of Cyberspace* (London : Centre for English Studies, University of London, 1996), pp. 93–104.

Walby, S., *Patriarchy at Work* (Cambridge: Polity, 1986).

Walkerdine, V., *The Mastery of Reason: Cognitive Development and the Production of Meaning* (New York: Routledge, 1987).

Walkerdine, V., and H. Lucey, *Democracy in the Kitchen* (London: Virago, 1989).

Walters, W., 'Social capital and political sociology: Re-imagining politics?', *Sociology*, 36:2 (2002), 377–97.

Walther, J. B., 'Interpersonal effects in computer-mediated interaction', *Communication Research*, 19 (1992), 52–90.

Warrier, S., 'Gujarati Prajapatis in London: Family roles and sociability networks', in R. Ballard (ed.), *Desh Pardesh: The South Asian Presence in Britain* (London: Hurst, 1994).

Webber, M. M., 'Urbanization and communications', in G. Gerbner, L. P. Gross and W. H. Meoldy (eds), *Comunications Technology and Social Policy* (Chichester: John Wiley, 1973).

Weber, M., *From Max Weber – Essays in Sociology*, ed. and trans. H. H. Gerth and C. Wright Mills (London: Routledge & Kegan Paul, 1970).

Weber, M., *Economy and Society*, ed. G. Roth and C. Wittich, 2 vols (Berkeley: University of California Press, 1978).

Webster, F., 'Is this the information age? Towards a critique of Manuel Castells', *The City*, December 1997, pp. 71–84.

Weeks, J., *Sex, Politics and Society: The Regulation of Sexuality Since 1800* (New York: Longman, 1981).

Weeks, J., *Against Nature: Essays on History, Sexuality and Identity* (London: Rivers Oram Press, 1991).

Weeks, J., *Invented Moralities: Sexual Values in an Age of Uncertainty* (Cambridge: Polity Press, 1995).

Weeks, J., C. Donovan and B. Heaphy, 'Everyday experiments: Narratives of non-heterosexual relationships', in E. B. Silva and C. Smart (eds), *The New Family?* (London: Sage, 1999), pp. 83–99.

Weeks, J., B. Heaphy and C. Donovan, *Same Sex Intimacies: Families of Choice and Other Life Experiments* (London: Routledge, 2001).

Wellman, B., 'Men in networks: Private communities, domestic friendships', in P. M. Nardi (ed.), *Men's Friendships* (London: Sage, 1992).

Wellman, B., 'Are personal communities local? A Dumptarian reconsideration', *Social Networks*, 18 (1996), 347–54.

Wellman, B., 'Physical space and cyber space: The rise of personalized networking', *International Journal of Urban and Regional Research*, 25 (2001), 227–52.

Wellman, B., and M. Guila, 'Net surfers don't ride alone', in B. Wellman (ed.), *Networks in the Global Village* (Boulder, CO: Westview, 1999), pp. 331–66.

Wellman, B., and S. Wortley, 'Different strokes from different folks: Community ties and social support', *American Journal of Sociology*, 96 (1990), 558–88.

B. Wellman, A. Quan Haase, J. Witte and K. Hampton, 'Does the Internet increase, decrease, or supplement social capital?', *American Behavioural Scientist*, 45:3 (2001), 436–55.

Werbner, P., 'The dialectics of cultural hybridity', in P. Werbner and T. Modood (eds), *Debating Cultural Hybridity* (London: Zed, 1997), pp. 1–26.

Weston, K., *Families We Choose: Lesbians, Gays, Kinship* (New York: Columbia University Press, 1991).

Westwood, S., 'Domestic labourers: Or stand by your man – while he sits down and has a cup of tea', in S. Jackson and S. Scott (eds), *Gender: A Sociological Reader* (London: Routledge, 2002), pp. 159–64.

Whelehan, I., *Overloaded: Popular Culture and the Future of Feminism* (London: The Women's Press, 2000).

Whitehead, S., *Men and Masculinities: Key Themes and New Directions* (Oxford: Polity Press , 2002).

Whitty, M., and J. Gavin, 'Age/sex/location: Uncovering the social cues in the development of online relationships', *Cyberpsychology and Behavior*, 4 (2001), 441–8.

Whyte, M., *The Status of Women in Preindustrial Societies* (Princeton, NJ: Princeton University Press, 1978).

Whyte, W. F., *Street Corner Society: The Social Structure of an Italian Slum* (Chicago: University of Chicago Press 1943).

Wilkinson, H., *No Turning Back: Generations and the Genderquake* (London: Demos, 1995).

Wilkinson, H., (ed.), *Family Business* (London: Demos, 2000).

Williams, W., 'The relationship between male-male friendship and male-female marriage: American Indian and Asian comparisons', in P. M. Nardi (ed.), *Men's Friendships* (London: Sage, 1992).

Willmott, P., *Friendship Networks and Social Support* (Cambridge: Polity Studies Institute, 1987).

Wilska, T. A., 'Mobile phone use as part of young people's consumption style', *Journal of Consumer Policy*, 26 (2003), 441–63

Wilson, E., *The Sphinx in the City: Urban Life, the Control of Disorder and Women* (California: University of California Press, 1992).

Wincapaw, C., 'The virtual spaces of lesbian and bisexual women's electronic mailing lists', *Journal of Lesbian Studies*, 4:1 (2000), 45–59.

Winstead, B. A., V. J. Derlega and M. J. Montgomery, 'The quality of friendships at work and job satisfaction', *Journal of Social and Personal Relationships*, 12:2 (1995), 199–215.

Wiseman, J., 'Friendship: Bonds and binds in a voluntary relationship', *Journal of Social and Personal Relationships*, 3 (1986), 191–211.

Witte, J. C., L. M. Amoroso and P. E. . Howards, 'Method and representation in Internet-based survey-tools: Mobility, community, and cultural identity in survey 2000', *Social Science Computing Review*, 18:2 (2000), 179–95.

Wittel, A., 'Towards a network sociality', *Theory, Culture and Society*, 18:6 (2001), 51–76.

Wittrock, B., and P. Wagner, P. (1996) 'Social science and the building of the early welfare state', in D. Rueschemeyer and T. Skocpol (eds), *States, Social Knowledge, and the Origins of Modern Social Policies* (Princeton, NJ: Princeton University Press, 1996), pp. 90–113.

Wood, B., 'Urbanisation and local government', in H. Halsey (ed.), *British Social Trends since 1900* (Basingstoke: Macmillan, 1988), pp. 322–56.

Wood, J., 'Groping towards sexism: Boys' sex talk', in A. McRobbie and M. Nava (eds), *Gender and Generation* (Basingstoke: Macmillan, 1984).

World Values Survey: http://www.worldvaluessurvey.com/.

Wright, P. H., 'Men's friendships, women's friendships, and the alleged inferiority of the latter', *Sex Roles*, 8 (1982), 1–20.

Yates, S., 'Sexes in battle of the texts', *Sheffield Hallam University News*, 9/11/2005. Available at: http://www.shu.ac.uk/cgibin/news_full.pl?id_num=PR862&db=05.

Yoon, K., 'Retraditionalising the mobile: Young people's sociality and mobile phone use in Seoul, South Korea', *European Journal of Cultural Studies*, 6:3 (2003), 327–44.

Young, M., and P. Willmott, *Family and Kinship in East London* (London: Routledge & Kegan Paul 1957). (Reprinted by Penguin in 1962.)

Zeldin, T., *An Intimate History of Humanity* (London: Vintage, 1998).

Index